STREET CAPITAL

Black cannabis dealers in a white welfare state

Sveinung Sandberg and Willy Pedersen

This edition published in Great Britain in 2009 by

The Policy Press
University of Bristol
Fourth Floor
Beacon House
Queen's Road
Bristol BS8 1QU
UK

tel +44 (0)117 331 4054
fax +44 (0)117 331 4093
e-mail tpp-info@bristol.ac.uk
www.policypress.co.uk

North American office:
The Policy Press
c/o International Specialized Books Services
920 NE 58th Avenue, Suite 300
Portland, OR 97213-3786, USA
tel +1 503 287 3093
fax +1 503 280 8832
e-mail info@isbs.com

Photographs kindly supplied by Ole Dyre Hesledalen

British Library Cataloguing in Publication Data
A catalogue record for this book is available from the British Library.

Library of Congress Cataloging-in-Publication Data
A catalog record for this book has been requested.

ISBN 978 1 84742 120 3 hardcover

Cover design by The Policy Press
Printed and bound in Great Britain by MPG Books Group

Contents

Preface

The book is about young black men dealing cannabis at a street drug market known as The River in downtown Oslo. The scene is characterised by violence, drug use and social problems, and the dealers are both socially and economically excluded from mainstream society. Young men in this situation are often depicted based on what they do *not* have: All are unemployed and have little formal education, some do not speak Norwegian well, and several do not have a legal residence permit. They are also feared by the general public – for good reasons. In this book however, our aim is to see further than this. After we got to know them, we also became aware of their energy, knowledge and competence, even if much of it was restricted to performances in street culture. Indeed many of them are violent, but they relate to others and negotiate disputes in numerous other ways as well. Generally we came to perceive these young men as more complex than what the academic literature typically describes. The violent street culture constitutes only one dimension of their lives.

The book has nine chapters. First, we describe different trajectories to street drug scenes and present and develop theory about street cultures. We also identify typical processes of marginalisation and exclusion at a more general level. We then present the young men at The River and their life in more detail, in chapters on drug use and masculinity, drug economy and street drug markets, and violence. The Norwegian welfare state structures their lives in complex ways, and this is described in Chapter Eight. The chapters are intended to be read successively, but for readers with a special interest they can also be read separately. Moreover, Chapter Three is probably of particular interest for readers concerned about theoretical issues. For others, more empirically oriented readers, it can be passed over.

A number of thanks are due, to numerous helpers, but here we only have space for some. An earlier version of this book has previously been published in Norwegian. The English version is completely rewritten however, we have gone into more depth in the analyses of the empirical material, and we also draw on a richer theoretical background. We are grateful for flexibility from the Norwegian University Press in this process. We also thank The Norwegian Research Council for funding in the process of writing the English version. Thanks also to Policy Press editor Karen Bowler and the publishers' consultants for useful comments and practical assistance.

Thanks are due as well to language consultant Chris Saunders who has helped us with transforming parts of the text from Norwegian to English and photographer Ole Dyre Hesledalen who is responsible for the pictures. Without Chris' nuanced work on the young men's street language and the Ole's illustrations from The River this would have been a very different book indeed. Thanks to the Sociology Departments at the Universities of Oslo and Bergen for housing us and to colleagues for inspiring discussions throughout the process.

Some ideas and parts of this book are previously published and further expanded upon in journal articles. Parts from: Chapter Two in 'Black drug dealers in a white welfare state: cannabis dealing and street capital in Norway' (Sandberg 2008a); Chapter Seven in 'Street capital: ethnicity and violence on the streets of Oslo' (Sandberg 2008b); and Chapter Eight in 'Gangster, victim, or both? The interdiscursive construction of sameness and difference in self-presentations' (Sandberg 2009c). Thanks to editors and referees, their comments to these articles have been helpful and inspiring for the work on this book as well.

Finally and most importantly we wish to thank the young men and the one woman at The River who shared their knowledge and life-stories. We asked for a lot, but had little to offer in return. Hassan, who will be introduced in Chapter Two, and others wanted us to tell their stories to the outside world. We hope our book can live up to some of their expectations.

ONE

Introduction

The street drug market known as The River area starts at this ball court. Here youths and students are playing basketball, table tennis, or just hanging around. The neighbourhood is an ethnically and socially mixed urban area.

The River

The river Akerselva divides Oslo – the capital of Norway – into its eastern, working-class parts, and the more prosperous west. From a distance, the area seems peaceful and cultivated. There are green parks and old brick houses – some of them former factories, remnants from the early industrial period. However, the area has a long history of poverty and social marginality. For the young minority ethnic men who are portrayed in this book, hanging out at 'The River', as they say, means selling cannabis.

A hundred years ago, the area was poor, inhabited by working-class families and even elements from the *Lumpenproletariat*. During recent decades, expensive flats have been built in rehabilitated former working-class estates. There are small design, architecture and advertising businesses, as well as art galleries, ethnic restaurants and fitness centres. The area is typical of many previously working-class areas in Western cities. It has numerous traces of poor living conditions and poverty, as well as traces of early industrialisation. However, recent gentrification processes have transformed the area into a popular and multicultural part of inner Oslo. The area around The River is usually called Inner Oslo East. During the last decade, poor segments of the population (especially immigrant groups) have moved from Inner to Outer East, to the satellite towns. Inner East now hosts a large number of young professionals and students. The typical migration pattern is that young, well-educated persons move from the western parts of the city to Inner Oslo East. The remains of the traditional working-class population and minority ethnic groups, who settled in the 1970s and 1980s, move to Outer East. Both the eastern satellite towns and the western suburbs now have an older age composition (see Bråthen et al, 2007).[1]

If you take a walk along the border of The River, you will see some young men hanging around, seemingly without anything to do. Now and then, a rapid conversation takes place with a passer-by, objects seem to be exchanged, there are nervous glances, and a minute later, the passer-by has disappeared, and the calm, almost sleepy atmosphere is re-established. They are actors in probably the largest open cannabis market in Scandinavia. The bulk of cannabis distribution takes place through other, more hidden, channels. However, The River provides the easiest *open access* to cannabis in Oslo. Most of the dealers are black and have an African background. The transactions are quick and instrumental, in order to agree on quantity, quality and price with as little small talk as possible, because there may be undercover police in the area.

Many of those who take a walk along The River will be asked, "Buy shit?" If you get the guy who asks to tell you about his life, you will hear a story about how 'being at The River' structures his life. Here he is hanging out. Here he is dealing *hash*. Here are his friends and acquaintances. For more than a year, we were also hanging out at The River. We were talking to and observing the young men. Our questions included: Who are the dealers? How is the dealing organised? Is violence an important part of their lives? Many of the dealers use slang and wear clothes influenced by hip-hop culture. What role does this music culture play? What are their relations with the police and the various actors and institutions of the welfare state? Gradually, however, our most important task became to describe how the dealers struggled to create meaning, to gain self-respect and to be accepted by society.

Street culture in a Scandinavian welfare state

We had been doing fieldwork at The River for a few months, and we were familiar with *Chris*. He was in his early twenties and was one of the more experienced dealers at The River. He had been dealing illegal drugs for years, and for some time he had also been a member of one of the established criminal gangs in Oslo. However, now he was only dealing cannabis on the street. When Chris spoke, he used many of the typical narratives of the young men at The River: as a "foreigner" it is impossible to get a job. The school system does not give foreigners an adequate education, and most of them drop out of school. Even if the Norwegian society seems tolerant on the surface, foreigners "do not really have a chance".

Once we were talking with Chris in a pub where we often did interviews. It was the second interview, and he had brought his cousin with him, who was five years younger than him. It was easy to see that Chris wanted to impress his cousin. We knew that his reputation in his family and among his relatives had been decreasing. We came to talk about violence in the streets of Oslo, and he told us in a boasting way that he was a great fighter. When we asked *where* he had learned to fight – whether it was at a training centre – he answered, "No, no, I have never been at any fucking training centre in my whole life. I have only been out on the street." We felt that the atmosphere was good, and we laughed as we commented, "So it has been 'the hard way'?" However, he did not smile back. He turned pale, got up, took his pint of beer and stared at us, obviously furious. In a loud voice, he cried out, "I have learned in movies how to kill a man." He held the glass in front of us. "Like this glass. You break it in the face of the 'motherfucker'!"[2] The situation suddenly became tense and unpleasant.

He probably felt that we had ridiculed him in front of his cousin. He must have felt that our "hard way" comment was a subtle and perhaps ironic way of questioning his claim of being a skilled fighter. Chris interpreted it as a joke made at his expense, and his response was to redefine the situation, turning it into a familiar game he knew we could not play. In the street, he was competent when it came to threats and violence. By introducing his street repertoire, he was able to take control of the situation. Threatening to break the glass in our face confirmed his street status, both for us and for his cousin.

We did not really know how to proceed with the interview. Still, after a break, we asked:

> *Interviewer:* 'Have you ever done that [killed a man]?'
> *Chris:* 'Yes … er … no, not with a glass.'
> *Interviewer:* 'But you have beaten up a few?'
> *Chris:* 'Yeah, once I took a bat and killed a guy. But he was a devil. He was Satan's kid. This isn't bullshit.'

Chris had probably never killed anybody. This expression was meant as a metaphor for having beaten somebody up. We were careful not to humiliate him in front of his cousin during the rest of the interview. The atmosphere soon calmed down, and we were gradually able to restore the more light-hearted tone we had at the start of the interview.

At first, we did not really understand what was going on in the interview with Chris. Later we realised that the episode had opened our eyes to the two main discourses that structure the lives of the young men at The River. In short, the dealers often presented and understood themselves as *victims* – partly of an impersonal and cold bureaucratic Norwegian system, sometimes even of direct racism. However, in their peer subcultures at The River, when dealing cannabis, their self-presentations and the way they understood themselves were different. Then, they were street-smart *gangsters*.

According to Goffman (1963), the pressure of normal conduct is present in everyone's life, but for stigmatised people, it tends to cause uncertainty and ambivalence. The response is frequent shifts between defensive covering and 'bravado'. Once we had this conceptual key, we could identify how The River dealers continuously moved between the positions of gangster and victim in an ongoing 'search for respect' (Bourgois, 2003a).

Thus, let us present our basic argument: the young men at The River develop a competence that we coin 'street capital'. This concept is similar to Bourdieu's (1984) 'cultural capital', but the competence, skills and dispositions involved are limited to a violent street culture. Cultural capital can be seen in three forms: institutionalised, objectified and embodied (Bourdieu, 1986). The dealers at The River have to develop skills related to the street; for example, knowledge of drugs and drug supply sources, the ability to deal, and the ability to fight. In the lives of the young men at The River, this is crucial. The most important form of street capital is the one that is embodied through the *habitus*. When Chris reacted as he did, it was his embodied street capital that disposed him to do so. He defended his street capital, which was the product of many years of living in a violent street culture.

In a welfare state, however, one needs more than street capital to survive on the street. One must also master the language and formal rules of the welfare state system. It is impossible to understand the lives of the young men at The River without situating them in the Scandinavian welfare state context.

The Human Development Index (HDI) is a comparative measure of life expectancy, literacy, education and standards of living for countries worldwide. For many years, Norway has held one of the world's top positions on the list, well ahead of countries such as France, Germany and the UK.[3] Norway is a rich country with a well-developed welfare state.

Social citizenship is the core concept of the welfare state. Above all, this idea involves the granting of social rights, and these rights are based on citizenship rather than performance. Conceptually, a *welfare regime* refers to a policy mix of labour market interventions, family support, public pensions and cash transfer systems. The Nordic social democratic welfare regime is characterised by a universal system of relatively generous social benefits (Esping-Andersen, 1990).[4] It has received much international attention because it seems to combine a strong safety net for its citizens with a competitive economy and strong growth.[5] However, surprisingly little is written about how the welfare system's beneficiaries develop strategies for dealing with the system, nor is there much written about the degree to which interaction with the system shapes their way of thinking, their daily lives and their identities.[6]

Chris and the other River dealers, for example, continually interact with the welfare state and its agents: they go to social security offices, they register as unemployed, they meet outreach field workers and most of them have a history in the educational psychology system. In all these settings, they must present themselves as legitimate claimants of granted social rights. This is nearly the opposite of the current situation the US, as described by Loïc Wacquant (2008) in his book *Urban outcasts*. The US ghetto is shaped by the erosion of the welfare state and the collapse of public institutions.

The cannabis economy

The dealers at The River sell cannabis. Now and then they also sell 'pills', amphetamines and cocaine, but it is the cannabis economy that structures their lives. It is difficult to evaluate the size of markets for illegal drugs. The standard yardsticks for legal markets cannot be used. However, all indications are that the cannabis economy is the largest and most important among the illegal drug economies – in Norway as well as in other Western countries (UNODC, 2006). Nevertheless, other underground economies, such as the ones associated with heroin or cocaine, have received more attention. The cannabis economy is structured in a different way from the 'hard' drug economies. It is based on a large number of participants and often undefined limits between dealers and friends in semi-private networks. Open access marketplaces, such as the one at The River, only distribute a small proportion of the total.

Over the last four decades, both global cannabis use and cultivation has increased in North America and Europe. Cannabis use has been growing faster than the use of opiates and cocaine. It is impossible to obtain precise estimates worldwide, but it is typically estimated that around 150 million people have used cannabis at least once during the last 12 months – far more than have used other illegal drugs (Leggett and Pietschmann, 2008).

In the European Union (EU), there are about 200,000 seizures of cannabis annually (Carpentier et al, 2008). In Norway alone, police have made approximately 5,000 cannabis seizures per year during the last decade,[7] even though small-scale cannabis distribution is not a police priority. Gradually, indoor cultivation and locally grown herbal cannabis have become an important supplement to imported hash, although not as much in Norway as in the Netherlands and the UK. During the last few years, however, a considerable number of cannabis farms have been discovered in Norway. The farms require large investments to set up rebuilt houses with irrigation systems, high-intensity sodium lamps, reflective foil on the walls and ventilation ducts through the ceiling.

The price of cannabis resin is higher in Norway than in other European countries (Carpentier et al, 2008).[8] Most of the cannabis is still imported from Morocco, which is the largest producer of cannabis in the world.[9] The typical route goes through Spain, which is the crucial transit zone for Moroccan hashish. A cannabis industry has developed during the last three decades, and smuggling networks have become faster and more professional. International connections with traffickers of other drugs have been established; for instance, with cocaine exporters from South America. Traffickers in other drugs are increasingly using routes established for the distribution of Moroccan hashish (Gamella and Rodrigo, 2008).

Cannabis is cheap in Morocco (Gamella and Rodrigo, 2008). The price may increase 50- or 100-fold before cannabis reaches the consumer. Many actors cash in on the profits generated by cannabis as it makes its way from the fields of Morocco to the drug markets of Northern Europe.

We will return to the cannabis economy later in the book. The sheer volume of the cannabis trade, the semi-accepted character of cannabis smoking, and the relatively mild punishment for those who are arrested for importing or dealing cannabis were all key factors in the lives of The River dealers. There is a high prevalence of cannabis use in the society, and this fact tends to minimise the perception of deviance as well as risk associated with the drug.

Oslo: a divided city

Oslo is a growing multicultural city of 550,000 inhabitants. Global migration patterns have had an increasing impact on the ethnic composition of and living conditions in the city. There are large groups from Pakistan, Iraq, Vietnam, Poland, Bosnia and Somalia. Humanitarian disasters have resulted in large groups of refugees and asylum seekers coming to Oslo. Nine out of 10 new inhabitants have a non-Western background. Today, this group numbers more than 100,000 (Bråthen et al, 2007).[10] At present, Oslo has inhabitants with 168 different national backgrounds, and 28 different languages are taught in the school system.

The living conditions in Norway are good. At the same time, social welfare *differences* are largest in Oslo – relative to other Norwegian cities and municipalities – in all of the important indicators, such as education, income, health, and mortality rates. In particular, the differences between the eastern satellite towns and the western suburbs are increasing. Immigrant families move to the eastern satellite towns, and ethnic Norwegian families move to the western suburbs. The result is an increasingly divided city, with large differences in living conditions in the midst of an affluent welfare state.

Health is a central indicator of living conditions. A composite measure of self-reported health was developed for a recent study of living conditions in Oslo, which included physical pain, ability to concentrate and sleeping problems among its items (see Bråthen et al, 2007, chapter 4). In Inner Oslo West, only 11% reported poor health. In the new satellite towns in Outer Oslo East, the figure was 26%. The same pattern was seen for living on disability benefits, being on long-term sick leave, or in medical rehabilitation institutions.

Another central indicator of living conditions is average life expectancy. There are large differences across Oslo, and they have been increasing. The outer western parts of Oslo have the highest life expectancy, and the inner eastern parts have the lowest. At the extreme is a life expectancy of only 68 years for one of the eastern districts (Sagene), which is 12 years less than the outer western district with highest life expectancy (Vestre Aker). There are a number of likely causes for these differences, including lifestyle factors such as physical fitness, nutrition and smoking patterns. However, increasingly, another source of poor health has been identified in recent research: *differences* in education and income. In addition to material living conditions and individual factors, the degree of social equality in an area may also have an impact (Roux, 2001).

From Africa

Most of The River dealers we encountered were black. Either they themselves or their parents had grown up in Africa. The majority of the dealers, and half of the dealers we interviewed, came from Somalia. A variety of other sub-Saharan African countries were represented as well, such as Eritrea, Ghana and Congo. Many journalists have reported on the cannabis dealing at The River, but this simple and very visible fact is rarely addressed. There is a strong connection between the skin colour and African background of the young men at The River, their living conditions and their everyday life in Norway, and the fact that they have come to monopolise the cannabis market at The River.

Most of the Somali in Norway came as refugees, which means they have escaped persecution or politically motivated violence at home. A minor wave of refugees came as a result of the war with Ethiopia during the 1980s. A larger group came as a result of the civil war, after the north-western region of Somaliland declared its independence in 1991. The year after, a humanitarian disaster and famine made the Somali known throughout the world (Gundel, 2002). The civil war led to a breakdown of societal institutions and the development of distrust and fear. Local clan leaders became regional warlords who resisted democracy (Luling, 2006). In recent times, full-scale war has ravaged Somalia, several of the major cities have been destroyed and there have been numerous civilian massacres. At present, there is no functioning national state, and the population is still among the poorest in the world.

The Somali are one of the largest immigrant groups in Norway, with almost 10,000 in Oslo alone. They are also one of the youngest immigrant populations, one that has been growing rapidly in recent years.[11]

Immigrants from Somalia are doubtless among those living in the most difficult conditions in Oslo. They have the lowest level of education, the highest rates of unemployment and the lowest income. Only one in 10 30–44-year-olds has a higher education. Only one in three is in the ordinary labour market, the lowest proportion among all ethnic groups in Oslo. In addition, the Somali report the lowest frequency of interaction with ethnic Norwegians.[12] A large proportion of the Somali males are also regular users of khat.[13] Moreover, a recent report revealed that the Somali also experience more racism and discrimination than any other group. One in three had such experiences while seeking employment during the last five years, and one in five had been harassed in the workplace. Forty-two per cent reported that they had been prevented from renting or buying a house because of their ethnic origin, whereas the figures for immigrants from Pakistan or Sri Lanka, for example, were less than 10% (Tronstad, 2008).

Although we should avoid stereotyping, there is no doubt that a considerable proportion of those of African origin in Oslo live at the margins of society.

Later we will go into more detail about how The River dealers' previous experiences as refugees and asylum seekers, their recent experiences in school and in the labour market, and the fact that they are black, can help us to understand why they ended up in the illegal drug trade. We will also go into detail about how they carried their minority ethnic status and refugee experiences with them, and transformed these difficulties to masculinity construction and identities that was advantageous on the street.

Approaching The River

Our study is based on ethnographic fieldwork at The River. The most important part of the fieldwork was qualitative interviews with the dealers. The milieu was fragmented and always in flux, but there were about 50–60 cannabis dealers at this street drug market during our study. We spoke to most of them and conducted in-depth interviews with 20 of them. Later, in order to gain a better understanding of the complex illegal economy, we also interviewed two top-figures in jail who were serving prison sentences for large-scale cannabis smuggling and 15 cannabis buyers.

The most important interviewees for this book, however, were The River dealers. They were between 17 and 30 years old. Nineteen were male and belonged to minority ethnic groups (mainly African).[14] The one female was an ethnic Norwegian. About half of them had refugee backgrounds; the others had grown up in Norway. All made their living dealing cannabis, and many occasionally dealt amphetamines and cocaine too. All had a police record and experience of using illegal drugs, and in different ways, they were all devoted to what Bourgois (2003a) has labelled 'inner-city street culture'.[15]

Unlike Bourgois's crack dealers, however, the cannabis dealers in this study had much more varied relations with street culture. Some were hardcore criminal offenders, fully committed to street culture, while others just 'flirted' with street culture to distinguish themselves among their peers or because they lacked any other means of generating income. In this way, our study reveals the flux and fluidity that are more generally observed in subcultures. Subcultures are not homogeneous and may be used by participants in very different ways. We will discuss these differences in more detail in the next chapter.

We chose to interview active drug dealers rather than ex-dealers in institutions such as prisons or therapeutic communities. The main advantage of this approach was that our research participants were closer to the events of interest and less influenced by institutional settings; thus, they were less prone to rationalising their behaviour (Wright and Decker, 1994, 1997). The disadvantage was, of course, that such an approach takes a lot more time and involves greater risk for the researcher.

Accessing The River was complicated, and we did it in several steps. First, we did some initial observational fieldwork to get to know the area. Later, Sandberg started working with a group of field social workers. He joined them as they walked around the area to develop contacts among the street dealers. We made some initial contacts this way, and these led to some interviews. After a while, however, it seemed as if contact with the social workers was more problematic than helpful for our fieldwork. It was hard to recruit research participants, and we began to worry that we might be hearing stories fashioned for the welfare state apparatus.

Thus, after a while, Sandberg started working alone. He lived nearby and had easy access to the area throughout the day. The objective was to get to know the dealers, and he spent a lot of time in the area. Making contact was easier this way, because when he came alone, the dealers would approach him to sell drugs. Sandberg looked like a typical customer – a white, middle-class student. After a while, he became a familiar face and was sometimes able to hang around with dealers while they were selling drugs. During this period, he observed both transactions and the social interactions among the cannabis dealers. Because of our steady presence in the area, we were able to interview some dealers several times.[16]

Interviews that we conducted away from the drug market became our most important data source. The main reason was that at The River, looking like customers, we kept other customers away. In the interviews, we had the time and opportunity to get details about the dealers' experiences and to hear stories without interrupting their business. We conducted interviews at nearby locations, such as pubs and cafes, sometimes in the dealers' apartments. The interviews typically lasted between one and a half and two hours. They were semi-structured and conducted in an informal manner, allowing interviewees to speak freely. We paid research participants the equivalent of €27 for participation.[17] We conducted most of the interviews in Norwegian, but some were done in English because some of the research participants did not speak Norwegian.[18] All interviews were taped and transcribed. We did not experience any problems with taping. During fieldwork on the street, we relied on field notes.

Pedersen participated in about half of the interviews, most often if they were planned in advance or if two dealers were interviewed simultaneously. Having two researchers present was helpful for discussions and motivation. It also proved helpful because we noticed, and were able to follow up on, different aspects of the conversation. It also made it easier to interview two individuals at the same time, which some of the research participants preferred because it made the interview less intimidating. However, the unstructured life that many of the research participants lived often made it necessary to do interviews on the spot, immediately after they agreed to do the interview.

Conducting interviews alone versus in pairs presented different challenges and advantages. On the one hand, some of the personal relationships Sandberg developed with research participants would have been difficult to achieve had he not been alone. On the other hand, the light-hearted and 'internal' talk recorded in some interviews when two research participants were present would probably have been more difficult to get in one-on-one interviews.

The interview data must be seen as being constructed by the interaction between the interviewer and the interviewee (see, for example, Kvale, 1996; Gubrium and Holstein, 2001; Silverman, 2001, 2004, 2005; Seale et al, 2004; Denzin and Lincoln, 2005). Surprisingly, however, when taken as a whole, the correspondence among interview constellations was more prominent than the divergence. The influence of particular interview constellations and contexts on the narratives and discourses elicited can thus easily be exaggerated. We tended to hear the same narratives repeatedly. The River dealers' language use was firmly embedded in pre-fixed narratives and discourses, as is true for everyone (see, for example, Kvale, 1996; Sarup, 1996; Roemer, 1997;; Gubrium and Holstein, 2003a).

This should not be surprising. After all, as emphasised by late constructivism, language is not constructed on the spot but structurally given.[19] Illustratively, while several narratives and discourses were easily identified in different interviews, it was difficult to pin down systematic differences between interview constellations. Moreover, the young men seemed to shift between narratives depending on the course of the interview and the questions asked. As illustrated previously by Chris, the discursive repertoire was especially apparent in the shifts between the discourse of a street subculture and more conventional discourse. This two-headed role playing game (Goffman, 1963) is the first step towards what has been described by Holstein and Gubrium (2000) as the practical and artful 'narrating of the self'. Meaning thus seems to be constructed locally, from minute to minute, but always in a way that reflects the 'discursive environment', 'families of language games' (Gubrium and Holstein, 2003b) and 'shared narrative formats' (Atkinson and Coffey, 2003).

Ethics

Doing research on people actively engaged in crime raises several ethical problems. We offered research participants confidentiality, which we have strictly maintained.[20] We also tried to avoid talking about specific people or future events in order to prevent situations where we could obtain information we did not want, such as details about previous serious crimes or future crimes.[21] A more difficult issue was the possibility of further stereotyping an already marginalised group. Most of the research participants were members of minority ethnic groups, and many were Somali, the most stereotyped minority ethnic group in Norway today. Studying their involvement in violence and street drug dealing further strengthens a negative public image. Still, we hope that by describing the practical rationality of street culture we can challenge some negative stereotypes and contribute to an understanding of the more complex mechanisms involved when minority ethnic groups get involved in crime.

In interviews, research participants enact narratives and construct themselves as particular kinds of moral agents (Atkinson and Coffey, 2003). When we study drug use, drug dealing, violence and socioeconomic problems, we run the risk that interviews will elicit (and thereby reinforce) research participants' destructive identity constructions.[22] As discussed previously, interviews that emphasised criminal activity, for example, may have increased the young men's identity constructions as 'gangsters'. Sometimes The River dealers explicitly reminded us about other more positive aspects of their lives; for example, that they were religious or had special skills in performing music or writing rap lyrics. Including all aspects of research participants' lives is impossible. Trying to avoid being one sided is nevertheless important, especially in studies of marginalised people. It may also help us avoid exaggerating differences between street culture and mainstream culture.

Finally, it was difficult not to make moral judgements when research participants talked about brutal violence they had been involved in, and we sometimes did. Most of the time it was just by phrasing follow-up questions in, for example, the following way: "But aren't you afraid that they will get serious injuries?"[23] The interview situation is not an ethically isolated island in society, and there are individual limits to what one can listen to without objecting. When research participants talked about drug-related problems, we sometimes intervened towards the end of the interview to suggest that they reduce their drug intake or to give them telephone numbers of welfare organisations that could help them. The major aim of the research interviews, however, was to give The River dealers an opportunity to tell (or co-produce) their stories, not solve their drug problems or to make moral judgements. After all, these young men are well aware that society condemns them, and if they wanted help, most of them could have got it elsewhere.

Notes

[1] See Bråthen et al (2007). The inner eastern parts of Oslo have been increasing in population, but there has been no relative increase in the proportion of immigrants. In the outer eastern parts, the increase in the immigrant population has been up to four times the general increase in the population (Bråthen et al, 2007, pp 50–60).

[2] Most of the interviews are in Norwegian and translated into English. However, "the hard way" and "motherfucker" were originally English. Street language in Norway often includes a lot of English expressions. These are often picked up from popular culture, movies and music in particular.

[3] See http://hdr.undp.org/en/statistics/

[4] Norway has traditionally been homogeneous in terms of ethnicity and religion, and has a relatively egalitarian class structure (Baldwin, 1990). The Norwegian welfare state also has some special characteristics, even within the Nordic welfare regime. During the

last few decades, the most striking feature has been growing oil revenue. While Sweden and other welfare states had to make heavy cuts in social benefits and services after the financial crisis in the early 1990s, Norway avoided radical interventions (Kangas and Palme, 2005).

[5] The social welfare system in the US, however, is often coupled with inequality, poverty and a weakly developed security net (Halvorsen and Stjernø, 2008).

[6] One reason may be that a number of studies indicate that – by and large – few develop 'welfare dependency'. In a recent PhD thesis, it was documented that most of those receiving social benefits are not being permanently marginalised in the working market but seem to respond positively to upturning business cycles and labour market programmes. Some groups, such as single parents, are more vulnerable to receiving long-term support than others. However, families with backgrounds from Third World countries have lower incomes than native Norwegians yet they do not seem to have a greater tendency towards benefit dependency than others (Lorentzen, 2006).

[7] See www.politi.no/pls/idesk/docs/f1499091601/narkotikastatistikk_halvar2007.pdf

[8] The saying at The River is that a gram should cost 100 Norwegian kroner (€12–13). However, usually the customers will get less than a gram in 'a piece', so if you buy small amounts, the real price will probably lie in the official EU statistics area, that is, around €20.

[9] Morocco is supplying over 70% of the cannabis used in Europe. The figures used to be higher, but we are seeing increasing levels of production in Afghanistan and increasing domestic production in a number of European countries, in particular the Netherlands and The UK (see Sznitman et al, 2008).

[10] Oslo has the largest proportion of immigrants in Norway; 25% of the city's population is now classified as immigrants or refugees. This figure includes immigrants from all parts of the world. If one restricts it to non-Western immigrants, the number is a little less than 20%.

[11] A number of reports on living conditions have been published, and several Somali women have written autobiographies or semi-fictional novels (see, for example, Storhaug, 2003; Norderhaug, 2004; Aden, 2008). Many of these are heart-rending reports of female circumcision, patriarchate gender regimes, child abuse and systematic exploitation of the state welfare system. Oppressed women and khat-smoking men, out of step with acceptable roles and norms, are commonly portrayed. A number of critical comments on these reports have also appeared, in particular from researchers in the area. They have argued that the stories are stereotypes, with limited generalisability, and that the reality of practices such as female oppression is more complex and ambiguous than they reveal. See, for example, one of the leading Norwegian anthropologists, Thomas Hylland

Eriksen, 'De andre fortellingene' [The other stories], *Aftenposten*, 10 September 2008. Thus, descriptions of African immigrants (especially Somali) have been controversial in Norwegian public debate.

[12] See www.ssb.no/emner/00/02/rapp_200805/. For employment, see pp 76–83. For general welfare, see Fangen (2008).

[13] It is difficult to evaluate the psychosocial consequences of chewing khat, but it has been suggested that between 50% and 70% of Somali men in Oslo are regular users of the substance, and that the habit costs up to €70–€80 a day; however, these figures are probably exaggerated, and more likely approximately 20% of adult Somali men in Oslo are regular users (Anniken Sand, *Aftenposten*, 8 November 2008).

[14] Ten of the dealers had a minority ethnic background from Somalia. The others had backgrounds from Congo, Eritrea, Gambia, Ghana, Kenya, Morocco and Pakistan.

[15] See the discussion in Chapter Three.

[16] Three dealers were interviewed twice, and one three times.

[17] It seemed respectful to recognise participation and time. Some interviewees lost income from drug dealing while talking to us, and most had financial problems. We also paid them because it can be argued that it is a cardinal rule of street life that you should never do anything for nothing (Wright and Decker, 1994). Paying most likely encouraged some of the reluctant participants. One of the interviews did not work because the interviewee was more concerned about the money than about the questions. However, in the other interviews, we did not get this impression. Sometimes interviewees even seemed to forget about the money as soon as they started talking about their lives, and we had to remind them towards the end of the interview that they should get paid.

[18] In one of them, we even used one of the other young men as a translator, because the research participant spoke neither Norwegian nor English.

[19] Late constructivism was inspired by, for example, Foucault (1970), Baudrillard (1983) and Lyotard (1984). It can be seen as opposed to early constructivism, which was inspired by, for example, Goffman (1959), Berger and Luckmann (1967) and Garfinkel (1967).

[20] We have taken several steps to secure confidentiality. We did not register surnames during fieldwork, and when transcribing the interview tapes, we removed names and other identifiable elements. After transcriptions were completed, we erased the tapes. We have also taken some steps to secure confidentiality in writing about this research. We have, for example, given the participants pseudonyms, changed some information about people that was not relevant to the analysis; and, on those occasions when we use a lot of

information from a particular research participant, we attribute the information to two individuals so as not to reveal too much about any one person.

[21] For example, in one case, when one of the young men started to talk about what 'really happened' in a notorious gang-related murder, we changed the subject. This was both for our own security and to avoid getting into a dilemma about whether or not to tell the police afterwards. It was, however, more common that we established at the beginning that this was not the kind of information we were interested in.

[22] A female, middle-level and apartment-based cannabis dealer we interviewed several times during another on-going study pointed to the complex relationship she developed with us during her interviews. She was a self-reflective person and gave us much important information. At the same time, she argued that it was difficult for her to continue with the interviews because she felt that she was important for us qua dealer, and that was a role that she gradually – not least because of the interviews – wanted to relinquish. We of course respected her wish.

[23] This is different from much probing done in other street studies. For example, in a study from St. Louis, when a research participant told about shooting someone in the back of the head in an act of retaliation, the interviewer's follow-up question was: 'A lot of guys, you know, they want that satisfaction of this guy seeing you do it' (Mullins, 2006, p 87, based on data from Richard Wright, Bruce Jacobs and Richard Rosenfeld's studies). The interviewee then changed his story so that the victim turned around when getting shot, and they made eye contact. Clearly, interview questions and probing influence the answers we get from interviewees. While our probing sometimes may have inspired conventional discourse and neutralisation techniques, the probing sometimes done in the North American street studies may have inspired exaggerated claims to street masculinity and what we coin 'gangster discourse' (see also Chapter Eight).

TWO

Trajectories to The River

The River divides Oslo into its eastern, working-class parts, and the more prosperous west. Recently gentrification processes has turned the neighbourhood into a popular and expensive area. Daniel, Usman and Hassan were three of the cannabis dealers we met at this street market.

Three groups of dealers

Most of the dealers we met had roots in sub-Saharan Africa, but some came from the Arab world. They ranged in age from 17 to 30, with most of them in their twenties. To the casual passer-by, there was little to distinguish one cannabis dealer from another. In reality, however, the differences among them were quite striking, as were their trajectories to The River. To capture this diversity, we present the life stories of three dealers – Daniel, Usman and Hassan – who represent three different groups of dealers. The concept of 'street capital' will help us understand these marginalised men's different trajectories to street drug dealing (see also Sandberg, 2008b). We will also present Mette in this chapter, the only female dealer we interviewed.

Daniel and his friends were the youngest group. Most of them came from dysfunctional families and had problems at school. They felt drawn to The River by a sense of adventure. The street drug market and street culture provided an arena for enacting alternative, tough masculinities. Usman was a part of an older group of dealers. Initiated into serious crime at an early age, even as children, they gradually lost the respect of the criminal groups, not least because of their own drug habits. The River gave them a place to enact roles of authority and leadership based on age and experience. The third group consisted of refugees. They were different in many respects, but they had all come to Norway in the relatively recent past and did not speak Norwegian well. Traumatising wartime experiences, problems getting residence permits and long periods at asylum centres had marked them. Hassan's life story is, in many ways, illustrative of this group.

Daniel: street capital as distinction

Daniel and those like him were the biggest group on the drug scene, at least during the summer. They were in the lower age range of our sample. They were interested in fashion and music, and some were doubtless considered trendy, cool and stylish. Some had come from other parts of the country, but most had grown up in the working-class suburbs of Oslo. Gradually, they started to drift downtown. Some had sold cannabis in their own neighbourhoods, but they saw The River as an opportunity to become autonomous and independent, and to make more money. Others came to The River with no previous experience of dealing drugs. They had smoked cannabis, often quite regularly, but they were uninitiated in the trade around The River. Friends or acquaintances introduced them to The River and its trade. Drawn to downtown Oslo by a sense of adventure, The River seemed to them a likely place to find friends and meet young people from similar African ethnic communities. These young men were generally not involved in serious dealing, nor were they connected with the city's established criminal networks.

Daniel was 20 at the time of the interview. He had been born in Ghana but raised in Norway. When we asked Daniel for an interview, we were already on speaking terms with him. He invited us back to the rented three-room flat he shared with his girlfriend. When we arrived, she lit some incense and showed us into the living room. Furniture was sparse: a small lounge suite, a dining table and chairs. The lights were off and the curtains were partly open. A pile of DVDs was stacked next to the television positioned against one of the walls. His girlfriend offered us juice while we waited. Twenty minutes and a few telephone calls later, Daniel appeared.

Daniel had spent his whole life in one of Oslo's working–class suburbs. He played basketball and was into hip-hop. Several relatives took turns bringing him up, but from his 12th year, he moved in with his mother. Daniel was unhappy with the change: "You can't just go and pick up a son you haven't seen in 11 years and expect to take control just like that [snaps his fingers]. It won't work." He and his mother apparently remained on good terms for a few years, but they started arguing after Daniel turned 14. For Daniel, the situation was not acceptable: "I don't like people talking about me – 'You're like this, this and this....' – but that's what Ghanaian mothers are like. It was irritating." The relationship deteriorated, and he was put into residential care 'to have a break'. He liked his foster parents and staying at the various institutions. His needs were met, and he was not forced to go to school. Eventually, he was moved to a children's home close to The River, in Oslo. It was a big place with "too many kids who were always misbehaving", he recounted, laughing. He became friendly with seven or eight of the institution's young population, and they started spending time at The River. Daniel continued:

> 'We used to hang out there every day. That was while I lived at the youth institution. We headed straight to The River after school. You eat your dinner, you're full up, you push off down to The River. On Saturdays and stuff, we used to hang around from six to 12 at night. Then we'd go for a drink at a club, like. You have to make money, you know. Not everybody likes asking people for cash all the time. So while you're there, you make your own money.'

Daniel remained a minor dealer. He cheated some of his customers by selling them bark or giving them less than what they paid for, partly to compensate for his inferior position. However, he was never forced to go to The River, either for drugs or for money. His additional income was pocket money.

> 'We went there to get money for going out and enjoying ourselves, see – to have a good time. No food, 'cause everybody's got food at home. You've got food at home, and those youth institutions, they've got food too. So we didn't need food and the like. It was only for clothes, maybe, and then cash for drinks.'

Daniel's story is similar to those told by some of the other younger dealers. They congregated in the city centre, needed money, and slowly began to see The River as a way of getting it. Some of them admitted that hanging out there was not a good idea, but The River was attractive, especially to young men with an African heritage. Pakistanis and other minority ethnic groups formed large groups in the Oslo suburbs. During childhood and early adolescence, the boys of African descent always remained a minority – even within the minority. At The River, however, they could meet others with the same ethnic background. For some of the Norwegian-African boys from the provinces, this was even more palpable. Many had experienced racism, and some told about confrontations with neo-Nazis. A more prevalent feeling among all of them, however, was the sense of not belonging, of being the only person around with an African background, or being the only black person. The River offered these identity-seeking young men precisely what they lacked: a sense of belonging and security. In this particular area, they were suddenly in the majority.

The actual selling of drugs seemed relatively small scale. One of the young men told us, "We often took a turn and played basketball. The minute we got hold of 200 kroner we beat it to cool off [laughs]. Then we went home to eat and watch a movie." The River, in other words, was part of a social round with friends, a place to hang out and meet peers. While the money was important, it was not the only incentive. The money made them interesting, and girls found them attractive, but it came with a bitter aftertaste.

> 'It's the wrong sort of attention, innit? It's not real. It's like … he dresses in that sort of gear, orders whatever he wants from the bar. You know what I'm getting at, it's like that's what the girls see. They don't see how long you've been freezing out in the cold to make the money. They just don't see it, see? It's the money, they only see the money.'

For the youngest dealers, The River was where things happened. A 19-year-old dealer who was used to selling drugs elsewhere said that he always returned because, "like, you know, there's always someone to talk to. And we do lots of cool stuff together." He later called it "the pull of The River". In their accounts, Daniel and the other youths often stressed the social aspect of The River. It was a place they could get together, not least of all during the summer months. There was action – police, fights and access to drugs. It was easy to get there and to scrounge cannabis from their friends. After the joint was lit, it was passed around, so that everyone got a share.

In their own minds, these young men were fearless and confrontational. Daniel and his like saw themselves as alone against the establishment, and on the banks of The River, they were power brokers. Life there was associated with coolness and protest, with free spirits who refused to be straitjacketed (see, for example, Willis, 1977). Connell (1995) calls it 'protest masculinity', highlighting its convergence with violence, opposition to school, crime, casual labour and insistent heterosexuality. The River was a perfect place to stage the form of masculinity characterised as 'live fast, die young' (Connell, 1995). In a context of social and economic poverty, the street drug market became a site for managing and dramatising masculinity. To appear as tough, hard and macho, and to avoid being 'punks' (Mullins, 2006) was important. Hip-hop was integral to this attitude. Some of the dealers were active hip-hoppers, but more importantly, hip-hop provided a source of role models and points of reference. The River dealers identified not only with African-American experiences of being marginalised and discriminated against (which is common in hip-hop lyrics) but also with the protest masculinity that defines gangsta rap, one of hip-hop's most popular genres.

Thornton (1995) has argued that 'hipness' is a form of subcultural capital, with several similarities to Bourdieu's cultural capital. Hipness is the cultural competence and skills that are acquired by members of a subculture and that raise their status. When Daniel and his friends were dealing at The River, this raised their subcultural capital, a form of symbolic capital available for marginalised groups who felt estranged from mainstream society. By participating in street culture, they went from being black losers in mainstream society to 'thugs' and 'hustlers' in hip-hop and street culture mythology. The use of illegal drugs contributed to this identity. As argued by Blackman (2004), drugs are important cultural commodities. Drug imagery and drug symbolism is used to sell ordinary products, from soft drinks to clothes and computer hardware. To a surprisingly high degree, drugs are – often with subtle references – presented as a part of young people's leisure and lifestyle (2004, pp 52–103). Most of the young men at The River came from poor families, but the easy money they made supported a lifestyle that ordinarily would have been impossible. The money funded their conspicuous consumption of drinks, drugs and expensive clothes as outward gestures (Jacobs, 1999).

Usman: street capital as status and power

Usman and others in his situation were older than Daniel and his friends. They were commonly in their mid-twenties, and born and raised in mainly working-class areas of downtown Oslo, close to The River. Several had records as juvenile offenders and were former members of local juvenile gangs. Most had also been involved in hardcore criminal networks, but had cut off these connections themselves or been ostracised.

We met Usman at a cafe in a central part of the city, a redeveloped working-class area east of the city centre. He wore sunglasses, had smoked cannabis before the interview, and spoke freely. The first thing he brought up was the difficulty he had repaying a 50,000 NOK (Norwegian kroner) (€6,250) debt. Usman came to Norway from Pakistan at the age of six. When we interviewed him, he was 22. He had been raised by an uncle who ran a take-away food shop. Their initially good relationship foundered because his Muslim uncle disapproved of him and his friends "using dope, beer drinking and screwing chicks". Usman thought his uncle incapable of understanding what growing up in Norway was like. He spoke of his childhood.

> 'I saw older Pakistanis, and the stuff they did was absolutely fucking unbelievable. It was just sensational. When you're that age, you think you're never going to die, you know. I was 12 and had just woken up, like, and they were six to seven years older. I knew they were scumbags, the lot of them, and did all this shit, like. They counted me in, and I earned big bonuses. I was a delivery boy, like, because I looked so fucking innocent. Once I was carrying a bag. Cocaine, five kilo. Right under the nose of the cops. They were raiding a building. So they let me go, like. I was just an innocent kid with an ice cream in his hand.'

After several similar episodes, Usman was soon working regularly for the older Pakistanis. This work introduced him to gang life, particularly the then infamous 'A' and 'B' gangs.[1] Family ties dictated connections, and children were recruited when they were relatively young. The younger they were, the less likely they would be to arouse the suspicion of the police. The reward was lots of money, trips abroad and the respect and admiration of older friends. Usman also worked for himself.

'I used to be a fucking hyperactive shithead, man. Did so much crap.
There were these cousins and me. We were Pakis in a country we didn't
belong to. Always together and always broke. All the others had these
wicked pants, so why not me? I ditched school and worked illegally at
a takeaway. So I earned dough there, and sold a bit of ganja [cannabis]
on the side. First we just smoked hash and downed pills [Rohypnol]
for the fun of it. So we starting thinking: if we got a blister pack to
sell … and we earned 5,000 coins in one bleedin' day. I was getting
famous! I knew a couple of chicks from the West side who called their
mates, and suddenly half the city was ringing for pills.'

Usman developed good connections early in his career as a dealer. He made a
comfortable profit on the Rohypnol and cannabis he bought at cut-down prices.
Customers from the wealthier areas to the west of the city were willing to pay
high prices. These youngsters had money to spare and often paid more than
normal street value. These early times were Usman's days of glory, which he looks
back on with pride and joy. Earning money and being connected with the right
people gave him a sense of power and invincibility. "I knew all the big dudes on
the street, and many of them gave me protection." He admits that luck played a
part, but he gives more credit to fate and a belief in God: "Every time I work the
field, I think of God and 'Allah save me!' He saves me." 'Field' is a war metaphor,
suggestive of how he sees his life. Fatalism and belief in destiny are well known
in the street culture literature (see, for example, Bourgois, 2003a).

However, within a few years, Usman's career had peaked and plummeted. He
lost his protection, stopped working, got heavily into debt after a couple of big
projects failed, and turned increasingly to drugs. He smoked more cannabis and
took more amphetamine. The latter was the biggest problem, he said.

'It's been really difficult. Used a lot of speed; my mind's all fucked up.
Physically too, I've lost weight. The whole family's noticed it, 'cause
when you do speed, you get thinner. You start looking like a fuckin'
junkie. It's obvious you're putting yourself on the line. You feel *so* tired,
and weird, and you get paranoid. Three days on speed, like, you're in
deep paranoia land. You can't sleep, and you hear voices, see things,
think things. It happens I take roofies [Rohypnol] and hash just to
wind down from the effect of the speed [amphetamine].'

Usman once occupied a central position in the dealer hierarchy. He earned good
money and had extensive connections, but at some stage, partly because of his
own drug habit, his debts grew to unmanageable proportions. He subsequently
lost his credibility in a social network dominated by big money, debt collecting
and frequent gangland confrontations. Several times Usman tried to regain the
reputation he once had, but he failed. No one trusted him. There was a sense of
contempt in Usman's story about The River.

'We realised that The River was for idiots. The River is what you fall back on when everything else fails. Dealing in large quantities is preferable in my opinion. You don't sell 100-gram sheets down at The River. You're a dickhead if you do…. The same if you're buying. The River is the last resort, when you can't show your face anywhere. It's where dickheads buy hash.'

Nevertheless, this was where we met him. He financed his escalating drug habit and honoured old debts by selling cannabis on the streets. One of the other young men called it the 'loan department'. It was always possible to make cash easily and quickly. When dealers' drug habits got them thrown out of the criminal establishment, The River was a last resort where they did not need a mobile phone, cash or regular customers to close a deal.

Usman and those like him existed on the margins of society, but they also existed on the margins of the criminal fraternity. At The River, however, their social networks, experience and know-how translated into social status. They knew the system and dealer network better than the younger dealers and the refugees, and were therefore more valuable. At The River, they were knowledgeable and experienced. In the legal economy, they were losers. Likely jobs for them in the white economy would be poorly paid, requiring few skills and of low status. The River, however, offered them social rewards, a possibility of status, money and, not least, respectability and admiration. Being at The River can thus be seen as a 'search for respect' (Bourgois, 2003a) for many of the older dealers who were raised in Norway.

Young men like Usman often had some work experience, spoke Norwegian fluently and had contacts in mainstream society, so if they wanted, they could get a legal job. Their socialisation, drug habits and lifestyle, however, made it difficult, and being part of a minority ethnic group certainly did not make it easier (Cross and Waldinger, 1997; Rogstad, 2000). Cultural capital is accumulated cultural knowledge that confers power and status (Bourdieu, 1984). For men like Usman, their cultural capital earned them neither power nor respect in mainstream society. Their embodied street capital (or habitus), however – the product of many years of crime – gave them respect, power and status in the social context of The River. Between amateur criminals, risk-seeking young people and recently arrived refugees, they could take up old leadership roles. The street market thus also gave them a sense of community.

Hassan: converting street capital to economic capital

During the winter, the largest group at The River were the refugees. With little chance of landing a job or gaining qualifications, they made a virtue of necessity by selling cannabis. Some of the refugees had a residence permit and some did not. Those without a permit were often non-returnable refugees from Somalia. The others were nationals of various countries.

Hassan was typical of many in the group. We met him in front of an old church (see picture in Chapter Nine) near The River on a winter's night. He was a tall, powerfully built Somali. He spoke no Norwegian and only poor English. He was frustrated: "Maybe you can write a book about how we feel or how we live. And you can explain to people, to the whole world, how we live and the hell we're in." At the appointed time for the interview, we asked one of the other Somalis we had interviewed several weeks previously to join us as a translator. This is Hassan's story as recounted to us.

Hassan was born in Mogadishu, Somalia, "the most dangerous place" after civil war broke out in 1991. A series of incidents compelled him to flee the country in 2003. It started with a football match:

> 'It was relatively calm that day, and we thought we'd play football. We hadn't played for several years. There was a war on, and it hadn't been quiet enough. My brother and I played together, but he got into trouble with some other boys. I said, "We don't want to fight, we don't want to do anything." I took my brother home. Later we sat and ate with the rest of the family. But the other kids, the ones we had been fighting, followed us, armed with guns. When they reached where we lived, they started shooting. Both my brother and I were hit, me in the side and my brother here [indicates chest]. My injury was serious, and I needed hospital treatment.'

He had lost a lot of blood, but to get treatment, his family had to pay in advance. He finally got in touch with them, and they sold off personal belongings to fund his operation. His problems were not over yet, however.

> 'They were still intent on getting their own back, 'cause, you know, if you hurt someone, the person you hurt can turn round and kill you. I was very afraid, but I decided to go to them, stop feeling afraid, like. I was thinking of taking revenge, before they came and got me. I got hold of a few guns and went towards their house. Because of my injury, walking was nearly impossible. It was dark, so they couldn't see my face. I didn't want anyone to know what I was doing, because those boys belonged to the biggest clan, and it could get my family into trouble.'

Approaching under cover of darkness, he fired a few rounds at the house. He hit one of his rivals before they started firing back, and then he made his getaway. When his family heard about the fight, they sold their home and got him out of the country. Several countries and a false passport later, he set foot in Norway. Life definitely looked brighter. "I liked Norway from the start because they treated me well," he says. He was given medical treatment for his injury. He was grateful for this, and it weighed heavily on his mind that he ended up being a cannabis dealer. For the first time in the interview, he attempted to say something without the help of the translator: "I didn't want to sell cannabis, do anything illegal. They helped me, treated me well. And … and I sell drugs instead."

However, he maintains that there was not much else he could do. After his discharge from hospital, his asylum application was turned down twice, and his benefits were cut in line with new immigration legislation. He lost his right to housing benefits and was forced to leave the asylum centre. Confused, he set off for Sweden and stayed with some friends for a few months. He was soon detained, however, and returned to Norway. The Schengen Convention requires all illegal aliens to be returned to the country of first entry. The Norwegian police picked him up at the airport, transported him to the largest police station in Oslo, and then set him down in the city centre, where he was left to his own devices.

Hassan was a non-returnable refugee. He was a failed asylum seeker, and Somali policy refused entry to non-voluntarily repatriated citizens. Returning voluntarily was not an option for him, because the clan he had clashed with would be out to retaliate. Moreover, rumours abounded in Somalia that refugees returned from Europe with money lining their pockets. He could be set upon and killed for either reason. Thus, living on the street in Oslo was preferable. He slept in parks in the summer when it wasn't too cold, and passers-by gave him food. Later, a welfare office organised a bed at a hostel where he shared a room with another refugee. Hassan survived on 60 NOK per day (equivalent to €7.5)[2] and reported that he sometimes fainted from hunger. Gradually, then, cannabis dealing at The River seemed like a more attractive alternative.

> 'It was easy. I got to know a guy at the hostel and he taught me. I was trained, two or three days, to see how it worked. They said, "Look, this is how we do it." They taught me to tell whether people wanted to sell or buy, about the uniformed police and plain-clothes police, so I could protect myself. I've never had any problems with customers to date. I only do business with Norwegians.'

When he came to Oslo the second time, he soon realised the financial potential of the drug scene. Within a couple of days, he had acquired the basic knowledge he needed and was ready to start dealing. Hassan's story was similar to that of many refugees. Non-returnable refugees were caught in a no-win situation and received harsh treatment from the government. Somalia was only willing to accept voluntary returnees, and the Norwegian government was doing its utmost to make life as difficult as possible in an effort to convince them that staying in Norway was simply not feasible. If they tried entering other countries in Europe, they were promptly returned.

We spoke to another non-returnable Somali, aged 20, who compared himself with the other young men at The River:

> 'I am staying here for several reasons. First, I don't have money. Second, I'm almost nobody. Because I don't have citizenship, I don't have my own clothes, a place that I can travel to, somewhere I can get a job. Nothing, nada, null. Actually, I'm nobody. The government, they just left me somewhere.'

He asked us several times during the interview what we thought he should do, and whether we had a job for him. The previous excerpt and our conversations with the other refugees all reek of desperation and despair. The refugees were depressed and felt abandoned. They were often homeless and isolated. Several times, they said that if they died, no one would know who they were. Some woke up at night screaming. Some relived violent incidents from the civil war in Somalia. Their accounts are similar to what psychiatrists call post-traumatic stress disorder. Loss of individuality and identity were also painful – the feeling of being 'nobody', as the young man mentioned previously states.

Although refugees who possessed residence permits and those who did not had different problems, their similarities justify grouping them in the same category. First, they had all come to Norway as teenagers or in their early twenties. They had all stayed at provincial asylum centres for two or three years, waiting for the authorities to deal with their applications. The centres had few activities, and they grew increasingly accustomed to lassitude. Because they were asylum seekers, they were not allowed to learn Norwegian, to get a job or even to qualify for a job. Whether they left the centre because they finally got a residence permit or because they were tired of waiting, they were ill prepared for the rigours of the labour market. The first few months at the asylum centre were not too bad, they told us, but the constant waiting soon became frustrating. Officials were often disrespectful, to the point of humiliation, according to some. The refugees had language problems and did not understand Norwegian customs and institutions. They also repeatedly felt that they were being treated poorly. According to Lindner, depression is a common response to humiliation, along with drug use, aggression and religious conservatism (Lindner, 2000, pp 374–5). Except for religious conservatism, we observed all these responses among the refugees at The River.

Another common experience of the refugees was the high cost of getting to the West: some had paid up to $5,000. Transportation was fraught with difficulties, such as dangerously overcrowded boats. The plan was to repay their families after establishing themselves in Europe. Their failure to do so caused widespread depression and embarrassment, especially when they had dependants waiting back home. Given their hopes of life in the West, ending up as petty criminals and members of a generally despised social group was hard to bear. Some came from wealthy families and were used to being shown respect. In Norway, they were disrespected for being refugees, and doubly so when they were petty criminals down at The River.

Hassan's and the refugees' habitus, which was moulded by their upbringing in a war-torn society, did not force them to become criminals. However, in the meeting between their habitus and Norwegian social space, small-scale drug dealing stood out as one of only a few ways they could make money. The refugees had little cultural capital (in the form of education, work skills and language abilities), but they knew how to fight and had seen a lot of violence. They therefore had experiences they could use in street culture. In a Bourdieuian framework, we can say that they had a habitus they could convert to a form of embodied street capital. Moreover, at The River, they could convert their habitus into economic capital in a way that would hardly be possible in any other social contexts.

Mummy's boys and helpless refugees

In media news coverage, the dealers at The River were seen as one group of 'Africans' or 'Somalis'. However, as illustrated by Daniel, Usman and Hassan, there are prominent differences between the dealers. Daniel and his friends, for example, had more in common with adolescents/young adults generally than they had with refugees who had recently arrived in Norway. The dealers themselves were conscious of the differences, and it affected their perceptions of each other.

Refugees were sceptical of the younger dealers. One of them expressed dismay over the "mummy's boys" who lived at home, received hot meals and clean clothes, and still frequented The River. In his opinion, they were to blame for most of the robberies that had given the area a bad name. They were just in it for the fun or to get money for drugs. To the refugees, the younger dealers were immature kids on the lookout for thrills. They had no good reason to sell cannabis, and they undermined the refugees' claim that dealing at the street drug market was a matter of survival. Thus, it was important for the refugees to distance themselves from both the young thrill-seeking boys and the dealers in larger criminal networks.

The Norwegian-raised dealers often felt sorry for, and sympathised with, the refugees. At the same time, they were upset about the continuing trickle of new refugees. "There are more refugees here than in the asylum centres," one remarked. They showed contempt for the distinctly "uncool", slightly older refugees. The latter had little of what Thornton (1995) described as 'subcultural capital': they did not set the trends in fashion or music, and they tarnished the image of The River as a "cool hangout". The younger dealers' identity construction of themselves as superior and competent was ruined by the presence of inept refugees. One of Daniel's friends remarked indignantly, "Why they come here is beyond me. To fuck the place up, or what? They're given a chance in life, like. Go to school, get a job. But they turn to crime instead." The young dealers raised in Norway were annoyed with the refugees because they were neither street wise (Anderson, 1990) nor conversant with the Norwegian society. "They can't even say 'hello' in Norwegian," said another, laughing. In Norway, the status of minority ethnic groups has previously been described as being dependent on successfully accommodating different cultures (Prieur, 2004; Vestel, 2004). Proficiency in both the minority and majority cultures, and in manoeuvring between them, gives one the most prestige. This is, for example, apparent in language skills. Thus, the refugees' status was low, even down at The River.

The last thing they'd do is hang out here

Usman and those like him had been members of criminal fraternities, but they fell from grace. Others, however, excelled. Promotion through the dealer grades was possible for people with a talent and an interest. One of the younger dealers, Ahmed, started selling at The River, but he was promoted to the job of smuggling large consignments of cocaine and cannabis into the country. Suddenly, he made big money and lived in expensive apartments. However, after a time, he found large-scale operations difficult to cope with. As he explained, "Instead of earning about 1,000 [NOK] a day, we were suddenly grossing 10,000 [NOK] every hour, like. It grew out of hand." Not the least of his problems was having drugs constantly on hand. Ahmed started passing free drugs around and used more himself:

> 'It's like – when you're sitting there with so much, you think, "It won't matter if I use a bit more, it won't make much difference if I take a bit more." And cocaine, you know, it's very addictive. So you've got, say, 50 grams of cola [cocaine], and suddenly four or five days later, it's gone, like, used up. And you owe money big time. So you take another consignment, and you buy that on tick too. In the end, you're in a bigger hole of debts and stuff.'

Ahmed's debts grew and grew. His own estimate was 200,000 NOK (€25,000), but his creditors put it at 600–700,000 NOK, he told us. Calculating the interest and prices of large quantities of illegal drugs is not easy. He found himself at the riverside again, this time to pay off his creditors. Ahmed's and Usman's stories illustrate an important point: those who aspire to a criminal career have failed if they are still hanging around The River.

Senior figures in the established criminal networks confirm this picture. A man in his forties who had been a top-level figure in the Norwegian cannabis market called The River a "slum". He said that the cannabis was of poor quality, and there was dishonesty and trouble. His connections, therefore, stayed clear of the area, and he could not really understand why anybody would care about The River people. From his vantage point – an elevated position in the drug market – The River was primitive and of no account. The "big boys" were somewhere else.

The public associate The River with drugs, deprived minority ethnic groups and antisocial behaviour. The cannabis dealers tended to agree. Many said it was difficult to make really good friends there. Drugs and debts were rife, and getting money was people's main preoccupation. It was an unforgiving environment, and most thought only of themselves. One of the refugees said he knew most of the dealers, but there was no solidarity among them: "People see each other, 'How ya doing?', and that's as far as it goes." When he had earned enough money for the day, he preferred to socialise with his own friends, people he had known for some time. Asked whether any of the young men at The River were his friends, he looked insulted. "You think I've got good mates here? I've got some good mates, but the last thing they'd do is hang out here," he said indignantly.

The River became a hard place to live because the dealers had a range of difficulties. One of the young men spoke about The River dealers more generally:

> 'Everybody's got problems. Some play the slot machines, some drink, some do pills. They've all got problems, but they don't talk about them. And they all solve their problems [by smoking cannabis and dealing drugs]. They think … some have a hashish problem, some have a family, others are on their own here. They have no family, no mother and father. And no one looks after them, sees them. They head off in the wrong direction.'

There were issues with housing, employment, addiction, gambling and family relations. On top of this, many of the refugees had problems with their residence permits and papers. However, given the relentlessly tough climate at the drug scene, it did not pay to air their problems in public. 'The code of the street' (Anderson, 1999) dominated, and the dealers tended to use what we later conceptualise as 'gangster discourse' when they spoke with each other.

Nevertheless, the young men were also altruistic and caring. As attested by Daniel, life at The River did produce friendships. Sometimes the bond was precisely that tough manner, and because they all had problems, they did not feel rejected or different. Abdil, one of the refugees, had befriended Mette. They had met in one of The Riverside parks, shared joints and were soon dealing together. Abdil called her his best friend, his soulmate. If one of them was thinking about something, the other sometimes started talking about it. They shared other things as well:

> 'If I've got this problem, I don't go round shouting about it. I don't wear my heart on my sleeve. I don't cry in public. I don't cry. Can't remember the last time I cried, you know. I do not cry, and I don't show people anything. That's the reason. Mette, she's like that too. Doesn't show anything.'

They were hard, and they were sensitive. They lived on the street, which in itself created a bond. Not talking about problems – of which they had more than their fair share – was a way of protecting themselves. Mette confirmed Abdil's version of their relationship. She said that with Abdil, she could talk about almost everything, apart from family problems. However, more important than the verbal communication was his support: "We support each other whatever the situation;

if we're out of 'startings', we start each other. Whatever happens, we help each other." 'Startings' is a few grams of cannabis needed to start the day as a dealer. In the event of a fight or violence breaking out, they also helped each other out. Although Abdil had grown up in a war-ravaged country in Africa and Mette had grown up in a peaceful community in southern Norway, they felt a kind of kinship, a bond of destiny. In Mette's words:

> 'We live the same life. Our lives are just as hard.… You need to think how you're going to make it. Think of money the whole time, and if you've got money, you have to think about food, about drink. And then you, kind of, live most of your life on the street.'

Despite their different backgrounds, they felt they were similar in many respects. They had found one another among the ostracised and had built a robust friendship. The River community was unforgiving, a place where interpersonal trust was difficult and risky. Nevertheless, dealers formed attachments and strong emotional ties. Some found friendship, others a sense of security in the area. That sense of refuge and belonging eluded them elsewhere.

A girl on The River

Mette was one of the few females who sold cannabis at The River. She was ethnically Norwegian and in her late teens. Raised in a small town in Norway, she got into trouble with her family, dropped out of secondary school and gradually drifted towards the capital. Mette soon learned about The River and its opportunities. She described the first time she came into contact with the cannabis dealers:

> 'Soon as you see them, and because you're a girl, like, when you meet them they're all over you trying to get you back home. Always trying to touch you up and all that stuff. But if you tell them to "bugger off" or give them a good shove so they know who they're dealing with, and I'm not interested, like, they give up sooner or later. They do really. So today everything's OK, on The River, like. I know every one of them now.'

For the young dealers, these first encounters aroused their sexual curiosity. After several rejections, they cooled off. Mette was proud of her success in her new role, claiming a place for herself on the men's turf. She sold cannabis, she mastered gangster discourse, and like the male dealers, she often became involved in trouble and fights. Sometimes it even seemed as if she had to be tougher than the men to be accepted. What men do is usually defined as masculinity. If we approach gender as praxis, putting biology aside, we can see how men can perform femininity and women can perform masculinity. From this perspective, it is possible to see how

Mette performed a form of masculinity that resonated with street masculinity (Mullins, 2006).

Although there were few girls selling cannabis, there were some at the outskirts of the drug scene. As part of the project, we also interviewed some Somali girls who liked being downtown.[3] Some were afraid of the area; others said that their fear was groundless because they were Somali and their fellow Somalis would not harm them. Several had been offered cannabis but had refused because they knew the boys would "want something in return". Nevertheless, personal relationships sometimes developed between some of these girls and the cannabis dealers, but they were always kept at arm's length. Here are Ahmed's words:

> 'They're not with us, because they don't want interference with the police. See? We tend to gather in a group, two or three of us. And the girls, they sit on a bench. Then they drift off, 'cause we forget they're there, like. We don't speak to them because they're not with us.... So they get miffed and get up and leave. It's funny, but that's how it is.'

Although they were acquainted with the young men, the few girls who frequented The River remained outsiders. They were excluded because they were not dealers and not devoted to street masculinity. The difference between Mette and these other girls underlines what other studies of street crime have found. Women sometimes seem to have a choice: either accept a place on the fringes of the group, or claim a place like a man, and be treated as such (Miller, 2001). If the girls have sexual dealings with the male members of the gang, it can muddy the waters. Mette discovered this when she paired off with one of the dealers. Suddenly he felt obliged to protect her and stopped her doing what she wanted. Accordingly, she felt she had forfeited some of her hard-earned respect. Being accepted as 'one of the boys' grew increasingly difficult, and the relationship foundered.

Most research into drug dealing is about men, especially studies of street culture. The evidence suggests a wider reality that these studies may have missed. Women are active in the illicit drug economy. Indeed, studies of criminal subcultures have been criticised for overlooking and failing to identify the roles and positions of women (Miller, 2001). Recent studies cast some light on female drug dealers, some of whom occupy positions of authority, operating without male protection (see, for example, Morgan and Joe, 1996; Denton and O'Malley, 1999). At The River, however, few women were to be seen.

The River dealers' street capital can be seen in their ability to identify plain-clothes police and avoid arrests (see also Johnson and Natarajan, 1995; Jacobs, 1996, 1999), their technical and mythological knowledge of illegal drugs (see also Lalander, 2003) and their ability to organise and make good deals when both buying and selling drugs (see also Adler, 1985; Bourgois, 2003a; Hoffer, 2006). The most important feature of street capital, however, is readiness to use violence (see Wolfgang and Ferracuti, 1967; Luckenbill and Doyle, 1989; Anderson, 1999; Vigil, 2002; Bourgois, 2003a). Street capital is gendered and closely linked to street masculinity (Mullins, 2006). This is probably why there were so few females dealing at The River.

Trajectories to the street

The trajectories described provide an indication of typical careers and life stories. For each of these groups, some economic and social motives also stand out as the most consistent keys to understanding why they started dealing drugs.

Daniel and those like him grew up in Oslo's outer working-class suburbs and had problems at school and in the labour market. Most of them were from rather poor families and they wanted money to buy clothes and drinks – conspicuous consumption to impress the girls. Money was a means to empowerment and control: when they had money, people suddenly took notice of them. At the same time, The River community also provided a stage on which to act out identities and dominance roles. Dealing became a 'tie sign' (Goffman, 1961) and created a bulwark against established society. The street capital they gradually accumulated functioned as a distinguishing mark. Street culture offered social contacts, new friends and membership of a hidden society. Within this culture, protest masculinity dominated (Connell, 1995). Protest masculinity is a marginalised form that reworks themes of masculinity in society at large in a context of poverty. It is a protest born of childhood experiences of powerlessness that takes form as an exaggerated claim to the potency that society attaches to masculinity (Adler, 1992). Gangsta rap can be seen as an exaggerated claim to the potency ascribed to black masculinity. Protest masculinity is a collective practice, and The River can be seen as a place for active and collective constructions of black protest masculinity.

Usman and those like him had both social and economic motives for dealing at The River. Spurned by the criminal fraternity, their social connections were cut, along with access to easy money. They had lost credibility in the established criminal networks and, accordingly, were seen as unreliable. At the same time, they had chronic financial worries. Years of crime had left some with considerable debts, and others needed money to finance their escalating drug habits. Dealing at The River offered a dependable income. However, they also had social motives. Without the income from dealing, they faced the lowest-paid and least respected jobs in the legitimate economy. At The River, the know-how and leadership abilities they had gained through many years of crime were appreciated. Between amateur criminals, risk-seeking young people and recently arrived refugees, they could hold sway. Thus, Usman and his like got a sense of community and respect from The River. Their street capital gave them status and power. Without the drug scene, they risked social isolation and loneliness.

Hassan and the other refugees had more plainly economic motives for dealing at The River. On the whole, making money was the overriding concern for the refugees. In short, they converted their habitus from war-inflicted countries into street capital and thus also into economic capital. The non-returnables were officially barred from the labour and education markets. In the highly regulated

Nordic welfare states the underground economy 'off the books' is also small, as compared with the US for example (Venkatesh, 2006). In the US it employs a large number of both legal and illegal refugees, but for the refugees at The River this was not an option. In this way, life for the excluded can be harder in more regulated economies.

Those with residence permits felt socially excluded from the labour market, and, with poor Norwegian language skills, it was difficult to get the qualifications that would gain them entry. After years of sitting and waiting in asylum centres, they were as poor as they were on the day they set foot in Norway in terms of wider qualifications, job training and education.

The wider picture shows how macro-structural characteristics push some groups into the illicit drug trade. Problems at school and the workplace, ethnic discrimination, and government asylum and immigration policies are all contributing factors. At the same time, the drug trade also has important enticements, such as the excitement, the opportunity for identity formation related to subcultures and, most importantly, easy money. This distinction between macro-structural and subcultural explanations will be important in the next two chapters as well.

We have described three trajectories to The River and its community of dealers. Of course, these routes are simplifications: the dealers resist compartmentalisation in many details. Nevertheless, speaking broadly, several of the young men who appear later in this book – Amin, Aser, Denis, Ebo, John, Mattar and Wari – share Daniel's trajectory to street drug dealing. They were young and excitement-seeking. Usman's trajectory is shared with Chris from Chapter One, Ahmed mentioned above and Rashid and Johs who will be introduced later in the book. All had failed in established criminal networks and ended up in, or returned to, The River. Finally, Hassan's trajectory was shared by Abdil, Abdullah, Ali, Mohamed, Omar and Sharif, all of whom were refugees.

Notes

[1] The minority ethnic gang scene in Oslo is liquid and constantly changing, but in the last decades there have been two main constellations. The first was labelled 'Young guns'. It merged with another group in the early 1990s, and became known as the 'A' gang. The second constellation developed as a reaction to this gang formation and was labelled the 'B' gang. Chris (introduced in the Chapter One) had been a member of one of these groups.

[2] The same amount was mentioned by several interviewees. It was 'emergency' support from the welfare office (see Chapter Four).

[3] Based on data obtained by MA student Mette Løvgren.

THREE

Street capital

Throughout daytime there is a multitude of people in this area, but after dark young ethnic minority men devoted to a violent street culture dominate. We coin the knowledge and competence you need in order to survive in this environment *street capital*.

Theoretical framework

The most important concept introduced in this book is 'street capital'. Street capital is inspired by Pierre Bourdieu, the French sociologist. Street capital is knowledge, skills and objects that are given value in a street culture. The concept is used to capture the 'cultural capital' of a violent street culture. We have already seen how the concept in a rather commonsensical way can help us understand why Daniel, Usman and Hassan started dealing cannabis. In this chapter, we hope to demonstrate further the fruitfulness of such a theoretical framework when studying, for example, practical rationality, the social and historical process of embodied dispositions, and the complex relationship between socioeconomic constraints and human agency.

Further, to capture the narratives that the young men live by, we will introduce two concepts: 'gangster discourse' and 'oppression discourse'. People are not fully committed to a subculture. When the dealers at The River switch between subcultural and conventional discourses, as Chris did in the first chapter, we see the fluidity and complexity of the subculture. This can be illuminated by contemporary discourse analysis, for which the French historian, sociologist and philosopher Michel Foucault has been an important influence. Bourdieu's and Foucault's theoretical frameworks are quite different, but they are still related. In this context, gangster discourse, for example, can be seen as the most important 'linguistic practice' (Bourdieu, 1991) of a violent street subculture where street capital is the dominant symbolic capital.

Our objective in this book is to combine insights from the theoretical frameworks of Bourdieu and Foucault in a study of street subculture.[1] Let us therefore begin by presenting some concepts from these two frameworks more in detail.

Social space, capital and habitus

According to Bourdieu (1977), modern society is constituted by an ensemble of relatively autonomous 'fields', with each field prescribing its particular values and possessing its own regulative principles.[2] 'Social space' is the multidimensional space constructed by the different kinds of power or capital that are current in the different fields. Agents and groups of agents are defined by their relative position in this social space (Bourdieu, 1991, pp 229–30). The 'field' has some interesting similarities with street culture as conceptualised by Bourgois (2003a): it 'presents itself as a structure of probabilities – of rewards, gains, profits and sanctions' (Bourdieu and Wacquant, 1992, p 18). Both the field and street culture are arenas for constant struggles for power, status and respect, and thus the main site for the practice of what Nietzsche (1968) labelled the 'will to power'.[3]

The dealers at The River were at the bottom of both mainstream society and larger criminal networks' hierarchies, and thus at the bottom of social space. They were, nevertheless, constantly involved in a struggle for legitimate power. For Bourdieu (1986), cultural capital is legitimate power. It is one of three forms of symbolic capital (recognised and legitimate authority).[4] The two other forms are economic capital (money and property) and social capital (social networks). Cultural capital has objectified, embodied and institutionalised forms. Of these three, the embodied form is most important for our study. *Habitus* is the individual embodied system of dispositions that is produced by historical and social conditions. It is based on past experiences, and early as well as statistically common experiences are particularly important.[5] Habitus is the practical sense or 'what is called in sport the "feel for the game"', that is, the art of *anticipating* the future of the game' (Bourdieu, 1998, p 25, emphasis in original).

We use the concept of street capital to describe better The River dealers' embodied skills and competence. Street habitus can be conceptualised as the relatively permanent and sometimes unconscious dispositions of individuals committed to street culture. It is the embodied practical sense that is seen in hypersensitivity to offences and frequent displays of violent potential. As illustrated by Chris in the opening chapter, Bourdieu's comments on intimidations are highly illustrative of the mechanisms of street culture: it 'can only be exerted on a person predisposed (in his habitus) to feel it, whereas others will ignore it' (Bourdieu, 1991, p 51).

Our use of the street capital concept highlights the practical rationality of street culture. Daniel, Usman, Hassan and the other young men at The River started dealing because they needed the money and had few other places to earn it. The street market was a place where they could pursue status and respect, which they were denied in mainstream society. In the cannabis economy, certain groups have realistic prospects of success, and in this way, crime and drug dealing are strategic choices. At the same time, early experiences embedded in The River dealers' bodies – wartime experiences, socialisation into criminal networks, and a feeling of estrangement from mainstream society – drove them into dealing. The concept of habitus addresses this tension between structure and agency in human behaviour (Bourdieu, 1990). Habitus is the structure within the actor, both enabling and structurally limiting different individual strategies.

The concept of street capital also reflects a tension between economic and cultural explanations of poverty and crime. This dichotomy has organised the North American debate about the so-called inner-city urban underclass. In short, liberals have argued that cultural values emerge from specific social circumstances and reflect class and racial position (Wilson, 1987, p 14), while conservatives have emphasised an autonomous 'culture of poverty' (Lewis, 1968) or 'culture of dependence' (Murray, 1984). As Bourdieu points out, inferior class position (socioeconomic structures) leads to the absence of cultural capital. Street capital results from having little to lose in mainstream society and is a form of power that the structurally oppressed can use. At the same time, while accumulating street capital, people develop and uphold a violent street culture. Street capital is thus shaped by socioeconomic structures, such as migration and discrimination, while also being a self-reinforcing cultural product. In this way, a street capital framework reflects the tension between agency and structural analysis, and includes insights from both cultural and economical studies (see also Sandberg, 2008a).

However, a theoretical framework of street capital and street culture also needs to conceptualise language use and to acknowledge the ways in which discourse shapes dispositions. In many respects, Bourdieu theoretically acknowledges the autonomous presence and creative force of language.[6] He nevertheless tends to end up with the same point of reference – objective fields and structures outside the discourse itself.[7] Thus, in an orthodox Bourdieuian framework, conceptualising a linguistic practice as gangster or oppression discourse is not theoretically problematic in itself, but it would probably be considered less important than studying the economic and social conditions that produced it.[8]

Discourse, narrative and subject position

We use *discourse analysis* to provide our framework of street capital with a more radical social constructivist component than what Bourdieu offers. In this way, we also describe how street culture can be a 'cultural tool kit' used strategically in interactions (Swidler, 1986).[9] Despite the great variety in discourse analytical approaches, Foucault's work has inspired most of them.[10]

He emphasised that statements are not 'pure creation, as the marvellous disorder of the genius' (Foucault, 1972a, p 146) but belong to an underlying system of meaning, or discourse. Chris, for example, introduced in Chapter One, could not freely choose how he wanted to present himself; he was strictly limited by the discourses available in his social environment.

A discourse can be defined as being 'made up of a limited number of statements for which a group of conditions of existence can be defined' (Foucault, 1972a, p 117).[11] Couched in slightly different terms, discourses organise social experience to make them comprehensible to individuals. The River dealers used oppression and gangster discourses to organise meaning, comprehension and self-presentation. A set of narratives that occurs with certain regularity can indicate a discourse. The discourse is the underlying system of meaning that makes it possible to produce, understand and use particular narratives.[12] Identifying wide-spread narratives may therefore be a fruitful empirical starting point for discourse analysis.

Discourses define 'the possible position of speaking subjects' (Foucault, 1972a, p 122) and thus the subjects themselves. These 'subject positions' (Laclau and Mouffe, 1985) emerge from discourses and determine what individuals can say in a given social context. An individual may inhabit several subject positions in several discourses, but they cannot determine which positions to accede to. Chris's subject position, for example, became that of a *victim* in oppression discourse and that of a *gangster* in the discourse of the street subculture. In this way, discourses systematically form the objects of which they speak (Foucault, 1972a, p 49) including when these objects are people.[13]

For Foucault, analysis of contemporary and historical society is analysis of discourses.[14] They define what can be said and thought at a particular time and place in history, and are also closely embedded in social institutions. When Foucault (1965, 1970, 1977) studies psychiatry, modern science or the prison – and their related professional practices – he describes how these social institutions create, reproduce and are the products of discourses.

Subcultures

Our study of The River joins the tradition of subculture studies. This is also the tradition we suggest can benefit from the concept we develop.

> Subcultures are groups of people that are in some way represented
> as non-normative and/or marginal through their particular interest

and practices, through what they are, what they do and where they do it. They may represent *themselves* in this way, since subcultures are usually well aware of their differences, bemoaning them, relishing them, exploiting them, and so on. But they will also be represented like this by others, who in response, can bring an entire apparatus of social classification and regulation to bear upon them. (Gelder, 2005, p 1, emphasis in original)

Gelder's definition captures an interesting tension in the conceptualisation of subcultures. Street culture, for example, can be seen as a response to external pressures, such as labelling processes and socioeconomic constraints; but street culture is also the product of creative strategies and active choices. For example, Daniel used street capital as a marker of distinction, and Usman used it to get status and power. Hassan, however, mainly used the opportunities available in street culture to get money. The concepts of street capital and gangster discourse bring these levels of analysis together. Street capital and gangster discourse emerge from socioeconomic marginalisation and stigmatisation. At the same time, these processes describe how individuals embrace and create a subculture for their own benefit.

Gelder's conceptualisation of subculture evolved from a long history of research. The first important tradition is the Chicago School of Sociology in the US during the 1920s and 1930s, and the second is associated with the Birmingham Centre for Contemporary Cultural Studies in Britain during the 1970s. Both traditions are still important for contemporary studies of deviance and subculture.

A social solution to social problems

The Chicago School's main interest was qualitative urban ethnography, especially among 'deviants' and 'marginal' populations, and it is here that we find the first conceptualisation of a street subculture (for an overview, see Plummer, 1997).[15] Park and his colleagues at the University of Chicago used methods from anthropology, but they were also inspired by the urban reporting in big-city newspapers, which had been emerging in the US since the late 1800s. The Chicago School approach differed markedly from the dominant tradition of 'library research', and it established the first school of ethnographic research in sociology. Fieldwork was often conducted in an informal and unsystematic way: 'Students were encouraged to explore the city on foot, to talk with the people and to note down their observations in detail' (Lindner, 1996, pp 80–1). Tensions within the Chicago School were not about whether to do quantitative or qualitative empirical research but whether the purpose of the research should be *reporting* (enlightenment) or *reforming* (social engineering). These tensions are still present in much social science research. In its empirical studies, the Chicago School was particularly concerned about the relationship between the physical environment and culture, often referred to as 'human ecology'. The zones of transition in

Chicago were particularly interesting, because they were in a constant flux. The zones were also problem areas, and studying them thus satisfied the sometimes conflicting ideals of reporting and reforming in the School. These areas, and the groups that occupied them, were newsworthy because they were exotic, and at the same time, it was obvious that they needed reform or social engineering.

Whyte's (1943) classic *Street corner society* was based on research in a Boston slum district, but it was heavily influenced by the Chicago tradition. Whyte used an ethnographic approach to study marginalised Italian street dwellers, and his book highlights one of the basic insights of the Chicago School: as with other zones in transition and marginalised communities, the 'street corner society' is not chaotic or disorganised, rather, the problem is the failure of the local social structure to fit in with the structure of surrounding society. Such an insight is as important today as it was when the Chicago School emerged, and it is fundamental to our understanding of social life at The River.

Cohen (1955) made the conceptualisation of subcultures even more explicit. He argued that marginalised groups of youths create a deviant subculture with hedonistic, autonomous and malicious values as a social solution to social problems. This was originally a critique of Merton's (1938) individualistic strain theory. Later, Cloward and Ohlin's (1960) returned to Mertons emphasis on the utilitarian nature of crime, but in a subcultural framework. They argued that 'serious delinquents' were looking for money to spend in the conspicuous consumption of 'fast cars, fancy clothes, and swell dames' (Vold et al, 2002, p 143). If legitimate opportunities were blocked, marginalised youths turned to illegitimate enterprises, but if illegitimate opportunities were also blocked, the consequence was a non-utilitarian delinquent subculture.

Anderson (1990, 1999), Vigil (2002), Bourgois (2003a) and Venkatesh (2006, 2008) have published influential contemporary studies of street culture that carry on the tradition of the Chicago School. In a study of gangs in Los Angeles, Vigil (2002) combined a subcultural approach with routine activities explanations (Felson, 1987). Routine activities explanations are based on space/time analyses, where motivated offenders, suitable targets and an absence of capable guardians converge at certain times and places to increase the likelihood of crime. The problem with the subculture approach, Vigil argues, is the lack of evidence regarding how norms are transmitted, leading to inferences about the subculture's values that are derived mainly from behaviour. The problem with routine activities explanations is the lack of ethnographic evidence (Vigil, 2003, p 229). Combining these two theories, then, he suggests a 'framework of multiple marginality'. The macro-historical forces at work are racism, fragmented institutions, and social and cultural repression, while the macro-structural forces at work are enclave settlements, immigration and migration. Combined with socioeconomic, sociocultural and social-psychological forces, these historical and structural forces trigger socialisation into street culture.

Vigil's multiple marginality approach has many similarities with our description of street capital, especially in its embodied form as street *habitus*. The dealing of cannabis at The River can be seen as the product of macro-historical and socioeconomic forces. This is particularly evident in Hassan's and the non-returnable refugees' stories, but economic and social exclusion (Young, 1999), migration and discrimination are also crucial to our understanding of Daniel's and Usman's trajectories to The River. We will discuss these marginalisation processes thoroughly in the next chapter.

Despite the usefulness of Vigil's approach, it also illustrates one of the criticisms directed at the Chicago School: it does not 'approach the casualness of the worlds' and suggests 'too much commitment, determinism, instrumentality, and stability in membership' (Irwin, 1977, p 18). More generally, marginalisation approaches also often fail to account for positive experiences within the subculture, or the 'seductions of crime', to use Katz's (1988) famous phrase. This criticism of the Chicago School partly follows its emphasis on violent juvenile gangs, offenders and homeless people, but it is also the direct consequence of the subcultural approach.

Opposition and resistance

The Birmingham School had a quite different and somewhat broader approach to subcultures than the Chicago School. French semiotics and Gramscian Marxism influenced theory, and researchers began studying a more diverse group of subcultures and their representations in mass media (for an overview, see Turner, 1990).[16] According to Gelder (2005, p 9), subculture studies are a response to the 'recognition that "society" is in fact host to an extensive range of social practices, some of which are "alternative" or "unconventional", others of which are transgressive or even oppositional'. The Birmingham School's neo-Marxist framework led it to emphasise the oppositional element in subcultures. The perspective of resistance and opposition is important for understanding street culture at The River as well, but it must be moderated.

The Birmingham School expanded the subculture theoretical framework of the Chicago School, but there are also many similarities. Willis's (1977) famous study of white UK working-class boys for example, has parallels in the Chicago School tradition. Miller (1958) argued that lower-class culture has certain focal values: getting into trouble with the police, showing toughness, manifesting street smarts (outsmarting and conning others), experiencing excitement, being lucky and maintaining freedom from constraint by authority figures. He argued that juvenile gangs reflect these class values.

Willis (1977) examined why working-class boys end up with working-class jobs. His approach was ethnographic, and he conceptualised a 'counter-school-culture', which shared many characteristics with the delinquent subcultures described by the Chicago School. For example, at the heart of Willis's counter-school-culture were cultural articulations – smoking, drinking, being street smart, stealing, having sex and fighting. These experiences gave the young men a fascinating aura of *difference*. Or as one of his research participants put it:

> ... we've been through all life's pleasures and all its fucking displeasures, we've been fighting, we've known frustration, sex, fucking hatred, love and all this lark, yet he's known none of it [directed at the 'ear'oles', young men devoted to school and middle-class culture]. He's never been with a woman, he's never been in a pub. (Willis, 1977, p 16)

As with Daniel and his friends, Willis's boys saw themselves as having exciting, fascinating and rewarding lives, as opposed to the boring lives of youths dedicated to school and middle-class society. This was how the boys got self-respect and respect from others. Willis's core argument is that the counter-school-culture creatively opposes school and middle-class values by imitating the male shop-floor culture of the factory. Moreover, and more importantly, when the jobs in the factory come to represent freedom, autonomy and transcendence, the working-class boys culturally reproduce class society.

Transferring this analysis to contemporary society highlights some interesting historical developments. In the same way as with Willis' boys, The River dealers associate manual labour with the social superiority of masculinity, while mental labour is associated with the social inferiority of femininity (Willis, 1977, p 148). In post-industrial society however (Bell, 1973), manual labour in factories is on the decline and 'feminine' service sector jobs are on the rise. For the young men at The River, the alternative to the drug economy was not jobs in the factory but in shops such as 7-Eleven. Service sector jobs do not affirm masculinity in the same way that manual labour does in working-class culture. For groups of marginalised youths in contemporary Western society, a violent street culture may therefore replace working-class culture as the main symbolic resource, and point of imitation, for both opposition and resistance.

In a brief section of his book, Willis also discussed the relationship between language and the oppositional culture. He writes that the young boys expressed their resistance as antagonism to the dominant bourgeois mode of signification and continued that 'language is no less rich in the counter-school-culture than in the conformist one' (Willis, 1977, pp 124–5). Gangster discourse illustrates this.

Willis's study of working-class culture has been celebrated as a classic, but is nevertheless controversial. It has, for example, been criticised for adopting the perspective of 'the lads' at the cost of the other boys and the girls, and thus accepting their worldview (Potter 1996).[17] The criticism is embedded in contemporary *discourse analysis*. Discourse analysis emphasise that self-reported data should not be regarded as descriptive of 'reality', but rather analysed as artful interpretative work in concrete interaction. Self-reported data are also mainly indicative of larger cultural discourses that 'speak through the subjects'. This far-reaching criticism is often called 'postmodern' and thus dismissed. The critique is nevertheless important, even though the discourse analytical solution may be too radical.

Willis's classic study is also at the core of some of the criticisms of the Birmingham School found in 'post-subcultures' studies. Bennett and Kahn-Harris (2004) criticise the Birmingham School for a failure to consider local variation in youths' responses to music and style.[18] They also argue that the increasing fragmentation of youth style causes a breakdown of the subcultural division. The post-subcultural approach favours other concepts over subculture, including 'scenes' (Irwin, 1977), 'tribes' (Maffesoli, 1996) or 'neo-tribes' (Bennett, 1999), 'lifestyles' (Reimer, 1995; Miles, 2000) and 'temporary sub-stream networks' (Weinzierl, 2000). The objective is to account for more cultural fragmentation, flux and fluidity, and to avoid homogeneous conceptualisations of cultures. The criticism from the post-subculture perspective highlights an important problem with all forms of subculture studies. A subculture theoretical framework has an inherent and almost necessary tendency to exaggerate the homological unity and consistency of the subculture and consequently also to exaggerate its differences from 'conventional' or 'mainstream' society (Jenkins, 1983).

In this study, despite these criticisms, we still follow the subcultural tradition in emphasising the structural level of culture. Bourdieu (1984), for example, convincingly demonstrates that culture is not a 'supermarket of style' (Polhemus, 1994) but strictly organised by a structure of class relations. Historical and social processes embodied in the individual habitus cause stability, inertia and social hierarchies in cultural taste and dispositions. Ethnicity and gender are similar limitations to culture. In the same way, but from another perspective, Foucauldian discourse analysis demonstrates how culture is organised in pre-structured narratives and discourses.

Tension between agency and structure, change and stability, and ambiguity and coherence is nevertheless present throughout this book. Bourdieu's main objective is to confront and overcome this tension by using the concepts of habitus and capital. After Foucault (who emphasise the structural level of discourse), discourse analysis has also included insights from the more agency-centred approaches of symbolic interactionism, ethnomethodology and social psychology.

Subcultural capital

Thornton (1995) introduced the concept of 'subcultural capital' to the Chicago and Birmingham traditions to describe the 'taste culture' of the UK club scene. She argues that the cultural hierarchies of the club scene are based on distinctions between the 'authentic versus the phoney, the "hip" versus "mainstream", and the "underground" versus media' (Thornton, 1995, pp 3–4). As with other subcultures, club culture members reinterpret the social world to elevate their social status relative to mainstream society. Inspired by Bourdieu's (1984) descriptions of the connection between taste and the social structure, Thornton describes 'hipness' as a form of cultural capital that can be both embodied and objectified. Moreover, it is also based on the 'second nature' of knowledge and convertible into economic capital (Thornton, 1995, pp 10–12). However, Thornton also questions Bourdieu's approach. She lists different forms of capital described by Bourdieu (cultural, economic and social), as well as some subcategories (academic, intellectual and artistic), and argues that they are effective and active only among the economic and cultural elite. By applying the concept of subcultural capital, she thus claims to challenge Bourdieu's hierarchical model of society and to reveal pockets of resistance, alternative taste cultures and alternative cultural hierarchies (see also Hall, 1992).

Thornton's study is important because it introduces Bourdieu to subcultural studies. Her study has of course inspired our conceptualisation of street capital, which can be seen as a more specific variant of subcultural capital. Unfortunately, however, she only describes the relationship between her approach and Bourdieu's in a few passages, and the descriptions are somewhat problematic. First, the autonomy of fields that Thornton calls for has already been described by Bourdieu (1993) in a study of the field of cultural production. Second, Thornton argues that subcultural capital clouds class relations, and she avoids the habitus concept. The concept of capital thus loses some of its essence and explanatory value. Third, when she simultaneously rejects the Birmingham School's emphasis on both development of theory and socioeconomic structures, she seems to accept the 'fantasy of classlessness' inherent in some subcultures (Jensen, 2006, p 265). This may not be a problem when describing clubbers, but it is highly problematic in studies of socioeconomically and ethnically marginalised groups. For these groups, class, gender and ethnicity are crucial limitations to the available choices of 'taste culture' and 'lifestyles'. Our approach, therefore, has even more important parallels in the contemporary literature on street culture.

Street capital

The two most important influences on the conceptualisation of street capital are Anderson's (1999) 'code of the street' (see also Anderson, 1990) and Bourgois's (2003a) 'inner-city street culture'. Anderson (1999, p 33) describes the code of the street as:

> ... a set of informal rules governing interpersonal public behavior, particularly violence. The rules prescribe both proper comportment and the proper way to respond if challenged. They regulate the use of violence and so supply a rationale allowing those who are inclined to aggression to precipitate violent encounters in an approved way.

Anderson continues by describing the code of the street as a 'cultural adaptation to the lack of faith in the police and the judicial system' and as emerging from a lack of jobs, limited public services, the stigma of race, drug use and the resulting 'alienation and absence of hope for the future'. As opposed to this 'negative influence' whose 'norms are often consciously opposed to those of mainstream society', Anderson sees 'the decent family committed to middle class values' (Anderson, 1999, pp 32–4). They represent what he describes as the 'code of decency'. Anderson presents impressive empirical research, and his studies have been important in contemporary studies of street culture. However, his approach has some serious flaws.

The most important is that he does not give the 'code' concept an explicit theoretical framework.[19] The way Anderson describes the code of the street, it seems to be just another word for a quite simplistic understanding of culture, as expressed by rules. We thus propose to use the conceptual framework of *street capital* instead. Street capital is masculine in its essence, and Mullins (2006) similarly describes 'street masculinity' as a form of 'gender capital'. As with street masculinity, street capital values violence, retaliation, fashionable clothes and female attachment, a common set of street culture values. Most importantly, street capital is a form of legitimate power, it is relational and it has the capacity to generate profit. We use the concept to describe better the embodied character of skills and competence on the street, as well as the practical rationality of street culture. This will explain stable orientations without conceptualising them as rules, and it will highlight the relationship between a particular culture and its historical and social conditions.

Bourgois (2003a) gave us an important clue to street capital when he described Ray, the leader of the crack dealers he studied in El Barrio. Ray mastered street culture in a way that enabled him to administer several illegal businesses effectively in the drug economy. These street skills, however, were counterproductive when Ray tried to establish himself in the legal economy. Bourgois (2003a, p 135) concluded that there are 'different "cultural capitals" needed to operate as a private entrepreneur in the legal economy versus the underground economy'. The dealers at The River tell similar stories, even though they are lower in the echelons of the drug economy. Their socialisation into street culture and the underground economy benefits their criminal careers, but it is counterproductive when they try to establish themselves in mainstream society.

In the same way that class habitus shapes the working, middle and upper classes, street culture shapes and constrains the bodies of the dealers. Street habitus creates cultural inertia and explains social reproduction and stability. Conceptualising street capital is thus an attempt to follow Bourgois and to describe the 'cultural capital' of a violent street subculture and underground economy. Street culture is described by Bourgois in this way:

> The anguish of growing up poor in the richest city in the world is compounded by the cultural assault that El Barrio youths often face when they venture out of their neighborhood. This has spawned what I call 'inner-city street culture': a complex and conflictual web of beliefs, symbols, modes of interaction, values and ideologies that have emerged in opposition to exclusion from mainstream society. Street culture offers an alternative forum for personal dignity. (Bourgois, 2003a, p 8)

Street culture is thus not 'a coherent, conscious universe of political opposition but rather a spontaneous set of rebellious practices that in the long term have emerged as oppositional style' (Bourgois, 2003a, p 8). Bourgois describes street culture as offering an alternative forum for personal dignity and resistance, and marginalised people as being 'in search of respect'.[20] Thus, he interprets the street subculture as active opposition and resistance in the same way that the Birmingham School interprets most subcultures. This form of resistance, however, destroys the participants as well as the community. Because drug dealing is the material base of street culture, that which makes it economically attractive, it becomes a lifestyle of violence, substance abuse and internalised rage (Bourgois, 2003a, p 9).

Street culture is difficult to escape. Embodied street capital, such as The River dealers' readiness to use violence, their knowledge of the illegal drug trade and their ability to avoid police attention, is of little use in mainstream society. Their careers, business dealings and intelligence are thus confined to street culture. In this way, both street capital and social capital (social networks) bind dealers and drug users to the illegal economy: Street capital is a form of cultural capital that can easily be converted into economic capital. To transfer street capital to other social arenas is harder.

Brotherton criticises both Vigil's multiple marginality approach and Bourgois's analysis of street culture for representing a paradigm of social reproduction that downplays change and agency. According to Brotherton (2008, p 61), resistance is present in social reproduction studies, but it is 'opposition without the possibility of any political or cultural transcendence, any meaningful link to larger movements of the marginalised or any indigenous self-renewal'.

Our emphasis on the dealers' use of different discourses in Chapter Eight answers some of Brotherton's critique. It also relates to the post-subcultural critiques of the Chicago and Birmingham schools. The interdiscursive changes between gangster and oppression discourse make it easier to explain why some of the young men at The River still managed to break with street culture – they mastered not only the culture and language of the street but also the culture and language of the welfare state apparatus and mainstream society.[21] Oppression discourse also has parallels in Mullins's (2006) descriptions of contradictory masculinity constructions. When the dealers self-presented as victims in an oppression discourse, they could easily be labelled as 'punks'. Still they managed to balance this position with a more masculine role as smart, violent and sexually attractive *men* in gangster discourse.

Gangster and oppression discourses

Another problem with Anderson's (1999) description of the code of the street is that it seems to refer more to particular immoral individuals than to a culture that can be used creatively. Anderson's framework does not allow ambiguity and lack of coherence in accounts, except for stating that code switching is possible. However, he describes code switching as something that mainly 'decent' youths do to survive on the street. Moreover, most of Anderson's accounts of street people come from 'decent' people, and in this way, the code of decency may very well reflect self-presentations in interviews rather than codes, culture or informal rules (see also Venkatesh, 2006). We have developed the concepts of gangster and oppression discourses to respond to this shortcoming in Anderson, as well as to the lack of conceptualisations of language use in the literature on street culture more generally.

The moral of gangster discourse is that individuals in street culture have more exciting and rewarding lives than individuals in conventional society. Gangster discourse creates fascination and fear by constructing difference, and the dealers at The River used it to get self-respect and respect from others. Oppression discourse on the other hand, includes personal narratives of unemployment, racism and psychosocial problems, often combined with stories about the government and city council being unwilling to help. Drug dealers at The River used this discourse to justify drug dealing and violence, both in self-understandings and in meetings with welfare organisations. The preponderance of welfare organisations makes oppression discourse particularly important in a Nordic context.

As with street capital, oppression and gangster discourses have parallels in the subculture literature. One of the most important is Wieder's (1974) ethnomethodological study of the convict code. On the face it, this use of the concept 'code' would appear to have many similarities to Anderson's. However, Wieder does not use the convict code as a mechanical code or guide but analyses it as a symbolic resource 'used to perform specific tasks' (Potter and Wetherell, 1987, p 73). Research participants' narratives are thus not used to explain the underlying 'rules' of street culture, as in Anderson's studies, but rather to study how these rules are used in practice. Wieder is not concerned with what the code is but rather what is achieved by using it and what function it has in concrete interactions.

Another important parallel, especially for oppression discourse, is Sykes and Matza's (1957) neutralisation theory. Sykes and Matza denounced subculture theory by questioning the extent to which 'delinquents' reject conventional values. They maintained that offenders and delinquents were aware of conventional values, understood that their offending was wrong and rationalised their behaviour ('self-talked') before offending to mitigate the anticipated shame and guilt of violating societal norms. They described five 'techniques of neutralisation': denial of responsibility, denial of injury, denial of victims, condemnation of condemners and appeal to higher loyalties (Sykes and Matza, 1957). The suggestion was that delinquents did not reject mainstream moral values but neutralised them so that they were able to commit delinquent actions.[22]

Gangster discourse also has parallels in contemporary studies of language use in street culture. For example, Jimerson and Oware's (2006) descriptions of how African-American men are 'telling the code of the street' and Topalli's (2005) description of how hard-core offenders are 'neutralising being good'. The most important difference in our framework, however – from these other approaches

– is an inspiration from Foucauldian discourse analysis. In this way, we introduce a post-structural understanding of language into a line of reasoning that has so far been dominated by voluntarism and a local understanding of the construction of meaning (as seen in symbolic interactionism, ethnomethodology and neutralisation theory).

Studying marginalised drug dealers

Several problems arise when we try to combine Bourdieu's and Foucault's theoretical frameworks, even for empirical and pragmatic purposes. The most obvious problems spring from the classic dilemma between radical constructivist (Foucault's relativist constructivism) and more realist (Bourdieu's structuralist constructivism) approaches to studies of social science. To suggest a compromise we must make some adjustments.

First, we must give language a more constitutive role than Bourdieu does. We must avoid his tendency to reduce language to a structure of class relations by adopting the method he sometimes uses in his more qualitative analyses, where language plays a constitutive role in constructing the social. Second, we must give the subject a different position in Foucauldian discourse analysis, making it apparent that the individual is not only a bearer of discourses, but also an active agent with an embodied personal and social history. We must also acknowledge the objective socioeconomic structures of social space. Perceptions are nonetheless never unmediated, and in social science the objects of study are never outside discourse.[23]

In such a 'dialectic approach' (Fairclough, 1992, 1995b) gangster discourse both constitutes and is constituted by street capital. Gangster discourse is embedded in a violent street culture but also upholds and constitutes the same culture. For example, unless the speaker of gangster discourse has symbolic credibility, through public displays of violence or street smartness, gangster discourse becomes only comic. Gangster discourse is thus dependent on embodied street capital to be effective.

The concept of street capital is obviously inspired by Bourdieu, and gangster and oppression discourses are most obviously linked to Foucault. His emphasis on how discursive practice forms the objects of which people speak is directly pertinent to both gangster and oppression discourses. The way discourses in the social context define the possible positions of a speaking subject highlights boundaries of constructions of identity and the self. As Goffman (1963) points out, these boundaries are especially crucial for marginalised and stigmatised groups. Street capital and gangster discourse emerge from an objectively given socioeconomic position, from the bottom of what Bourdieu conceptualises as social space. Paradoxically, oppression discourse also gets its symbolic value from this position in social space. The concept street capital is used to analyse the capital augmentation of marginalised people, and the concepts gangster and oppression discourses to analyse their interpretative work.

Our study challenges the hierarchical and authoritative approach that is explicit in Bourdieu's social space and more implicit in Foucault's episteme and discourse, and it allows more room for resistance and opposition to emerge from the subculture.[24] Symbolic capital augmentation and autonomous linguistic practice take place far from the educational system. Moreover, and in line with the understandings of subcultures highlighted by the Chicago and Birmingham School, linguistic and embodied street capital gets its symbolic value by being *opposed* to the educational system and mainstream society. As subcultural capital, it has long defined itself as extra-curricular, as knowledge that cannot be learned in school (Thornton, 1995, p 13).

As with the subculture, however, resistance is limited and field specific, and the solution is in many ways 'magic' or 'imaginary' (Cohen, 2005). Street capital and gangster discourse are obviously not equal to legitimate symbolic capital and language. They are even counterproductive if one's aim is to advance in mainstream society. As illustrated by Daniel, Usman and Hassan life-stories, the tragic paradox is that The River dealers' accumulation of street capital and use of gangster and oppression discourses further escalates the marginalisation processes that originally engendered their social and economic exclusion. However, this does not imply that such a symbolic universe is of little relevance: refusing to analyse the autonomy, linguistic practice, and symbolic capital of people at society's margins only adds to their marginalisation.

Notes

[1] This does, of course, present several challenges, including the issues of realism versus constructivism, practice versus discourse, and the constituting force of language. We will, however, argue that the advantages for empirical research are greater than the disadvantages.

[2] Bourdieu introduced the 'field' as a concept late in his career, and it may best be described in the study of cultural production (Bourdieu, 1993). Examples of fields are education, the academy, artistic production and organised religion. The field can be defined as 'a network, or configuration, of objective relations between positions. These positions are objectively defined, in their existence and in the determination they impose upon their occupants, agents or institutions, by their present and potential situation (*situs*) in the structure of the distribution of species of power (or capital) whose possession commands access to the specific profits that are at stake in the field, as well as by their objective relation to other positions' (Bourdieu and Wacquant, 1992, p 97).

[3] However, street culture is not a field in Bourdieu's understanding. For example, the street lacks formal institutions, and its autonomy can be questioned (Jensen, 2006). Moreover, Bourdieu's (1984) cultural capital is characterised by transferability in social space. On the street, capital accumulation is specific to street culture, and having street habitus will be disadvantageous in other social arenas. Thus, the long-term 'effectiveness' of street capital is limited. Nevertheless, Bourdieu emphasised that theory is only a 'temporary construct

which takes shape for and by empirical work' (Bourdieu and Wacquant, 1992, p 161). We followed this pragmatism when developing the concept of street capital.

[4] Bourdieu's concept of symbolic capital was developed from his studies in Algeria but later used in studies of the modern French society. Symbolic capital 'is to be understood as economic or political capital that is disavowed, misrecognised and thereby recognised, hence legitimate, a "credit" which under certain conditions, and always in the long run, guarantees "economic profit"' (Bourdieu, 1993, p 75).

[5] Habitus consists of 'a set of historical relations "deposited" within individual bodies in the form of mental and corporeal schemata of perception, appreciation, and action' (Bourdieu and Wacquant, 1992, p 16). It can also be defined as 'a system of durable, transposable dispositions, structured structures predisposed to function as structuring structures, that is, as principles which generate and organise practices and representations that can be objectively adapted to their outcomes without presupposing a conscious aiming at ends or an express mastery of the operation necessary in order to attain them' (Bourdieu, 1990, pp 53–4; see also Bourdieu, 1977, p 87). Habitus is produced by historical and social conditions, and in this way, street capital is similar to Anderson's (1999) and Bourgois's (2003a) claims that the code of the street and street culture is a response to socially marginalised positions.

[6] See, for example, 'social science has to take account of the autonomy of language, its specific logic, and its particular rules of operation' (Bourdieu, 1991, p 41).

[7] In the following quotation Bourdieu addresses conversation analysis, ethnomethodology and symbolic interaction: 'The "interactionist" approach, which fails to go beyond the actions and reactions apprehended in their directly visible immediacy, is unable to discover that the different agents' linguistic strategies are strictly dependent on their positions in the structure of the distribution of linguistic capital, which can in turn be shown to depend, via the structure of chances of access to the educational system, on the structure of class relations' (Bourdieu, 1991, p 64). Bourdieu argues that the production of meaning cannot be understood locally, as the outcome of individual strategies or free acts of creation (1991, p 56). Meaning is embedded in economic and social conditions (1991, p 44). The object of study must thus be the 'relationship between the structured systems of sociologically pertinent linguistic differences and the equally structured systems of social differences' (1991, p 54). A similar objectivist argument is important in Bourdieu's critique of structural approaches, such as those of Foucault and discourse analysis. 'It can only be an unjustifiable abstraction … to seek the source of understanding of cultural productions in these productions themselves, taken in isolation, and divorced from the conditions of their production and utilization, as would be the wishes of "discourse analysis", which situated on the border of sociology and linguistics, has nowadays relapsed into indefensible forms of internal analysis' (Bourdieu, 1988, pp xvi–xvii). He also ridicules Foucault for refusing to look outside the 'field of the discourse' (Bourdieu, 1993, pp 33, 179–81). Bourdieu also explicitly states that 'the factors which are most influential in the formation of the habitus

are transmitted without passing through language' (Bourdieu, 1991, p 51). In this way, he both explicitly and implicitly downplays the constitutive force of language. He downplays that linguistic practice or discourse is itself a part the struggle for 'the constitution and classification of social relations'' (Chouliaraki and Fairclough, 2000, p 402).

[8] This is, however, only what Bourdieu explicitly says about language. A quite different way to read him is to 'bracket' what he says about language and to emphasise instead what he says about other aspects of social life (Hanks, 2005, p 69; see, for example, 'The Berber house' (Bourdieu, 1973), and *Masculine domination* (Bourdieu, 2001). Sometimes Bourdieu's description of the field, which he sees as organised in relational opposites, is also influenced by French structuralism. Bourdieu does, for example, sometimes describe the field as 'a language game in which certain ends are pursued with certain discursive resources according to established guidelines', and as 'a set of beliefs and assumptions that undergird the game' (Hanks, 2005, p 73; Bourdieu, 1985). In this understanding of the field, he is close to a theoretical position that most schools in discourse analysis would share.

[9] Thus, Bourdieu's conceptualisation of the field is sometimes better described as a culture, a set of discourses or an order of discourse, when analysing interpretative work. It can even be argued that the order of discourse is 'the specifically discoursal organizational logic of the structure of a field, and analysis of the former can be seen as part of the analysis of the latter' (Chouliaraki and Fairclough, 2000, p 407; for a more thorough discussion, see Chouliaraki and Fairclough, 1999, pp 114–16).

[10] Foucault (1970) describes how language in the dominant scientific discourse (episteme) went from representing objects to becoming a system of its own, giving words meaning only in relation to a system of words or a system of categorisations. *Discourse analysis* originates in very different sciences and, consequently, has different developments. Empirical discourse analysis has been important in such different fields as linguistics, the social sciences and psychology, inspired in each case by philosophical post-structuralism. We can trace the origins of contemporary discourse analysis back to influences as different as Chomsky's generative grammar, Austin's pragmatics, Sack's conversation analysis and Saussure's semiology (see Potter and Wetherell, 1987; Potter, 1996; van Dijk, 1997; Jaworski and Coupland, 1999; Wood and Kroger, 2000; Schiffrin et al, 2001; Jørgensen and Phillips, 2002). Jørgensen and Phillips (2002) classify discourse analysis into discourse theory, critical discourse analysis and discourse psychology. Discourse theory evolved in the social sciences and emphasises discourse as structure, as is seen, for example, in the post-structural writings of Foucault (1972a, 1972b, 1978) and Laclau and Mouffe (1985). Critical discourse analysis evolved in linguistics and the social sciences. It carries much of the post-structural philosophy of Foucault but opens up a larger space for individual agency. The most coherent description of this tradition is in Fairclough's work (1992, 1995b). Finally, discourse psychology evolved in social psychology. Unlike discourse theory and critical discourse analysis, it emphasises the production of meaning from actors in concrete interaction (see Potter and Wetherell, 1987; Potter, 1996).

[11] It is important to distinguish this poststructuralist understanding of discourse from a linguistic approach. In linguistics, 'discourse' signifies the use of language. A discourse will therefore embrace all textual production within a thematic or textually limited area. Fairclough (1995b, p 54) refers to this appreciation of discourse as 'spoken or written language use'. To crowd the landscape even more, 'discourse' is used in everyday speech, and by philosophers like Jürgen Habermas, synonymously with 'debate'; that is, an exchange between several implicated parties aimed at achieving consensus.

[12] Foucault continues: 'what they [the discourses] do is more than use these signs to designate things. It is this more that renders them irreducible to the language (langue) and speech. It is this more that we must reveal and describe' (Foucault, 1972a, p 49). Foucault's aim was to study the regularity of statements to uncover the regularity of a discursive practice. In Foucault's view, conditions for the production of statements can be understood by the concepts positivity, historical a priori, and the archive (Foucault, 1972a, p 126–31). The positivity of a discourse is its expression in texts. The historical a priori is that which makes such a positivity possible. The systems of statements produced by the different positivities, in accordance with historical a prioris, make up the archive (Sheridan, 1980, pp 102–3).

[13] Such a determinism or structuralism in early discourse analysis has triggered a lot of criticism for its failure to suppose agency or active subjects, as has the vague descriptions of the relationships among discourse, practice and materiality. Bourdieu and contemporary discourse analysis appears to have answered these two problems in a more coherent fashion. For a more throughout discussion of the relation between Bourdieu, Foucault and the concept introduced in this book, see Sandberg (2009a).

[14] 'We shall not pass beyond discourse in order to rediscover the forms that it has created and left behind it; we shall remain, or try to remain, at the level of the discourse itself' (Foucault, 1972a, p 48).

[15] See Park et al, 1925; Thrasher, 1927; Wirth, 1928; Shaw and McKay, 1929; Whyte, 1943; Cohen, 1955; Cloward and Ohlin, 1960; Becker, 1963; Yablonsky, 1966; Suttles, 1968; Keiser, 1969; Miller, 1973, 1975; Moore, 1978, 1991; Horowitz, 1983

[16] See for example Cohen, 1972; Hall and Jefferson, 1976; Willis, 1977; Hebdige, 1979.

[17] Potter, for example, criticises Willis for taking the boys' 'evaluative descriptive constructions and treating them as factual versions of their social world' (Potter, 1996, p 99; see also Marcus, 1986; Atkinson, 1990). A social group's categories and individual self-presentations are thus taken as objective pictures of social relations and 'selves'.

[18] Other critiques include failure to provide accounts of girls in subcultures, equating youth consumerism with working-class resistance, having a structuralist theoretical bias, failure to recognise the role of media, and having a too-limited definition of youth only

as an age category (Bennett and Kahn-Harris, 2004, pp 6–11; see also Muggleton and Weinzierl, 2003).

[19] For example, it is unclear whether he uses code as it is used in traditional linguistics, as the product of an 'irreducible inner logic' (Hanks, 2005, p 75), as it is used in post-structuralism, as 'a perspective of quotations, a mirage of structures' (Barthes, 1972, pp 20–1), or, as Bourdieu uses it, merely as a synonym for culture (Bourdieu, 1977, pp 23, 81). This uncertainty is reflected in questions about whether the code of the street is a logic of the street, a way to 'read' the ghetto, or even how it relates to other important concepts such as street culture or the subculture of violence (Wolfgang and Ferracuti, 1967).

[20] *In search of respect* is the title of Bourgois's (2003a) book.

[21] See also Sandberg (2009b, 2009c). Interdiscursivity is derived from Bakthin's (1981) intertextuality, interdiscursivity describes the process when a speaker or a text draws on different discourses to create legitimacy and meaning. Spoken or written that evokes different discourses increases the space of interpretation, and the reception will be more ambivalent and sometimes more effective (Fairclough, 1992, 1995a).

[22] Subsequently, additional neutralisation techniques have been suggested; for example, justification by comparison (Cromwell and Thurman, 2003), the defence of necessity (Klockars, 1974; Minor, 1981; Coleman, 1998) and techniques of risk denial (Peretti-Watel, 2003). Many of the central statements in neutralisation theory have since been questioned. Some examples of these questions are whether high norm acceptance is necessary for neutralisation effects, whether prior norm violations decrease the impact that neutralisation exerts on deviant behaviour and whether the use of neutralisation techniques actually predicts deviant behaviour (Fritsche, 2005).

[23] To put a spin on Bourdieu's criticism of Foucault for not looking outside the 'field of discourse' (Bourdieu, 1993, pp 33, 179–81).

[24] Despite their differences, Bourdieu and Foucault agree that the educational system and middle-class society are at the centre of discourse allocation and capital accumulation. Bourdieu, for example, states that 'the sociology of language is logically inseparable from a sociology of education' (Bourdieu, 1991, p 62), and Foucault states that through education, individuals 'can gain access to any kind of discourse' (Foucault, 1972b, p 227). Bourdieu's emphasis is on the elite, and he tends to focus on the educational system. When he writes about language, it is typically about 'legitimate language'. Maybe Foucault also has a bias towards the educational system and academics because he only studies written texts. Even though his understanding of power is that it evolves from 'everywhere', the discourses he describes are produced by the elite.

FOUR

Marginalisation and resistance

Drug dealers sought shelter under this bridge in bad weather. In an attempt to stop drug dealing it was closed off. It had no effect. Processes of social marginalisation are more important than spatial concerns, to understand the dealing of the young men at The River.

Under the bridge

It was a bitterly cold winter's night. We had been walking our planned route along The River but had finished earlier than expected.[1] Not many people were around, and we were cold, tired and looking forward to a dry room and something hot to drink. Towards the end of the round, we spotted the light of a fire under a bridge. We knew that the dealers at The River and some ethnic Norwegian street addicts often sought sanctuary there in bad weather. They were burning planks found in the vicinity. The warmth of the fire made it a good place to shelter from the elements, but the light it emitted was not so good for avoiding the police. A young man lay sleeping under a blanket on an old mattress. He was oblivious to the world, muttering only indistinctly from time to time. Beside him a man sat writing in a notebook. "I write down everything that happens to me," he said.

Three young men stood round the fire, talking and keeping the fire going. Further away, near the entrance to the bridge, some slightly older ethnic Norwegian drug addicts huddled together. The scene with the old bridge, the glow of the fire, the mattress, the young dealers and older addicts could have been cut from one of Charles Dickens's stories of London's underworld in the 19th century.

We spoke for a while with the dealers, but they soon lost interest. Their attention was caught by a quarrel between the older addicts and the young men about how the fire should be tended. Some of them were intoxicated and aggressive, and the mood was unpleasant. One man was particularly agitated, storming back and forth while others attempted to pacify him. We had been warned that some dangerous psychologically unstable individuals frequented the area. It was pouring with rain outside, and everyone knew that the police would appear at any minute and douse the fire. The temperature would plummet, and most of them had nowhere to go.

We have already described what makes life at The River appealing to some people – easy money, drugs, thrills, and leadership roles. One of the young men called it "the pull of The River". Here under the bridge, however, as we sheltered from the weather, we were reminded again that no one could *really* want to lead this type of life. After the first exciting phase, life at The River settled into a pattern of fights over minor sums of money, humiliating confrontations with the police and social services authorities, and a never-ending struggle to maintain self-esteem and the respect of others. As the notion of street capital points out, we need to understand the dealers' situations in the light of wider social and economic processes. Nobody ends up like this by chance.

In this chapter, we will identify how experiences in school, in the job market, with racism, and as refugees are important to understanding why the young men ended up dealing drugs at The River. In addition, we will show how many of them developed strong subcultural identities over time. As 'foreigners', they capitalised on a kind of 'otherness', and from a subordinate position they developed counter-strategies. These strategies built self-confidence and ethnic pride. However, they also reinforce processes of marginalisation.

Marginalisation in a Scandinavian welfare state

Even though most studies of street culture include marginalisation processes in their analysis, some do so in a more coherent and detailed fashion than others. For example, in his study of advanced marginality, Wacquant (2008) mentions six properties of the 'rising regime of marginality'. These include wage labour as a new vector of social instability, functional disconnection from macroeconomic trends, territorial fixation and stigmatisation, spatial alienation, loss of hinterland, and social fragmentation.

Wacquant's study has many parallels to Wilson's (1987) classic, *The truly disadvantaged*. Wilson argued that historical discrimination and migration kept the urban African-American population relatively young and made them vulnerable to industrial and geographical changes in the economy. In times of downsizing of traditional industry and increasing unemployment rates, the black middle class also disappeared from the ghetto. The result was poverty and social isolation, and the creation of an 'urban underclass'. According to Wilson, this underclass also developed a destructive culture that reinforced their socioeconomic marginalisation. Similarly, as described in the previous chapter, Vigil (2002, 2003) proposes 'a multiple marginality framework'. Socioeconomic, sociocultural and social-psychological factors are all important, and they take their particular shape through the influence of immigrant experiences.

In the UK, Young (1999) describes a movement from inclusive to exclusive society. His thesis is that late modernity is characterised by large groups of people being economic excluded from the labour marked, socially excluded in civil society and further excluded by an ever-expanding criminal justice system. In a rich, detailed ethnographic study from a housing estate in North of England, McAuley (2007) describes how these processes of exclusion are interwoven with modern consumer society. 'At the heart of young people's experiences of exclusion', he states, are 'the images of crime imposed on their poor community' (McAuley, 2007, p 7).

Most studies of marginalisation and social and economic exclusion use a relativistic approach: deprivation has to be defined contextually. Poverty, for example, refers to a lack of the resources necessary to participate in the normal way of life in the relevant social system (Merton, 1959; Hallveröd, 2004).[2] Nordic welfare states routinely have more evenly distributed patterns of income than do other European countries.[3] Norwegian data indicate that although many people may experience periods of low income, few remain in that position for long (Epland, 2005).[4] A large proportion of those defined as 'poor' also seem to be rather well integrated into social networks (Dahl et al, 2008). Moreover, the majority of those who receive social benefits in Norway seem to do so for short periods only.[5] Immigrants, especially those from African, Asian and Eastern European countries, receive more social assistance payments (and for longer periods) than people born in Norway. There is no difference between these groups, however, in their likelihood of re-entering the welfare system (Hansen, 2008). Nordic welfare states do not have very high occupational mobility (Hansen, 2006). However, all evidence points to rather small differences among people when it comes to income. Relatively few people are permanently marginalised, and 'welfare dependency' is also low.[6]

In sum, the street drug markets described in other studies are usually situated in more marginalised areas than the cannabis trade at The River (May et al, 2005). Processes of marginalisation are nevertheless crucial to understand the involvement of people from minority ethnic groups in criminal gangs and crime in Norway (Andersson, 2003). Even if relatively few are permanently marginalised in Scandinavia, The River dealers were in a high-risk group: they had poor education (or none), little experience in the workforce, criminal records, and high levels of drug use. They also had experienced racism and discrimination, which increased their alienation from mainstream society.

Education

Usman, who we profiled in Chapter Two, grew up in inner-city Oslo. School, he told us, was a constant pain. "I just couldn't get myself to go to school at all." He was extremely restless. However, there was more to Usman's story. "We weren't any good at school anyway," he said. Usman was not the only one in his peer group to fall short. By the age of 13, Usman had reached a conclusion: "Fuck school." Almost a decade later, he had the same opinion, and most of the dealers at The River shared this experience.

Broadly speaking, regardless of the outcome measured, we find rather stable educational patterns for minority ethnic groups in Europe. Their educational qualifications tend to be substantially lower than those of the majority groups. The most disadvantaged are people of Turkish, Pakistani, Caribbean and African ancestry.[7] Compared with other European countries, the educational disadvantage for minority ethnic groups seems to be small in Norway (Marks, 2005). Nevertheless, minority ethnic children in Norway do encounter specific problems in school (Støren, 2002), and a recent Norwegian study concluded that there is much ground to cover before ethnic inequalities in education become a thing of the past (Fekjær, 2006).

Much of this can be traced to social class. Many minority ethnic people are children of less-skilled labour migrants. Non-Western minority ethnic groups occupy lower class bands overall and consequently have a poorer showing in the statistics. Some of the parents have also suffered decreasing social status, which they have found to be humiliating. However, there are additional problems, and a recent review concluded that mechanisms beyond socioeconomic background are needed to account for the minority disadvantage in education.[8]

Most of the dealers at The River who grew up in Norway came from a problematic family background. Few had been living with both parents, and their parents were often unemployed and living on social security, they told us. Some of the dealers were teenagers when they came to Norway, and this made it even harder to learn the language and succeed at school. For the refugees, experiences of war were additional barriers to success.

Wari came to Norway as a 10-year-old. Asked if there had been problems at school, he insisted there had been none: "I just didn't like school." He did admit later that it had been difficult to keep up. Another dealer, John, came to Norway from Somalia as a 13-year-old. When we met him he was 21. He had been on the run in other African countries, and he enjoyed living in Norway, but it was demanding. He went to a specialised school first, to get some basic skills and learn Norwegian. He then began studying mechanics at upper secondary school, but he found it difficult to fit in.

'I'd been there for a couple of years before I was thrown out. It was
a bit of a hassle, like, with the whole class, because I wasn't the only
one, it wasn't just me, there were three others, like. The only people
who couldn't get a handle on this mechanical stuff, and all that reading
and stuff, that was us. The rest of the class were ordinary Norwegians,
like. The teacher told us: "Do this, do that." But it don't work like that,
because we never understood what "this" and "that" were!'

John took a break from school, then he gave up and dropped out altogether. Clearly,
his relations with the teaching staff could have been better. He spoke Norwegian
poorly and was not always easy to comprehend. However, his pride prevented
him from asking his teacher for help until it was too late. John told us that he was
not good at learning "mechanical stuff". He presented it as a personal problem,
but there was more to it. According to him, the ethnic Norwegian students did
well while the "foreigners" had problems.

The dealers at The River had experienced more barriers in the educational
system than majority ethnic adolescents with similar working-class backgrounds.
Probably, we are faced with a complex mosaic of factors. In European debates on
this issue, poor language skills, differential aspirations and low social capital have
all been suggested as contributing factors. One Norwegian study attests to the
complexity of the problem. Bakken (2003) found that minority-language students
often did a great deal of homework, enjoyed parental support and aspired to a
university education, yet they still performed poorly. This was in part due to the
parents' low social class and education levels and the students' limited access to
books and computers. Furthermore, Bakken argued that the educational system
provides the knowledge and cultural capital of the *Norwegian* middle class. If
students are not socialised in the Norwegian language and culture from infancy,
they will find it hard to succeed at school.

In addition, in many European countries, neighbourhood social deprivation
(but not ethnic segregation per se) seems to have a negative impact over and
above that of parental social disadvantage (Heath et al, 2008, p 229). Most of
the dealers at The River grew up in the satellite towns east of Oslo. The schools
in this area serve low-income families, have high rates of immigrants, and have
students who earn much lower grades than students in the rest of Oslo (Hansen,
2007). In all the dealers' life stories, this was a clear thread: an irrelevant school,
with disciplinary problems, which early on gives way to adventurous experiences
in local peer groups.

Work

None of the dealers had a permanent job during the time they sold cannabis
at The River, but most had some experience working. Typically, they held jobs
in the retail and transport sectors. According to what many of them said, they
wanted to work but were excluded from the labour market. Discouraged, apathy

took the upper hand. When John dropped out of the education system, he tried getting a job.

> *John:* 'I came to Oslo, applied to get on a training programme. I was told to use a computer [at the job centre], like, that's the only thing we can help you with. How many jobs d'you reckon I applied for?'
> *Interviewer:* 'Don't know.'
> *John:* 'The drawback, if you're name sounds foreign, like, you don't get a job.'
> *Interviewer:* 'Not even an interview?'
> *John:* 'No. You send off your application form, they see your name, and they don't want to see you. I want to work, obviously, but if you can't find work and you've got nothing, what are you supposed to do, like? I can't go and live off benefits. Not for me. I want to work. I want to earn my own money.'

We asked him where his money came from, and after an embarrassing but brief silence, he told us what we already knew: "I stand here and sell."

People from minority ethnic groups have a harder time finding work, said the dealers at The River. They do not get job interviews, and if they do get a job, they are the first to be made redundant. John saw a connection between unfair treatment and selling cannabis as an alternative means of survival. He needed money but was not prepared to "live off benefits". Because he felt he was effectively barred from doing legitimate work, The River became an option.

Ali shared this feeling of being excluded from the job market. He also believed he had trouble finding a job because he was black and had a foreign-sounding name. He told us repeatedly that he *wanted* to work. We asked him if he thought that he was unable to get a job because Norwegians are racists. "Not all," he said, "but a lot." It was particularly noticeable when he applied for work. If he applied in writing, he would not be considered because potential employers could see he was a foreigner from his name:

> 'I saw this job, and I applied, and gave them my name. I waited two weeks, then I got: "The vacancy is filled". But before I sent that application, I changed my name, to trick them, like, and filled in a Norwegian name and sent it off to them. I've done that three times so far. Every time I write a Norwegian name, I get the job, but if I give them my real name, so-and-so, they say "The vacancy is filled". I call myself Knut Arne, Bjørn, I'm tricking them. They say, "Come to an interview."'

Ali said that he did this experiment "three times in the recent past". Other young men at The River also told us such stories, and it may be a kind of urban legend. Nevertheless, the stories we heard typify what many of the dealers at The River had discovered for themselves. They are handicapped from the start. Their skin colour, name and religion are all wrong. That is why the labour market will not have them. Most Norwegians are not racists, in their opinion. Even people who do nurture racist ideas are not necessarily consistently racist. However, the young men did feel that Norwegians prefer to keep their distance and are generally sceptical. All other things being equal, a person from the majority ethnic group will be preferred.

Research on European immigrant adolescents has focused more on education than on their experiences in the labour market. However, given the strong general links between education and success in the labour market, it is not surprising that there are strong parallels in these areas. Thus, most interesting are the 'ethnic penalties' experienced by minority ethnic groups in the labour market relative to peers from the majority population with the same education (Heath and McMahon, 1997).

As in most Western countries, studies in Scandinavia find wide income gaps between non-Western immigrants and the majority population, whereas differences among people from culturally and economically similar countries are small. In Norway, the rate of unemployment in groups of African descent is six to seven times higher than among ethnic Norwegians (SSB, 2006). Immigrants from Somalia have one of the highest unemployment rates (Østbye, 2004).

Nevertheless, when it comes to unemployment rates and segregation, there is still a considerable difference between Norway and other societies. Currently, unemployment does not exceed 16.5% for people of African descent (as against 2.2% for non-immigrants). So even in these groups, the vast majority of people are able to find jobs – even if many work outside the ordinary job market or in job-training programmes. Almost all Norwegian-African young men complete secondary school, get a job and start a family. As yet, Norway has been spared the massive marginalisation affecting certain groups in, for example, the US (Massey and Denton, 2003). The young men at The River must therefore be considered exceptions in their groups.

Studies of labour market participation indicate the importance of a number of semi-observable factors pertaining to immigrants.[9] They include formal qualifications (training, work experience), informal skills (social relations, adaptive capacity), language skills and knowledge of Norwegian culture. Circumstances loosely captured by the controversial terms 'welfare state dependency' or 'culture of poverty' may also play a role: apathy, resignation, personal insecurity and short-term horizons. However, ethnically based discrimination is probably the most important factor. Discrimination is usually taken to mean the devaluation of immigrants relative to the majority population, all other factors being equal.

The use of various controlled tests is one way to measure discrimination, and the evidence presented by Ali represents a street version of the method. The method requires research confederates to pose as jobseekers, one of whom claims affiliation with a minority ethnic group while the other claims to be a member of the majority. Other factors such as education, professional experience, age and sex are kept constant (Cross and Waldinger, 1997). In countries where such studies have been conducted, about 30–40% of minority ethnic applicants were discriminated against.

The low relative rates of employment can be attributed to a complex interplay of immigrant- and market-related factors (Røed and Bratsberg, 2005). The thesis we propose is that when young men with immigrant backgrounds are marginalised in a number of situations – in the family, at school, among peers, in the job market – they seek out street culture and street capital. This capital should be understood as resistance or opposition to both the mainstream Norwegian culture and the minority ethnic cultures of the young men's parents.

Little money

Some of the relatively newly arrived refugees with residence permits had a hard time finding jobs and tried selling cannabis to see what they could make. One of them was Sharif. He wanted to get on, but it was hard. Comparing himself with the other dealers at The River, he said, "Some of those kids hanging out there don't give a fuck about tomorrow. The only thing on their mind is what's going down today." For himself, he wanted more than "hanging out here, make yourself a couple of coins and run away". However, it was easier said than done. He was hampered by the lack of ready money:

> 'I've been served a debt recovery notice. That's the mother of all shit, mate. You see what I'm saying, my life has come to a big stop. No job, no school. Nothing. I can't get help from them. Only thing I get is bills, bills, bills. What am I supposed to do with bills? I haven't got a job. How do they expect me to pay?'

Facing mounting bills, Sharif saw no other option but The River. Public authorities frustrated him; they treated him badly and refused to help.

Most of the young men had done casual work. As described previously, some felt they were treated badly in the workplace. Aser had worked as a cleaner, telephone seller, and crew member at McDonald's. None of them were permanent jobs. At McDonald's, his wages were paid by the municipal job centre. According to the agreement, after training he would get a normal job. That job never materialised, however. After two months of waiting, the only offer was to sign on for yet another month of training. We asked him how it felt. "Two months I worked for nothing, and I didn't get a job. I was angry; I said no, I'm not taking any more of this." He was frustrated, and told the job centre that if he were taken on, he would stay on. If a vacancy turned up, they told him, they would call him. They never did.

However, the picture is more complicated than just frustrations with the authorities. The River tempted him even when he had a job. "You earn much less at McDonald's than you can make down The River," said Aser. Rashid was similarly tempted. It was "the lure of The River," he told us. That explained why he and others hung out there. We asked whether he thought that workplace discrimination could explain why the majority of the people at The River were from minority ethnic groups. Exasperated, he said:

> 'It's 'cause they don't care. They don't want the grief of being tied down with a job and told where to get off all day. If you sell dope and live like that, see, you're your own boss.... They like being in control. It's only about individuals, see, nothing to do with skin or colour or shit like that. Some of them may use it as an excuse, but that's their business.'

Dealing cannabis is a way to make "easy money". For young men who are used to being treated badly at work and in school, the chance to be their own boss can be liberating. Discrimination can also be an excuse, as Rashid states. However, past incidents and experiences were instrumental in creating a disposition in him and others for criminal activities.

The refugees regularly mentioned a sense of isolation and alienation. Many felt as if they were the only ones in this situation. They told us about missing what they had left behind, loneliness and dislocation. Many saw themselves on the fringes of the mainstream community, and they had few ties. Some of the boys who had grown up in Norway also shared this sense of social malaise, often starting while they were still at school.

Racism

Some of the young men at The River had experienced blatant racism. Aser told us what had happened once when he went to a disco with a friend. This was a long time ago, many years before he started dealing at The River. An ethnic Norwegian girl had come over to them and asked if she could sit with them. After a while, she asked them if they would like to dance. Aser told his friend to "watch out, don't say anything". However, they did eventually move to the dance floor. At that point, a group of boys approached. "We were dancing, they turn up and say, 'You've got the girl,' and started causing trouble. We didn't want any trouble. 'You can have your lady,' we said. When we left, they started hitting us." Aser rang the police. When the police arrived they told Aser that the group was a well-known gang of racists. They had used the girl as bait and an excuse to cause a fight. Aser had been involved in similar incidents later as well. "When they see me, they do like this," he said, drawing a finger across his throat in mock execution.

People had also taunted Ebo, calling him "Negro" and "blackass" and telling him to "go back where he came from". He did not give it much thought, he told us. Nevertheless, it had obviously upset him. "Those 30- to 40-year-olds will always be racists in Norway. Even in 50 years," he said. Crime, violence and forming a gang have previously been reported as possible responses to episodes like these (Prieur, 2004; Andersson, 2005).[10] Their distress at feeling left out, which they expressed as hostility to all things Norwegian, was a key factor in their social exclusion.

Ebo and Aser did experience racism first hand, but their descriptions were the exceptions. Rather, most of the young men at The River answered general questions about racism relatively vaguely. Left to speak freely, however, they filled in the spaces between some of the contours, mentioning more vague incidents in the neighbourhood, at school, downtown, in shopping centres, at work, and with state officials and authorities – incidents where they thought they had been insulted, ridiculed or denigrated.

People from minority ethnic groups in Norway do *not* usually report ethnically based discrimination. In one study, more than eight in 10 minority ethnic people had no such experience in the previous year. Surprisingly, however, those with full-time jobs were most likely to experience discrimination (Rogstad, 2004). This is unexpected in that we tend to think of the workplace as inclusive and protective, as a place that promotes economic and social cohesion. One reason why discrimination might be more frequently experienced in the workplace is *exposure*. When people from minority ethnic groups form isolated groups and live in areas seldom visited by ethnic Norwegians, conflicts with and biased treatment by the majority will obviously occur less frequently. Without some intermingling or contact, open discrimination is less likely to take place.

The dealers at The River had contact with ethnic Norwegians in welfare state positions, and they had regular interaction with police from the majority ethnic group. They experienced a kind of 'otherness', which was encountered in a hierarchical structure, from a subordinate position. It formed the basis for hidden discrimination, which (along with the feeling of being excluded) may possibly be even more widespread and hurtful than undisguised racism. "Some people cross to the other side of the road," Denis told us, "because you're walking there. You notice things like that." John felt it whenever an ethnic Norwegian disregarded him. It was worse when it was impossible to avoid the people involved, such as in interactions with other pupils, teachers, employers or colleagues. In these situations, it was impossible for the young ethnic minority men to use their acquired street capital to force people to show respect.

A Negro in the kitchen

Denis had been seconded to a restaurant for on-the-job training. He liked the work, believed he was good at it, and worked hard. However, he felt insecure all the same. Two of his fellow workers, the two he worked with most often, let fall abrasive remarks every now and then. "I'm still the Negro in the kitchen," Denis said. "I'm not saying they're racists, like, but you get the feeling that's the way the wind's blowing, and I'm the only African guy there. And sort of, like, you know, I pick it up, you know." Without addressing him directly, they dropped hints about what they suspected him of doing, including smoking cannabis.

'They were jawing together and saying that hash was hopeless, you know, being totally negative about the weed. "You don't smoke hash then, do you Denis?", carrying on like that they were; but he knows I smoke it! But he knows I'm not going to make an issue out of it 'cause I'm there on job training and, like, you know, 'cause like, you'd have to be out of your mind to do that, wouldn't you? It was absolutely out of place to ask me that, anyway, see? They could've asked me in private.'

Denis felt put down by his co-workers, if only indirectly. At the same time, it was easy to see that these fellow workers had got hold of an important aspect of his everyday life. Denis smoked cannabis on a daily basis, and at least one of them knew this. However, regular cannabis smoking would lead to social sanctions in any work environment, regardless of one's ethnic background. Had Denis been an ethnic Norwegian, he would probably have *interpreted* the situation differently. He did not speak about it in terms of discrimination at first, but delving into the details of what happened, the power and ethnic dimensions emerged more distinctly.

Denis told another similar story. His fellow workers often started talking about "people being robbed downtown". What they had in mind was clearly minority ethnic youth, he thought:

> *Denis:* 'Like, you know, they go on about people downtown getting robbed and stuff, they keep on about things I know they don't usually talk about! It's just 'cause I'm there, you know. I know I can be grumpy, like. That's why I say to me self, why waste energy feeling fed up, 'cause if I start off, and say something like, "Oi, I don't like what you're saying, mate," like, I know I couldn't stop the ball once it started rolling. I wouldn't be able to stop myself.'
> *Interviewer:* 'So if you start, you can't stop yourself, is that it?'
> *Denis:* 'No, I wouldn't be able to leave it at that. At the end of the day, I'd be the one looking stupid, like. Typical. Black guy turns up and causes mayhem.'

Denis bases his interpretative framework on ethnicity. *Because* he is black, he cannot retaliate. He has been unfairly treated but cannot protest. If he does, it will only cause trouble and more hostility. Because he is black, he is to blame. He is the one *causing mayhem*. Denis was usually a cool, laidback type of guy. He was energetic, lively and charming. However, there was bitterness in his voice when he spoke about these episodes. He felt humiliated, rejected and insulted.

Denis was a leader in the eyes of his peers. At work, he felt patronised. Everything he had learned on the street urged him to take a stand, to retaliate. He knew that a response from his street repertoire would temporarily boost his self-esteem and standing among his peers. However, at the same time, he knew that it would destroy his working conditions at the restaurant. Unlike some of the other young men, Denis was highly aware of these issues.

> 'To tell you the honest truth, a lot of the stuff there I wouldn't put up with for a second, you know. I'd never let somebody talk to me like that or take the mickey about something I was touchy about. But that lot, you know, if I sort of behave like I normally do, it's me who gets the rap. Whether I'm right or not, I lose out.'

Denis describes what our concepts of street habitus and capital try to capture. Marginalised people's practical rationality may further escalate the very same marginalisation processes that originally engendered their social and economic exclusion.

The white gaze

Unlike many other international studies of street drug markets, a distinctive feature of the drug market at The River is its proximity to a white middle-class residential area. The interface between an increasingly gentrified and prosperous part of town is more conspicuous here than in studies from other countries. The dealers at The River are consequently more exposed to the majority population. Because they have contact with such a wide range of buyers, few can be turned away at a glance. People who look 'straight', even parents with small children, buy cannabis. Most passers-by are not customers, however. What happens when they pass the dealers? We observed this numerous times. Some people look apprehensive, and many shift their attention elsewhere. Some return the young men's gaze – briefly, and expressing no interest – before walking on. Some look at the dealers contemptuously.

The dealers meet potential buyers, but they also meet fear and indifference, and, from some, condescension. These brief encounters establish certain fundamentally different social positions. Every time the dealers at The River solicit a potential buyer, they are constituted as 'the Other'. Many of the dealers wear baggy clothes and jewellery, and some look dissipated and worn out. It is easy to see that the refugees are new in Norway. Some people consider them exotic, others find them dangerous, but they are always seen as *different*.

To understand the seller–buyer interaction in these contexts, we need to invoke the wider historical and global context of Western hegemony, where difference is ordered hierarchically. Some have argued that terms such as 'immigrant' (*innvandrer*) are neutral in the Norwegian language and simply refer to lexical understanding. Others, argue that 'immigrant' is not only a word in the dictionary but also a rhetorically powerful concept. While its denotation is neutral, its connotations are negatively charged. In the dictionary, the term denotes all who come from outside Norway, including, for example, Swedes and North Americans. In the streets and in the mass media however, a more restricted use has emerged, an implicit code based on Third World origin, dark skin and working-class background (Gullestad, 2006, p 175).

Non-returnable asylum seekers

So far we have discussed marginalisation processes related to the educational system, the labour market and discrimination and racism. The so-called non-returnable refugees, however, have more specific problems, as illustrated by Hassan's story in Chapter Two.[11] He had no permanent dwelling, little money and was not allowed to go to school or to work. Omar was in the same situation. Both were critical of the authorities. Omar was dejected when he said, "Either the state has to give us a positive [response to the asylum application] or bring us back to our homeland and let us die there. That would be much better. You can't call this living." However, he did not want to return. "Haven't a clue why they laid on the pressure. They've given dozens of Somalis permission to stay in Norway. We're no different from them. So why are we treated differently?"

What upset Omar the most was not being allowed to work or go to school. Nor could he understand why so many other Somalis had been approved while he was rejected. He continued, "It's a hard life. I dunno what I'm s'posed to do. I'm mixed up. I'm just waiting for the gods to help, 'cause I've got no one else. I got no one to help me."

Most of the non-returnable asylum seekers at The River were from Somalia. Several of those we met had traumatic memories of the war. One told us:

'Every now and then it just bursts: bang! I'm standing there once, like, on the corner to sell weed, and my head starts hurting, my mind sees the old pictures. I said, "This can't go on." Called a mate and said I'm coming over. So I sit there all night thinking, is this a dream? I say to myself, "You sleeping or is it real, this thing, ordinary life, like?" 'Cause I'm thinking, "Why did I ever come here, what am I doing standing here?" You can believe me or not, but that's how my mind is working.'

Experiences from the war had made a great impact on him. He was confused and afraid, and he was not sure whether we would believe him. Another remarked, "I'm thinking, what's the point of living, like." He had no family in Norway, but he had made some friends. "And me mates tell me, like, cool it, burn some rope [smoke cannabis], you haven't done anything really, this is nothing. Why you wanna stress like that, take it easy, like."

Several of the refugees were traumatised, and cannabis softened their memories of war. However, several also told us that the drug could intensify recollections of traumatic events.[12] All the same, in a chaotic and difficult situation, cannabis and other drugs provided a free space for many, a chance for a break. Being in the company of other smokers and a street culture environment, many felt they could build new identities and, in this way, be respected and appreciated.

A policy field in the making

In the late 1990s, the number of asylum applicants was increasing in Norway. The annual figures used to be around 5,000 a year, but in 2002, it rose to 17,000. Restrictive measures were introduced to reduce the inflow, and they succeeded. However, asylum seekers remained in Norway, even if their applications had been rejected. Judged by the authorities' standards, it was safe for them to return to their countries. However, it was impossible to force them to leave, for two reasons: many came from countries with which Norway had no repatriation agreement (including Eritrea, Ethiopia and Somalia), and many had unclear identities, making it difficult for the police to establish where they should be returned (Brekke, 2008). A number of the young men at The River belonged to this group. They were non-returnable asylum seekers.

They were in a complicated situation. They were given neither job training nor help to learn the language while they waited for the authorities to consider their applications. It was unclear whether they had any rights to benefits from the welfare state, and in 2004, they lost the right to reside in asylum centres.[13] When we met the non-returnable refugees at The River, they described stressful circumstances. Several of them desperately lacked food, housing and money. What would happen if they approached the social welfare office? Would they receive support? Would they receive support on the condition that they agreed to leave? Would such contact increase the likelihood of forced deportation by the police?

Some of the young men at The River eventually tried to get help from the social security system, but area offices were unable to agree on the 'emergency assistance' tariff. The Oslo City Council decided in the spring of 2005 to provide board and lodging for non-returnable asylum seekers. In practice, however, it meant a bed at a shelter and not much money to live on. Some of the young men we interviewed said they had to get by on 60 NOK a day. Probably, they were referring to the social security tariff. With a change of government in 2005, non-returnable asylum seekers were allowed to stay temporarily at a reception centre. However, for young men with a taste for money and drugs, returning to the tedium of life at a reception centre could prove a very long road indeed.

The non-returnable asylum seekers felt they were "put on the street", and political leaders and high-level administrators let it be known that they should not receive any help. However, at the local level, a number of welfare state agents were in a bind: they felt that the lack of support for asylum seekers contradicted the core ethical principles of the welfare state, so they could not refuse to help them. Thus, political dilemmas that are usually handled at the political level were left to social and health policy workers in the field (Brekke, 2008). This was probably a new experience for a number of them. Suddenly, they were agents of social exclusion, asked to do the opposite of what they were trained to do:

---

now, they were supposed to reduce the asylum seekers' chances of becoming self-reliant. We saw few traces of these dilemmas on The River however. Most of the non-returnable asylum seekers there never really got the chance to discuss their possible rights.

Abdullah was 30 years old. He had come from Mogadishu, Somalia, where he had been working as a driver, but he told us it was dangerous: when someone wanted a car, they simply shot the driver. After almost three years in Norway, he did not speak Norwegian and his English was very poor. He explained to us, "Here is no life... They say, 'Your case is closed, final decision.'" He felt that he had no options. He was not allowed to work, learn Norwegian or go to another country of the European Union. Sharif, one of the other Somali non-returnable asylum seekers was desperate:

> *Sharif:* 'I don't see future, any future. It's just black. It's a black world. When I go back to my country, then it is still war.'
> *Interviewer:* 'So you're kind of trapped in a situation where you can't go back?'
> *Sharif:* 'Yeah, I don't know where I belong now. Somalia is no good now. Here is a little better. It's no civil war. A little bit better to get my bread. But not really better. I don't see any future.'

Abdullah and Sharif were unable to influence their own situations, and they were unable to contact the appropriate bureaucrats in the welfare system who could help them. Drawing on traditional conceptual tools for analysing power in sociology, we would not characterise them as having *little* power. Rather, they felt they were at a long distance from all relevant actors and all arenas where power is practised – they were *powerless* (Hernes, 1978).

In the Chapter Eight, we will return to the large differences between the young men at The River in this respect. Some of them had a well-developed competence when it came to knowledge of the welfare state and its support system. Some even bragged about their ability to drain resources from the state. However, others lacked this competence, and the non-returnable asylum seekers did not even have fundamental rights in the welfare state.

The non-returnable asylum seekers' situation is an extreme version of what other marginalised groups have to put up with.[14] Initially, the government took a tough stand on this question. Gradually, however, the course was adjusted, and the new social-democratic government in 2005 was partially responsible for this. Still, tensions related to these asylum seekers have not been resolved. The situation for this group really demonstrates how strong despair can be, even in a welfare state.

As we mentioned in Chapter Three, economic opportunity structures play a decisive role in the development of criminal subcultures. Classical works of sociology tell us, moreover, that social networks and identity building reinforce opportunity structures. Street culture is a haven for people whose everyday lives are troubled by uncertainty and a sense of alienation.

The River as refuge

Discrimination in education and the labour market, racism, poverty and immigrant experiences formed the framework for the interactions we observed at The River. Drug dealers are constituted as 'the Others'. Their position relies on a hegemonic structure in which they are subordinate and alien. While this status leaves a lasting mark on the dealers, they attempt to mitigate it by turning it into something else. Their counter-strategies include looking dangerous, in control and stylish. Street capital is a defence against being relegated to a subordinate, downtrodden position. The dealers at The River create their own subsociety, in the same way as previously described by researchers in both the Chicago and Birmingham Schools. They develop a street culture with its own rules, norms, rewards and sanctions.

When these young men seek refuge in subcultures like the one at The River, they also limit their exposure to school and workplace harassment. The River offers an escape route, a retreat from a world where they are always on the bottom. Environments like this become a free space, one where a sense of community may be found. For some, socialisation during childhood and adolescence was completely devoted to the creation of this type of free space and to developing the skills and knowledge required to survive in it.

The subculture represents resistance and opposition, a response to pressures felt by adolescents from certain social classes, areas or environments. The Birmingham School of Cultural Studies was particularly preoccupied with working–class youth. Their parents were being squeezed out of the traditional industries, and, not least, out of old working–class areas. A latent function of the subculture is to formulate the inherent structural contradictions in the parents' and the boys' situations. The youngsters want control over a delimited social space and territory where they feel at home (Cohen, 2005). The same is true of the dealers at The River. However, the subculture is a symbolic response as well. In London's East End, the consumption culture of the mods (Vespas and parkas) and the skinheads' stylised 'working–class look' played on various types of class tensions. The mods formulated tensions in capitalistic consumption. The skinhead aesthetic represented a retreat to puritanical identification with an imaginary working–class community. For the young minority ethnic men at The River, hip-hop was the most important cultural point of reference.

Old street culture, new ethnicity

The street culture at The River revolved around crime. Terms like 'respect' was central and upheld by publicly staged acts of violence. This is nothing new. It is depicted in the classics introduced in the previous chapter, and there have been gangs for many decades in Norway (Hauge, 1970). The difference today is that Oslo's street culture has acquired an ethnic dimension. The 'foreigner' has acquired a distinctive role. The public is increasingly inclined to associate people from minority ethnic groups with crime. One reason is that minority ethnic youth do in fact commit more crimes, according to the statistics (Skardhamar, 2006). Nor is there any doubt that the type of gang criminality gaining ground today was virtually unknown in Norway a few years back. The Pakistani community in Oslo is predominant in this respect.[15] However, we must also see recent years' developments in light of the popular cultural landscape. Gangsta rap made a hero of the gangster (Moshuus, 2005b).

A few years ago, things were different. Anthropologist Viggo Vestel carried out fieldwork in a multi-ethnic suburb in Oslo in the early 1990s and again late in the decade (Vestel, 2004). The minority ethnic boys changed their production of style during the 1990s. Many left uncertainty behind and grew into self-aware producers of potent signs. The reception of styles changed too. Fashions, greeting gestures, music and complete style packages dispersed from immigrant areas to larger youth groups. Young minority ethnic boys did not adopt the style of affluent West Oslo youth uncritically. They created a local style instead. Teenage boys started wearing gold rings, black silk shirts, leather jackets and gold necklaces. Inspired by gangsta rap, they idolised a flamboyant, macho image. It alluded to designer clothes, influence and wealth but in a modified form. Using Bourdieu's terminology, it was a sort of distorted symbolic capital. Rather than signalling empowerment based on educational qualifications, wealthy parents and cultural capital, it aspired to caricature. The caricature rests on another form of power – physical, brute power, developed in the street.

A study of heavy drug use echoes the tendencies that Vestel discovered. Another anthropologist, Geir Moshuus, gained access to a shooting gallery in an old, dilapidated building in the centre of Oslo. Even within this marginalised community, people from minority ethnic groups were looked down upon. The counter-strategies they developed were to enact street personas, embracing key elements of popular culture. Gangsta rap was an important source of inspiration. Moshuus (2005a) says that the oldest informants would not have referred to themselves as 'gangsters', although it seemed increasingly acceptable to the young. Over the course of his fieldwork, gangsta-style street culture spread throughout Oslo. The marginalised men formed new collectives that helped them 're-code their marginal positions in relation to the surrounding street worlds' (Moshuus, 2005a, p 279). He further demonstrates how this adaptation involves identities that are already in place in Western societies – for example, the 'gangster' and street culture, and not an 'immigrant honour culture', as is often portrayed by the media (and sometimes supported by research; see, for example, Lien, 2001, 2002; Bucerius, 2007). This time, however, the gangster hero was black.

The most important historical development in this respect was the *mainstreaming* of hip-hop and rap. In listening to and identifying with hip-hop, minority ethnic men went from being losers in a white Norwegian mainstream society to black heroes in hip-hop mythology. This was important for the young men at The River.

A cultural expression for marginalised people

Hip-hop culture articulates ethnic and class tensions and is a product of African-American urban culture. It is 'overwhelmingly and fundamentally black American' (Perry, 2004, p. 2). That was probably the reason why The River dealers identified with it. They were not American, but they were black. Some were performers; others just liked to listen. One of the guys said, "It's all there in the music, like. It cheers me up, gets me going." It was relaxing but encouraging as well. Daniel and Mattar emphasised how hip-hop gave them a sense of freedom. Daniel explained, "The main thing about hip-hop is we can say whatever we want. Nobody's going to kick up a fuss, like, 'cause we got the music, innit." They discovered a language and taught themselves to master it. They grew in self-confidence and enjoyed a wider repertoire of self-expression. This was particularly apparent among the younger dealers who were raised in Norway, but many of the younger refugees also enjoyed the music. Philosopher Antonio Gramsci (1992) argues that a critical and reflective mindset can emerge in groups without academic traditions. Popular culture can be an arena of this 'organic intellectualism'.

One of the most committed hip-hoppers at The River was nicknamed Tupac. He had a large pendant inscribed with Tupac Shakur's initials, and he often rapped his songs while hanging in the area. Hip-hop can be divided into different genres (for example, party rap, jazz/bohemian, mack and reality rap; see Krims, 2000). Reality rap emphasises 'keeping it real' or 'telling the true story'. When this reality is drug dealing and gang life, it is often called gangsta rap, and Tupac is seen as one of the founders of this version of hip-hop.[16] Of all the rap genres, gangsta rap in particular gave the guys something society could not. They felt their lives were hard and a constant battle to preserve some sense of self-respect. Like the 'thugs' or 'hustlers' described in gangsta rap, they sold drugs, were chased by the police and lived on the street at times. Gangsta rap also allowed them to revisit difficult childhoods and feelings of alienation and oppression.[17] McAuley (2007) similarly describes how hip-hop resonates with life experiences of social and economical exclusion, also for white youths in deprived urban areas in England.

Hip-hop has also given a new meaning to the 'street' concept and new interpretative matrices for processing events on the street. Philip Lalander (2005) studied Swedish-Chilean young men and concluded that the street is an arena where problems from home are resolved, a place of excitement, and something authentic and real. These characteristics speak to the fascination that street culture has, both for its participants and for outsiders. He further described how the construction of a mythological street culture is connected to music styles such as hip-hop. By strongly demarcating between the street and other social worlds, they vent sorrow and disappointment and create dignity.

Music cultures can be a source of pride for marginalised people. Listen, for example, to Ebo and Denis when they talk about hip-hop and growing up in one of Oslo's suburbs:

> *Ebo:* 'Everybody listened to hip-hop, one way or another. But, as I said, there were a lot of funny people there. They weren't all fans. Like Turks and the like, they listened to techno and that sort of stuff, see. There was like long techno period too, I remember it. [Denis laughs] Lasted forever, you know, wherever you went they played techno....'
> *Interviewer:* 'So you two were trendsetters?'
> *Denis:* 'We listened to hip-hop at home, not other places. On the CD player or cassette player, you know. You didn't go to the youth club to hear hip-hop, like. They played techno.'

Many of the dealers at The River were innovators of popular culture. Ebo and Denis found inspiration abroad and invented their own musical style, distinct from the Norwegian ethnic style as well as from that of the 'Turks'. They also formulated the element of opposition within hip-hop as an attitude of scepticism of everything Norwegian; long-term exposure to racism encouraged some to express this scepticism more aggressively. Others spurned the Norwegian culture by emphasising its distinctiveness. It became popular in hip-hop lyrics, for instance, to call ethnic Norwegian people 'potatoes' and pronounce the word *norsk* (= Norwegian) as *torsk* (= cod). By playing on the uninspiring blandness of cod and potatoes, which also is traditional Norwegian food, minority ethnic boys seemed like exotic seasoning in comparison. In a society where individuality is prized, a different ethnic background can sometimes be an advantage. By seeing Norwegian-ness as a *sign* with insipidness, the minority ethnic boys became exciting.

As hip-hop became mainstream, Ebo and Denis's popularity with the girls also increased. They also started a hip-hop group. The girls loved the band, and word spread far beyond theire immediate circle of friends and acquaintances. At performances, girls tugged on rappers' clothes. When the performance was over, the girls wanted to go backstage. "You can't say no to something like that, can you?" remarked Ebo, chuckling.

In a study of masculinity and gangsta rap from Denmark, Sune Q. Jensen (2007) described the complex way that minority ethnic men capitalise on their 'otherness' by embracing the stigma of being both 'dangerous' and sexually alluring. He further argues that 'dangerous' is an integral part of 'sexy' and that playing the dangerous foreigner is a strategy not only for relating in the street but also for attracting girls. Being perceived as dangerous can be seen as cool and therefore sexy (Jensen, 2007, p 324). Such role playing often emerges from socioeconomic oppression; still, it can be done just because it is an attractive possibility. Ebo and Denis's story illustrates how a music culture can open doors for marginalised groups. Thanks to their connection with an increasingly mainstream youth culture, their status changed radically. The young men's music-based mechanisms of change may well resemble those of other youth cultures, such as rock, techno or even the flower power movement of the 1960s.

An imaginary solution

What we see emerging is a pattern in which some of the young men at The River became pioneers within a broader youth culture. The Norwegian-Africans were recognised as *genuine* – authentic – because they were black. Their connection to the mythological 'street' in gangsta rap, through dealing drugs and hanging out at The River, further increased this identification, as did their experiences of socioeconomic marginalisation and racism. In this way, The River dealers' approach to gangsta rap may have been less a playful act (which is often the case for mainstream listeners) and more a way to cope with life. For example, when we asked one of the dealers whether it was hard to get money, he replied, "It is 'get rich or die tryin', you know," which is the title of 50 Cent's breakthrough album. Another dealer stated, "I don't know, man. It is a hard life. That's why I say 'thug life.'" The latter expression is the title of a legendary Tupac album from the mid 1990s.[18] Without resources to manage conventional life, and feeling estranged from white middle-class society, the interwoven mixture of life at The River and hip-hop mythology became a subcultural refuge.

Keyes (2004) argues that hip-hop has several positive functions for deprived adolescents. It gives them a chance to express themselves, to exert social control, and to build self-confidence and ethnic pride, and it enables political opposition. Unlike in institutionalised politics, the young men at The River found a space within hip-hop where they could express themselves. Self-confidence, appeal to the opposite sex and a sense of being hip trendsetters echo in many ways what Thornton (1995) describes as 'subcultural capital'. Subcultural capital can even be translated into economic capital, she argues, via recording contracts and work as DJs, or in clothes design, fashion or music journalism. In most cases, however, subcultural capital does not translate into money or jobs – at least, not for people who do not already have social and cultural capital such as social networks, middle-class socialisation, education and the necessary language skills.

Cohen argued in the 1970s that the subculture's 'solution' to socioeconomic marginalisation is 'magical' or 'imaginary' (Cohen, 2005). Most importantly, the subculture does not take the struggle to the arenas where the power is. It does not enable the participants to cope with difficult situations or the unpleasant sides of mainstream society. Rather, it encourages them to seek refuge in a place where other rules apply and where harassment and discontent can be reinterpreted. This has its advantages, but it becomes increasingly harder to deal with real problems. The subculture is a double-edged sword. It can help the participants transform failure into something else. For instance, supported by images from gangsta rap, young men can turn the loss of a legitimate job (and the need to sell cannabis at The River) into an expression of freedom and resistance. The alternative would be to compromise one's street habitus and to practise the behavioural codes of the workplace – privileging discipline, good manners and nice language. Many would feel as if their identity were under siege if they made such a compromise, while others might even consider it a betrayal (Bourgois, 2003a, p 145). This is an important tension for marginalised and stigmatised groups. On the one hand, subcultures can strengthen self-confidence and empowerment. On the other hand, subcultures exacerbate isolation from mainstream society.

Notes

[1] Field observation by Sveinung Sandberg with an employee of the Outreach Service (*Uteseksjonen*), November 2005.

[2] Researchers may, however, transform this assertion into a variety of research strategies when studying poverty and marginalisation. A conventional approach is to define as poor those whose income remains below 60% of the national equivalent disposable income. However, the results will depend on the shape of the income distribution of each country and not on absolute income. A way to solve this problem is to compose units that are larger than individual countries; for example, set a common poverty line for all Nordic countries, or merge European countries together (Kangas and Ritakallio, 2007).

[3] The income differences between regions are also relatively small (Kangas and Ritakallio, 2007).

[4] To investigate patterns of chronic poverty, one needs to follow people over time. When 'poverty' is defined as 50% of the median income, only 0.6% of the adult population remained in this position over a six-year span. (Epland, 2005, p 11). In a personal communication, Epland suggested that a 'permanent poor' group would amount to approximately 20–30,000 people of a Norwegian adult population of 3.6 million.

[5] However, there is variation, including some long-term periods, and a large proportion of those who exit social assistance later re-enter (Hansen, 2008).

[6] This has also been a finding in many previous studies in this area, starting with Duncan et al's (1988) classic.

[7] However, there are differences between the groups, and a few minority ethnic groups outperform the majority population. For example, those of Indian ancestry perform well in both Norway and Britain, and those of Chinese ancestry in Britain (Heath et al, 2008).

[8] Heath et al (2008) contains an update on the literature on immigration and education and occupation in Europe. The patterns are surprisingly identical in the US (see Kao and Thompson, 2003). Both reviews suggest that half or more of ethnic disadvantage can be explained by social background.

[9] It is a complicated field to study. Discrimination takes many different forms; it is morally illegitimate, and illegal to some extent, making it difficult to investigate (Rogstad, 2000, pp 41–8). Differences that remain after controlling for education and experience could possibly be explained by factors that are difficult to observe but not distributed randomly.

[10] There is no reason however to deny the young men's tendency to pin the racist label on everyone they had clashed with, including teachers, social and child welfare officers. It increased the legitimacy of the conflicts they had. The dealers also tended to use offensive terms to describe ethnic differences among themselves.

[11] The non-returnable asylum seekers shared many of the same experiences, though their individual circumstances were highly dissimilar. According to the Norwegian Foreign Ministry's definition of 'non-returnable' asylum seeker', the applicant must have cooperated with the Ministry and their return found to be impossible or the applicant's identity unknown. The Equality and Anti-discrimination Ombudsman (*Likestillings og diskrimineringsombudet*) stresses rather the asylum seeker's personal perception of his or her returnability. We call them non-returnable because they have had their applications turned down but have not been forced to leave the country. In most cases, this was because their 'country of origin' would not accept them. Some of them may have been in hiding from the police, although it is unlikely in our view, because contact with us was established very easily. After we completed our data collection, the authorities began to send refugees back to Somalia.

[12] Such reactions have, to our knowledge, not been described in the literature. However, there is agreement in the literature that brief psychotic episodes may result from cannabis use and that there is increasing risk for more lasting serious psychiatric reactions, at least after chronic cannabis use (see Chapter Five).

[13] Both measures were criticised by the United Nations Committee on Economic, Social and Cultural Rights (www.nakmi.no/nyheter/artikkel.asp?NyhetID=400&SpraakID=1&SeksjonID=2).

[14] The interviews with this group were painful. Several appealed to us for help. After discussing it, we decided not to intervene with the authorities. The reason was that this would restructure our relations with the group completely. We understood early that many of the stories they told were aimed at positioning them in a welfare state context and that it would be impossible for us to get the kind of information we wanted if they also saw us as possible suppliers of benefits. Rumours about this would also rapidly spread at The River. However, in some cases, we took time to describe the welfare state system and helped them identify the relevant institutions and actors.

[15] The so-called A and B gangs in Oslo are at the core of these developments; both are built around young adults, and adults from minority ethnic communities. They have huge economic resources in an organised system held together by family loyalties.

[16] Even though he was shot dead in 1996, the American gangsta rapper, actor and social activist Tupac Shakur was the most admired artist among the young men at The River. They often said he was different, deep, the greatest or had everything.

[17] Tupac is probably the best example of this combination of gangster attitude, personal lyrics and political opposition. The lyrics to *Dear Mama* are a good example of emotional lyrics, while street culture references are seen in, for example, one-liners such as, 'I'm suicidal so don't stand near me' (from *So many tears*) and 'I ain't a killa but don't push me, revenge is like the sweetest joy next to gettin' pussy' (from *Hail Mary*). His radical political stance is evident in quotations such as 'They got money for wars, but can't feed the poor (from *Keep ya head up*) and 'instead of a war on poverty, they have a war on drugs so that the police can bother me' (from *Changes*). His life story reflects these same tensions (see Dyson, 2001).

[18] He translated it to 'The Hate U Gave Lil' Infants Fuck Everybody' (Light, 1996, p 29). This is a good example of the close relationship between the gangsta image and political radical critique in gangsta rap.

FIVE

Drugs and masculinity

This is the view from one of the main dealing spots. Several streets cross and there are always customers passing by. Here The River dealers were also using their drugs, a practice interwoven in the young men's masculinity constructions. It was, for example, important not to be regarded as 'dependent'.

Drug competence

Most of the young men at The River grew up in Norway and started smoking cannabis with their peers in their early teens. The initiation into cannabis use was a rite of passage; it signified the end of childhood. It was a gateway to thrills and adventures and meant a gradual incorporation into new networks. Cannabis use became a key element of a youthful subculture. It was an activity far from parents, teachers and conventional values.

However, the importance of cannabis – and partly also other psychoactive substances – went wider. Cannabis gradually became a key element in their 'street capital'. The most important activity at The River was dealing cannabis. To be a good dealer, one needs skills, especially the ability to differentiate between cannabis from Pakistan, Nepal or Morocco and 'skunk', which is grown in Europe. This competence depends heavily on a deep and personal knowledge of the psychoactive effects of cannabis (and other drugs). Moreover, the various substances have different symbolic meanings, and these meanings and values change over time. It is said that in Greenland, there are innumerable concepts describing the different kinds of snow. The dealers at The River were able to talk about their use of drugs and about being stoned with a rich, multifaceted language, in great depth and very persuasively.

The most important norm regulating their *use* of drugs was that they had to maintain control: they could not be seen as 'dependent' or as using too much.[1] If they failed, the street capital they had accumulated over many years would be at risk.

Getting stoned

It took a while for some to learn how to smoke cannabis, while others picked it up quickly. This is how Daniel and Mattar described their first experiences:

> *Interviewer:* 'So you took to cannabis from the start? What did you like about it?'
> *Mattar:* 'Getting stoned.'
> *Daniel:* [laughs] 'No, I just enjoyed the sensation, the feeling, from the start.'
> *Interviewer:* 'Did you get high that first time? Or did you need more time to get the hang of it?'
> *Daniel:* 'I got stoned the first time.'

Getting stoned or high means becoming intoxicated, but there is more to the concept. It implies getting intoxicated in a responsive, powerful and clear way. Alcohol will not make a drinker stoned. The hallucinogenic properties of cannabis make the substance different. The user needs to open up to the experience and learn to *interpret* what the signals mean. Getting stoned is a learned social skill.

Social scientists soon realised how complicated the process of learning to use cannabis can be. In an early work, sociologist Howard Becker (1953) discussed the time required to achieve the desired effects. To get high, to enjoy the effect, the user needs to negotiate three steps, he says. The user must (1) learn to smoke in the proper way, (2) learn to perceive the effects and make the connection with using the drug and (3) learn to enjoy the effects, the central point being the gradual appropriation of a framework for experiencing and interpreting the effects – it does not happen by instinct. The stories Becker heard had one thing in common: few of his informants got high the first time. Being high is a learned behaviour, and it takes time to learn.

Daniel became stoned the first time he used the drug. He thought it was a kind of gift; either he was simply lucky or he had a natural talent. Daniel and Mattar both started smoking in their early teens and soon developed a regular cannabis habit. When we interviewed them, they were in their early twenties, and they still smoked regularly. Cannabis signified leisure, sociability and fellowship, and others shared their views. The young men at The River remarked on the sense of fellowship and pleasure they got from smoking – a relaxed, mild sense of inertia. The substance continued to have a place in their everyday lives as they grew into adulthood. They enjoyed lighting up. Many of our research participants told us they had smoked a joint before the interviews. It was part of their normal, everyday routine, and most had also had periods of really intensive smoking, often several grams a day.

We interviewed Daniel and Mattar at Daniel's place, a flat his brother rented and paid for partly with his housing benefit. The furniture was spartan, but it was clean and tidy. They had high-end stereo equipment in a corner, a modern TV and DVD player, and a good selection of DVDs. They were self-assured and coiled themselves up on the sofa while they spoke intensely about 'hash': Saturday afternoon, high-grade quality hash, the usual group of seven or eight friends (all males), a good film in the DVD player, the whole evening to look forward to, and joints passed round. They told us that on Saturdays afternoons, they used to be in party mode. Later in the evening, they would set off for the city hoping to meet girls. The main difference between The River dealers and the majority of youth in Oslo was that their drug of choice from early on was cannabis, not alcohol. As such, it distinguished these boys from most ethnic Norwegian adolescents.

The so-called 'normalisation thesis' has played an important role in recent debates on illegal drug use, particularly in the UK (Parker et al, 1998). The argument is that illegal drug use once was associated with individual pathology and social marginalisation, but that it has increasingly become an integrated and unremarkable part of ordinary young people's lives. Evidence from Norway in this respect is ambiguous: On the one hand, parental socioeconomic status seems to play a minor role as a factor behind adolescent illegal drug use. However, poor parental monitoring and care seems to be important, and from early on, one can observe associations between illegal drug use and educational and conduct problems (Pape and Rossow, 2004). With increasing age we see an increasing social marginalisation even of recreational users of illegal drugs (Pedersen, 2009).

Although many young Norwegians try cannabis, few are regular users. However, for the young men at The River, it had pride of place. Cannabis can have a wide variety of effects, they say. It can make you gregarious and extroverted. Some describe feeling things more clearly, or emphatically, especially musical experiences. They get 'high' or 'stoned', and many use the word 'chill' to describe the experience, suggesting a laidback, easygoing mood. The word 'chill', in this context, is actually derived from chillum, the name for marijuana pipes in Jamaica (Booth, 2003). Daniel also claimed "pot makes you think better", because "it opens your mind". Thinking becomes less inhibited, and people feel less weighed down by pressures and disruptive or confusing ideas. This was Usman's description:

> 'You're smoking, like, and you're off on a high, y'know. I could just prattle on with this guy, totally normal, like, the whole time, y'know. I dunno, I sort of dig the feeling, the effect. You don't get all wound up, you don't get all hyper, with them. You wind down, like.'

Drugs are at the centre at The River, and the dealers there have a sophisticated drug vocabulary. Cannabis is not just cannabis, it is 'moroc', 'kif', 'ganja', 'tjall', 'gallar','shit' or 'skit'. They know where it is manufactured, its grades, its strength, its price range, techniques for using it and its various effects – including knowledge of its harmful effects and about tolerance, dependency and abuse. This knowledge represents an important form of street capital.

They use drugs, and they do so for many reasons. The most cited one is also the simplest: being high is an exquisite sensation; it makes you feel good. The point is simple but not obvious either to the scientific community or the general public. We often hear drug use described as self-medication or as a means to escape a painful reality. However, these were not the reasons given by these young men – at least not in the first place, and not in relation to cannabis. They considered cannabis to be a 'soft drug'. They drew a clear distinction between cannabis on the one hand and 'pills', amphetamines, ecstasy and cocaine on the other. Most had experimented with all these substances, but cannabis was their drug of choice.

You feel like a king

The young men's stories about cannabis revolved around the pleasures of taking it and learning how to get stoned. They started out – in their early adolescence – with cannabis, like other adolescents start drinking. They told us about the thrill, about pushing boundaries and stepping into the adult world. Alcohol, however, is legal in Norway; cannabis is not. This explains the dramatic differences between the potential consequences of alcohol and cannabis use. Alcohol may be dangerous, of course, but alcohol consumption is legal, and it mimics substance use in mainstream culture. Cannabis, on the other hand, can easily draw peer groups to illegal and criminal networks.

Rashid is an example. He grew up in an Oslo suburb and started staying out at night in his early teens. His mother was alone and unable to care for him adequately. He started sleeping in basement storage rooms in the neighbourhood with friends. In these storage rooms they had their first experiments with hash, which culminated in them being apprehended by the police.

> 'The whole stairwell stank to high heaven. A neighbour came in; it stank so much he rang the police. The police used to come with a dog, and they always found us. Everyone was taken into custody, all of us crammed into the same cell. When we were put in the cell, we still had hashish and marijuana on us, which they hadn't found. So we sat there smoking a joint, in the lockup. And we weren't nicked for it. See, when you get away with something like that, it makes you feel like a king, you know. You feel so fucking superior.'

Starting to smoke cannabis was one of the most important events of Rashid's early teens. Not only was the effect good, it was also an effective way of transgressing norms and pressing limits. Cannabis provided material for an anti-mainstream subculture, and it could be used to build a more adult identity. When Rashid and his friends started smoking cannabis, they announced to the whole world that childhood was history.

These beginnings are similar to other adolescents' experiments with alcohol. They find a spot for themselves where their parents cannot see them. It is about flirting, sexuality, and learning what it feels like to drink or take drugs. The unsupervised sites of their initial drug experiences may also be places where sexuality and masculinity are tried out as well. Alcohol can lead to serious problems for all young people. Physical injury, accidents and violence are common effects of drink, and there is evidence that heavy drinking at a young age may predispose some to alcohol problems later in life (Dawson, 2000). However, alcohol is legal and does not socialise young people in the same way that cannabis may – to a life of crime or into the illegal drug economy. Cannabis is part of an illicit economy, and it may play an import role along the road in deviant identities.

In Rashid's story, the police eventually came with their dogs and took him and his friends into custody. Having chosen cannabis as their drug of choice, they were gradually drawn into an alternative subculture where identity building was in opposition to the police and mainstream society. To get hold of supplies, cannabis users come in contact with the illegal economy. Many of The River dealers developed early connections with older dealers who had criminal records. In the previous chapter, we described the stigmatised and marginalised position of many of The River dealers. Early experiences with cannabis and social contacts in criminal networks opened up a new world for them, one in which they could be the champions. It also started the slow development and nurturing of a street habitus. This embodied system of dispositions, skills and competences became useful for them later when they got more involved in violent street culture and began dealing drugs at The River.

The darker side

Cannabis was not seen as a dangerous drug, at least not at first. The dealers at The River told similar stories: having learned how to use cannabis to get high, it became an enjoyable and relaxing experience. At the same time, however, many of them mentioned the dangers of overuse, resulting in increased tolerance and dependency. Wari smoked about 10 grams of cannabis a day at times.

> *Interviewer:* 'Say you smoke a lot of hash, d'you notice any problems?'
> *Wari:* 'When I smoke in quantity, I get beyond stoned. I can't get high any more, it just won't work. The joint doesn't affect me; I get stoned in my head, y'know. Need something stronger, but that's bad, isn't it?'

Wari had learned to use the drug, learned to appreciate its effect. However, he also said that its effect was diminishing. He had built up a tolerance to it, so that the same dose produced a steadily weaker response. Amin, one of the other dealers, discovered how dependent he was on cannabis, after first being arrested.

> 'I smoked more and more. So when I was in jail, I got abstinence symptoms because I couldn't get any weed. The first few months sitting in Block B, like … you're indoors 23 hours a day, you get one hour outside. You're locked in the whole time.'

His cannabis abstinence symptoms were painful both physically and mentally. They made his time in prison, with its ban on visits and correspondence, harder to bear. A number of the dealers at The River told us about their dependence on cannabis.

A cannabis dependence syndrome has been documented in recent years, even if terms such as cannabis dependence are contested, not least from a sociological perspective (see endnote 1). Epidemiological studies indicate that the risk of cannabis dependence seems to be around 10% among people who have ever used cannabis, and around one in six among people who begin smoking in adolescence (Room et al, 2008). Poor parental bonds, problems at school and early-onset behavioural problems are all risk factors (Hall, 2006; Jenkins, 2006). In other words, cannabis seems to be most dangerous for those with the most problems to start with. This put the young men at The River at a particular risk for developing a problematic pattern of cannabis use.

The dealers' ambivalence to cannabis was rooted in its possible harmful effects. Rashid was more sceptical about cannabis than most of them. He claimed he had stopped smoking. He wove his experience into a frame story, describing how cannabis gradually takes control and affects one's interpersonal relationships. He described the long-term effects in the following way:

> 'Depressions, thinking, what the fuck, where am I going to get the money? You have to drag yourself out of the depression without doing anything stupider than you already have. People dig their graves deeper and deeper. You dig, you dig, you dig. When you meet people you owe something to, you run in circles round the issue. But you're only chasing your own tail, see. You can't escape. That's the vicious circle.'

Rashid was prone to depression, and he was confused. However, what is remarkable were the close connections he made among what he perceived as depression, his need to get hold of money and the character of his social network. He associated cannabis with broken promises and outstanding debts. Earlier in the interview, he stressed the connections between cannabis tolerance, dependency and nerves. When he spelled out his reasons for deciding to quit, he lighted on the problems cannabis caused in his daily life. Cannabis use became a signifier for everything that went wrong, including his school problems and trouble with the police, but also for an unforgiving economic environment. Admittedly, the drug has an enjoyable effect and provides a good income. Because both the income and use are illegal, however, cannabis throws an ordinary life into crisis. Above all, it complicates relationships with people who have lent you money.

Most of the young men said they used too much cannabis. They knew a lot about the dangers and the costs. They talked about tolerance, dependency and the sense of apathy that comes over you if you smoke too much. Some of them had had 'nervous attacks'. More importantly, however, they had started to get involved in criminal networks. Rashid gave one account in the excerpt included previously. Often, the circle cropped up as a metaphor for their problems. Some of them also believed that cannabis remained stored in the body, and that even when you stopped using it, traces remained, possibly "for many years". Rashid was convinced of the drug's harmful effect on male fertility: "All that shit, stays inside you for ages, mate. Your sperm gets polluted, you can't even get children. Quality drops. You drop."

Rashid's information possibly stems from research quoted by the media, but the information circulates on the street as well. He expanded the danger to the reproductive system into wider, existential consequences: when your sperm are damaged, you are damaged as well. He believed that having children becomes impossible, and thus the quality of your life project suffers.[2] The young men's stories about cannabis are thus not only about joy, pleasure and subcultural revolt but also about reduced fertility, damaged masculinity and failure.

In Christopher Mullins's (2006) study, the most clearly recognised subordinate masculinity on the street was labelled 'punk'. A punk demonstrably failed to live up to the demands of street masculinity. The category of punk is linked to both femininity and male homosexuality. Punks were regarded as soft, womanly, a 'bitch' or a 'fag'. Drug addicts were also considered punks. One of Mullins's informants described robbing addicts as "taking candy from a kid" (2006, p 68). There was no risk of retaliation. In Mullins study a heavily addicted crack user described how crack dealers frequently threatened him.[3] Because the crack dealers used marijuana regularly, he tried to invert his subordinate relationship with them by arguing that their cannabis use was no better than his own use of crack. However, he did so in vain, because street wisdom in St. Louis, Missouri, did not equate the use of cannabis with crack when it came to posing a threat to masculinity. All the same, using *too much* cannabis and showing signs of dependence were seen as a threat to street masculinity and street capital at The River.

Cannabis use was a symbol of childhood's end and entry into adulthood. With first-hand knowledge of its varieties and effects, cannabis became for some a game about testing boundaries and building semi-criminal identities at the margins of mainstream adolescent groups. Many continued to smoke cannabis and began to sell it as they matured into young adults. Sometimes they managed to create social settings where they could enjoy themselves, where drug consumption was tied to a much-longed-for sense of well-being. However, most of the young men at The River had also begun to see that a price had to be paid.

Cannabis was the most important drug at The River, but the dealers also used alcohol and other illegal drugs. A complex web of cultural norms, ideas about psychoactive effects, and stories about dangers and dependency governed the dealers' patterns of drug use as well as their opinions about different drugs.

Alcohol: unclean for 40 days

Bucerius (2007) studied a group of street drug dealers in Frankfurt who were quite similar to the dealers in our study – young minority ethnic men with Islamic backgrounds. She argues that their distinct concepts of purity/impurity were important in helping to determine which drugs they sold and to whom they preferred to sell drugs. They preferred cannabis to harder drugs and tried to avoid selling to other Muslims, especially women.[4] They also treated money from the drug business as '*Haram Paras*', or impure, and it could not be spent on the family or durable goods or be saved for the future. Symbolic boundaries between drugs are important for all users and dealers, religious or not, and there is a general tradition of spending 'criminal money' quickly. However, there are some important culturally specific characteristics of the drug trade for users and dealers with an Islamic background. This is most clearly seen when comparing cannabis with alcohol.

Many of The River dealers with a strong Muslim identity were ambivalent about drink. This is what Daniel and Mattar had to say:

> *Interviewer:* 'So if you're a Muslim, what would be worse, smoking hash or drinking?'
> *Mattar:* 'There's nothing in the *Qur'an* about hash. It's only your health that's on the line. So as far as that's concerned, it's mostly pig meat and alcohol.'
> *Interviewer:* 'But doesn't the *Qur'an* have a ban on drink?'
> *Mattar:* 'Yep.'
> *Interviewer:* 'But nothing on hash?'
> *Mattar:* 'Not on dope, no, nothing like that.'
> *Interviewer:* 'So if you compared them, is hash less risky than drink?'
> *Mattar:* 'Drink is much more dangerous.'
> *Daniel:* 'When you're a Muslim and drink, it takes 40 days before you're clean again.'
> *Mattar:* 'You're not clean. Can't pray to your God. Must not eat pork either.'

Most of the guys at The River were raised as Muslims, although the role that religion played in their lives varied considerably. They frequently discussed Islam in a rather detached manner. Culturally speaking, alcohol still carried a stigma for them, and it was usually mentioned together with pork. In Islam, both make one unclean. Most of the dealers at The River regarded cannabis as something completely different from alcohol. Adolescents in their early teens considered cannabis to be more risky than alcohol, but they did not share this opinion.[5] From early on, they had a lower threshold to experimenting with cannabis.

How does this picture comport with standard interpretations of the *Qur'an*? The answer is not obvious.[6] The following appear to be the key passages:

> 5.90:You who believe liquor and gambling, idols and raffles, are only the filthy work of Satan; turn aside from it so that you may prosper.

> 5.91: Satan only wants to stir up enmity and jealousy among you by means of liquor and gambling, and to hinder you from remembering God and from praying. So will you stop? (Chapter 5: 'The Dinner Table')[7]

The word 'alcohol' is not used in the original Arabic text. *Khamr* is the term. What counts as an intoxicant seems to extend beyond alcohol, and some would doubtless include cannabis and *khat* under the *khamr* umbrella.There are, however, historical and cultural differences, and the ban is always subject to local adaptation and interpretation.Alcohol is proscribed across the board by Islam and, as a rule, its prohibition is strictly enforced. In contrast, several Muslim countries appear to have a more liberal tradition regarding cannabis.[8]

Generally, people from minority ethnic groups face a range of overlapping and cross-cutting normative values and expectations. Bauman (1997) argues that new alliances and cultures have hybridised Europe and may challenge old norms and values in European countries, as well as those from South Asia or Africa, for example.The process of reinvention and renegotiation hybridises ideas and practices all the time (Bauman, 1997). Still, a number of studies conclude that the Muslims' ban on alcohol seems to be rather durable.Abstaining from alcohol seems to be regarded as 'rational' and 'logical' by many Muslims living in Western countries. Many negative aspects of non-Muslim societies, such as prostitution, premarital pregnancy and the spread of HIV, are attributed to the disinhibiting effects of alcohol (Bradby, 2007).This is probably one of the reasons why the use of cannabis is as widespread, relatively speaking, as it appears to be among Muslim adolescents in Norway.[9]

It may also partly explain why many of the cannabis dealers at The River had an Islamic background. Cannabis is forbidden by secular law, but alcohol is forbidden by religious law.This increased the risk of early experimentation with cannabis for some groups of minority ethnic youths relative to other minority groups or the ethnic majority, and the early introduction to an illegal economy made it easier to become dealers later.

Rohypnol: heroin's little brother

The young men at The River also made a very clear distinction between cannabis and other illegal substances. This is what Wari said:

> *Interviewer:* 'So there's no one that doesn't smoke?'
> *Wari:* 'No, they all smoke. At least the guys I know.'
> *Interviewer:* 'But from smoking hash to taking pills [Rohypnol; see later], isn't that a big step?'
> *Wari:* 'Yeah, it is. I've tried coke, and I tried amphetamine once. Pills and ecstasy and whatnot, they don't agree with me. So I stick to hash. It's the best, man!'

European youths in their early teens view *all* illegal substances as dangerous. By their mid-teens, however, views begin to differentiate (McIntosh et al, 2003). While they continue to view substances like cocaine and ecstasy as 'narcotics', they now rank cannabis more or less on a par with alcohol and tobacco (Pearson and Shiler, 2002). This corresponds with what we found among our research participants at The River, although they had already adopted this view of cannabis in their early teens.

Distinctions between different illegal drugs were closely linked to the accumulation and symbolic construction of street capital. Cannabis was in a class of its own, and the young men were more afraid of other illegal substances. Still, they both used and sold them. Amphetamines and cocaine played an important role, but 'pills' were most important. All types of pills can be bought on the streets of Oslo. One of the most popular used to be the sleep-inducing drug Rohypnol, or *hyppere*.[10] It ranked as one of the country's most sold benzodiazepine for a time, and authorities have seized large quantities from illegal sources, especially former Eastern bloc countries. Several of the young men at The River told us about Rohypnol's ability to increase perceived energy levels and temper tendencies towards self-criticism. One of them said: "One pill, and you feel like nobody can get the better of you. You can run through the window if you see a cash register or machine, fruit machine." The pills provided courage when they had burglary on their minds, or some job requiring more than the usual amount of courage.

A number of studies indicate that Rohypnol may foster feelings of aggression in some individuals (Bramness et al, 2006). In addition, a large number of 'drunk drivers' have been found to be under the influence of such pills in Norway.[11] For that reason, the chemical group (Flunitrazepan) that includes Rohypnol was upgraded from a class B to the most strictly regulated class A drug group. The customs authorities, police and manufacturers ran a coordinated campaign, and the Rohypnol brand was eventually pulled off the market. Police statistics illustrate the drug's waning popularity. Within a few years, the seizure rate fell dramatically (KRIPOS, 2006).

The young men at The River had also debated Rohypnol intensely. Most had grown sceptical and stopped using it. Amin said:

> 'Yeah, two or three years ago, there was a lot of it around, but not nowadays. None of my mates use it at all, it's just not in circulation. No one uses it anymore. It's past its sell-by date, to put it like that. Because in reality you get really fucked up. And you know it. Totally annihilated.'

Usman, whom we introduced in Chapter Two, had sold and used large quantities of *hyppere*. We interviewed him several times, and he had already begun to show signs of abuse, including facial swelling and disconnected speech. He looked like a 'fallen gangster' trying to maintain his image. It shone through the cracks, however, that his career was faltering, and much of his everyday life was devoted to his personal drug habit. He had started taking Rohypnol pills as a teenager because, as he said, they helped him "chill out". It made him create 'a place of his own'. The drug made him vanish. Sensing its danger, he had tried to cut it out entirely over the past few years. This is what he said about the effects:

> *Usman:* 'Rohypnol I like, but it ruins your memory, man. Like, I was in the security cell, you know. You know, before they throw me in, I unscrew the little bottle. And 20 pills. I swallow the whole fucking lot. Bang! I'm out, don't remember a fucking thing. Wake up in the morning. "What am I doing here?" I say. Can't remember nothing.'
> *Interviewer:* 'So you think Rohypnol's a dangerous drug?'
> *Usman:* 'Man, its heroin's little brother.'

Other young men also used the expression 'it's heroin's little brother', and we wondered what explains this unusual metaphor? None of our respondents had used much heroin. However, they were, of course, aware of the risks associated with it. Perhaps the key to the metaphor lies in heroin's assumed danger. For although Rohypnol may induce aggressive behaviour in some, it helps you turn your back on the world and withdraw to a private place. Originally a sleeping drug, it has a powerful sedative effect. Several studies describe heroin as 'the perfect drug' if what you are after is withdrawal from the world, peace, quiet and rest (Lalander, 2003).

In the previous quotation, Usman talks about retreating from everyday reality. However, at the same time, people claim that Rohypnol increases the potential for aggressive or violent behaviour. In this way, Rohypnol could be used to boost street habitus and 'artificially' to fortify street capital – something heroin hardly ever does. If you go out after taking Rohypnol, you risk losing your self-control and getting into fights. Most likely, then, the metaphor embraces more than Rohypnol's sedative, heroin–like effect. Because heroin is *the most dangerous drug*, the 'little brother' metaphor likely refers to the dangers of Rohypnol as much as to the highly satisfying effects of the drug.

Cocaine: the ultimate high

In Norway, cocaine has typically been linked to the high-living and self-indulgent partying of small groups of individuals, although the prevalence rates are increasing. The media have portrayed the typical user as a young, wealthy adult in a creative job or in the entertainment business. Several of the young men at The River spoke a great deal about cocaine. Cocaine was seen as an exclusive, privileged drug. Rashid's account of how he made his own crack was illustrative:

> *Rashid:* 'Right, when you've bought coke to snort you can make it yourself. You mix it with ammonia and water and let it crystallise. Everything that's not coke is washed out by the ammonia. The crack you get in the US isn't half as strong as what you get here in Norway.'
> *Interviewer:* 'What's the difference between snorting and smoking?'
> *Rashid:* 'Holy shit, man, it's colossal! You snort a line and you're in flight. It is the ultimate high: 10 times better than the best high. It's so addictive, you know.'
> *Interviewer:* 'How does that feel?'
> *Rashid:* 'Like you're the boss, mate. You can half kill yourself and you wouldn't notice or care. It's over the top. Like mushrooms. Vikings and mushrooms. That tells you something. Vikings and mushrooms. How come little Norway, the Vikings, are known all over the world? They made a mark, and so few of them. Got the right herb [chuckles].'

Rashid knew what there is to know about the production of crack. He was pleased with himself as he told us how he goes about making it. His method was efficient and meticulous. His frame of reference was the US – although US crack, he maintained, was not as good as what he made himself. He also gave an expert's account of the intense effects of crack: "Ya riding high!" He even saw a connection between cocaine and the most heroic parts of the history of Norway – Vikings and mushrooms. For the Vikings, 'possession of the right herb' was the crucial thing. It explains why they conquered the world. He described cocaine as a dangerous, addictive drug, but the frame story relied on something else. He had an initiate's esoteric knowledge of a drug not many people in Norway know much about. Rashid took us into a world full of symbolic markers – complex, but also prestigious. Later he compared the effect of intoxication with a spiritual experience, "same as the Indians", and then he compared the brain with a "big factory where the chemicals need controlling". His ability to combine various narratives to tell mythological stories about drugs was fascinating. It must have taken a lot of time to acquire both the technical skills and the mythological knowledge Rashid displayed. In most of the young men's street capital, such knowledge and skills were important.

Cocaine is becoming accepted in ever-wider circles across Europe (EMCDDA, 2006). It is mainly snorted. It can also be converted into 'freebase' cocaine and smoked. A third form is 'crack', which Rashid described previously. It has been called the fast-food version of cocaine. Small doses suffice, and the drug is sold in small dose-sized packets on the street. Because the volumes are small, a single package of crack is relatively cheap. Its immediate effect has been likened to an intense orgasm. It is a well-documented fact that users can binge on the drug for extended periods, often compulsively. It has a powerful but short-lived effect, and shorter still when smoked. Cocaine is generally regarded as one of the most addictive drugs, and crack is even more addictive than traditional powder cocaine (Morris, 1998; Nutt et al, 2007).

A study in European cities found that cocaine use was most prevalent in three groups:

- well-adjusted youths who take drugs and are active in the party scene;
- socially marginalised groups, such as homeless people, prostitutes or those found in open drug scenes;
- opiate-dependent patients in maintenance treatment who also use cocaine.

The last of the three groups uses cocaine occasionally instead of opiates (Haasen and Prinzleve, 2004).

When the crack epidemic hit the US in the early 1980s, the hardest-hit groups were the most disadvantaged and marginalised populations, often minority ethnic groups living near city centres. Bourgois's (2003b) thesis is that crack consumption patterns are based on the systematic discrimination and exclusion of minority ethnic groups. Ethnic exclusion is less prevalent in Europe, he maintains, which reduces the impact of the drug (Bourgois, 2003b). Although the number of cocaine seizures is rising fast in Norway, this is not the case for crack (KRIPOS, 2006). In that sense, the Norwegian statistics seem to corroborate Bourgois's thesis.

Stories about drug use, pleasure and pain

We have already described how sociologist Howard Becker (1953) argued in 'Becoming a marijuana user' that it takes time to learn to get high. Psychiatrist Norman Zinberg (1984) developed this perspective further in his study *Drug, set, and setting*.

Zinberg discovered that reluctance among physicians to prescribe morphine – even to terminal cancer patients – affected the patients' perceptions of the drug's effectiveness. They sensed their doctor's hesitation and incorporated it into their interpretation of the relatively ill-defined effects produced by morphine. This prompted Zinberg to investigate the social setting's significance for the use of psychoactive drugs. His most contentious finding was that it was possible to live with a controlled consumption of, for instance, morphine and heroin, given an appropriate setting.

It was contentious because it countered the reigning paradigm, which held that the pharmacological properties of drugs largely determine their effects and risks. Zinberg looked instead at the degree and nature of social control. He proposed that this control has two dimensions. The first is social sanctions; that is, rules stating when and how a particular drug can be used. The other is related to social rituals, such as how a drug is obtained and administered, the choice of setting and the procedures to avoid undesirable effects. Rituals augment and symbolise sanctions. In combination, sanctions and rituals affect perceptions not only of a drug's effects but also of the risk of harm or injury involved in taking the drug.

Zinberg's approach introduced a new paradigm in drug research, but he had relied on a number of earlier studies pointing in a similar direction. Lysergic acid diethylamide (LSD) grew increasingly popular as a recreational drug in the 1960s, and it was believed to increase the likelihood of psychotic episodes. In time, it became clear that the effect of LSD was subject to wide variation. The relationship between LSD use and incidence of psychotic episodes was shown to be more tenuous than generally assumed. Becker (1967) had already suggested that the rise in the number of people admitted to hospital for psychotic episodes could be explained by the fear and panic spread by the media. One had seen the same thing in the 1920s, although the drug then was marijuana, he argued. When the panic subsided, so did the number of psychotic episodes attributed to the use of cannabis.

In the wake of work carried out by Becker, Zinberg and others, it is generally accepted today that drug effects have to do with 'learning'.[12] The effect of a particular drug depends only partly on its pharmacological make-up. Knowledge of the correct dosage, social setting and how to interpret signals is necessary to enjoy the effect.

No doubt, many of the young men at The River teetered on the edge of a serious drug problem. Some had received professional treatment. Their situation was reflected in their stories as well. They told us stories about cannabis use from their early teens. They told us about the thrill and pride of 'being stoned'. Many described how drugs, and in particular cannabis, marked the end of childhood and the inclusion in a new and fascinating subculture. They described the complicated process of learning to enjoy the effects, and they emphasised the bonds of friendship and coolness typified by the subculture. All the same, none of the young men prettified drug taking, and they revealed complex and ambivalent attitudes towards them. Generally, however, in the many hundreds of pages of interview transcripts, it was harder to find stories about the pleasures of drugs than those about the pain and costs. The young men at The River probably possessed a more sensitive vocabulary to describe the pleasures of drugs than we managed to elicit.

There may be a number of reasons for this. Many of them had had a traumatic childhood. Racism and repression had been integral to their lives in Norway.

Some obviously tried to medicate the pain and sadness away. At the same time, we believe they told us more about harm than pleasure because of our own social role as social scientists. Zinberg (1984) described how patients sensed a physician's concern about opiate use, and that this concern influenced their interpretation of the drug effects. We can extend this argument. The young men at The River had probably experienced a wide variety of drug effects. When they told us about them, they produced one type of story for the sake of Norwegian officialdom, authorities or the welfare state. They produced another type on the street.

Rashid, for example, gave us an extended 'lecture' on the harm caused by different drugs. When he told us about cocaine, we asked if he had quit. He replied incisively: "No, no, are you crazy?! I enjoy a line or two now and then." There are many stories, and all may be 'true', but some are more likely to be told in specific social contexts.[13] We will return to this in Chapter Eight.

Sissified

As we mentioned previously, the burden of cannabis was particularly heavy for the dealers' masculinity. As is generally agreed today, there is no universal form of masculinity. Perceptions of masculinity (and femininity for that matter) are in constant flux. Connell (2002, p 5) quotes Simone de Beauvoir: 'One is not born a woman. One *becomes* one'. The principle applies to men, too. One is not born a man, one learns manliness, and in that way *becomes* a man (Connell, 2002). Gender has to be recreated constantly in daily relationships and behaviour. Even groups, pastimes and places can be gendered in this sense. It follows, then, that The River is a gendered scene. It is a place for young men working constantly on formulating convincing, legitimate forms of masculinity. Still, the requirements for this work are uncommon. For marginalised young men like those at The River, masculinity has to be created on the basis of an already existing inferior status. We have shown that the young men felt (and were) excluded from school and work (see Chapter Four). The street culture at The River supplied the raw material to transform structural inferiority into masculinity and sexual superiority. Habitus, style and, not least, violence were important. However, drugs played a role, too. The effect of drugs could be associated with hardness, toughness and virility, attributes perceived as masculine and important. However, drugs *in excess* were dangerous. The young men were concerned that cannabis might destroy their sperm. Other drugs can "sap your lifeblood". A "junkie" is never masculine, never a real man. Too heavy on the drugs, "you lose your balls". These were common threads in the stories.

Amin reflected about the consequences of smoking too much cocaine base:

> *Amin:* 'I smoked every day. A stroll round the river, me and a couple of me mates. People passing by, we clobber them and take their money. I was fucking addicted man. Until one day I was put in jail. I got to know my current girlfriend. She got me to cut it out, the coke, I mean.'

Interviewer: 'Isn't it strongly addictive, cocaine?'
Amin: 'Yeah, you get hooked in no time.'
Interviewer: 'So what made you realise you were hooked yourself?'
Amin: 'Ah, 'cause I just had to have it every day. Like me mate says, come on, let's go downtown. I was hooked then.'
Interviewer: 'Could you describe what it was like, the effect?'
Amin: 'It's not like weed, it's not like anything. I don't know. It feels great, yeah … you get, I dunno, like [chuckles].'

At first, this sounded like a story about acting tough and violently, both of which gave high status at The River. However, the subtext reads differently. They were not robbing people for rational reasons, based on calculation and free will. Amin did it because he had to. He needed the money because he was addicted to cocaine. He saw himself as a weak man, one who needed his girlfriend's help to break free of the obsession. It was the opposite of a highly gendered street capital or street masculinity, as Mullins (2006) coins it.

Wari had also had a serious crack habit. Every time you use it, he said, "it leaves a small hole in your brain". The dealers agreed about the effects of coke and crack. These substances gave them an exquisite sense of well-being but at a high price. They suffered, especially in terms of their masculinity and toughness. At first, it would make them strong and hard, and possibly even make them feel invincible. However, as the cocaine took hold, they were left with nothing but a hard *shell*. It slowly took its toll and hit them where it mattered most. It sapped their strength, control and courage, and turned them into "sissies". This is what Rashid had to say:

> *Rashid:* 'Take cocaine and you stay in control. You're untouchable, like, somebody comes and knocks you senseless, you don't notice a thing. You get up and give him back what he gave you, you get up and knock him flat. But at the end of the day, you're all sissified, like. That's the long and short of it. You turn into a sissy.'
> *Interviewer:* 'Why?'
> *Rashid:* ''Cause you're so used to being on top, so when it doesn't work like that anymore, that's when you start changing. What you used to use inside your body when you took cocaine, it gets used up after a while. So you're losing stuff all the time. I'm so pissed off about people who use cocaine, they all turn into wimps. They can be tough, they can still be strong, but your courage – it eats away your courage.'

'Wimp' and 'sissy' are gendered, belittling epithets, the same as 'punk' (Mullins, 2006). We could possibly read these words as metaphors for the loss of a major concern to the young men – everything that gives them status, prestige and respect on the street. This pattern is frequently described in the street culture literature too. 'Addicts' lose all dignity and self-respect. They are at the bottom of the street hierarchies. This is especially so for chronic crack heads (Jacobs, 1999).

All drugs may undermine one's autonomy. Cannabis can lead to dependence, sapping one's strength and even damaging one's core masculinity. Ecstasy can lead to psychosis, Rohypnol to memory loss. Coke and crack can turn dealers into sissies and wimps when they are not taking them, and then their street capital will be gone. The exit will be blocked too. "This ain't no life," is an oft-repeated sentiment. In the long run, what ties the dealers down is their drug habit. Rashid put it in the following way:

> 'All I can say is that a lot who used to hang out here, they're gone. The only ones left are the addicts, hanging out 'cause they've got to get cash somehow, to pay for the next trip. They're really desperate.'

It is a precarious balancing act. Life at The River is tantamount to perpetual exposure to drugs. The dealers have to prove they are ready to take risks fearlessly, including risks with drug use. Drugs can also supply the courage they need for violence or robberies. Status and prestige, however, can evaporate in the face of a destructive dependence running out of control. Drugs taken in excess threaten one's masculinity.

This tendency is visible not only at The River but also in street culture more generally. Drug dependence has traditionally been seen as rather feminine – ever since the late 19th century (Keire, 1998). There seems to be a cultural continuity here, beginning with doctors in the 1870s giving women morphine to numb the pain of "female troubles" or "to turn the wilful hysteric into a manageable invalid" (Keire, 1998, p 810). Historian David Courtwright (1998) describes how this female drug addict of the late 19th century (who had started taking drugs for medical reasons) was replaced at the turn of the century by a young man from the urban lower classes. However, this new character was not very masculine. He might often be a pimp, living off 'immoral women', or he might be 'a fairy', selectively adopting feminine signifiers – 'plucked eyebrows or bleached hair and an exaggerated walk' (Keire, 1998, p 814).

There are few studies of the historical development of illegal drug use in Norway, but there is much to indicate that there has been a similar undercurrent. Cannabis for example, was originally used to prevent spontaneous abortions and 'female bleeding', and opium (in the form of laudanum) was used as a painkiller (Lilleaas, 1987). When the first drug abuse clinic was established in 1961, women played a central role among the medically based opiate and barbiturate abusers. Physicians and nurses had high rates of drug use relative to the general population, and even for the small group of people with a 'disorderly lifestyle' who became patients, there is little to indicate that they were hardened criminals or violent men (Pedersen, 1994). The use of alcohol is more strongly associated with masculinity in Norway.

Controlling the limits

Sociologist Philip Lalander (2003) claimed that the drug subculture can be conceived of in terms of a role game, one that takes time to learn, and where participants in the subculture are the players. The drug subculture offers excitement, social networks and fast rewards.[14] Practical and technical knowledge of buying, selling and using drugs (and of their effects) is a prerequisite. As one learns, one evolves a particular outlook on the world and life. 'Action skill' is Lalander's term for it, and coping with risk is one of the key elements. Status within the group depends on 'living the action'. It is the sign of a real outsider, a person who has opted for an exciting life. Using drugs is the clearest expression of this way of life. Drugs are also linked to the game's highest reward. You do not have to wait. Drugs deliver pleasure after pleasure, and represent the antithesis of a routine life in mainstream society. However, to sustain drug use, players must develop 'control skills'. They must go from being impulsive, playful players to being experts at the game. The desire and pleasures once associated with drugs and the street may vanish. At the same time, their craving for drugs becomes increasingly imperative. What used to deliver freedom may slowly turn the players into addicts.

This paradox is reflected in the lives of all the young men at The River. As we mentioned previously, Rashid reflected on the effects of drugs more than most.

> *Interviewer:* 'What's it like, taking the different drugs?'
> *Rashid:* 'Depends on the person. One person can smoke weed for 10 years and never, ever get into trouble. He can take amphetamine and get so high he can fly. People react differently. Drugs demand a lot of experience. You can get something positive out of it, which you can use in your life. Either you work with it or you work against it.'
> *Interviewer:* 'What can you do with it then, what may the effect be?'
> *Rashid:* 'At the start maybe [you can benefit from it] but not later. By then, you don't care about anything or anyone. There are always consequences. You miss out on a shitload of stuff, man, when you're doing drugs, like. Like on the inside, your mind's starved – nothing ever happens. There's so much you lose out on. Thing is, you don't notice what you're missing. Already too far gone, you don't see the edge. Everything's numb. Things just keep going, like. That's when it's gone too far. You have to know where the edge is, it is so important.'

Rashid's story was extraordinary for its metaphors. The most important thing was that drugs could give him a positive experience, an experience he could put to good use. However, he had to learn how to do drugs. "Either you work with it, or you work against it." For him it was crucial – and difficult – to learn one's limits, otherwise suddenly, things may go too far. This may lie at the heart of street capital and street subculture as well: learn how to do drugs, get to know the effects and identify one's limits. Dealers such as Rashid have to test their limits and know how to play with them, but they must not lose control. The day they lose control, their street capital vanishes. From there, it is only a small step to a life on the washed-out junkie scene.

Notes

[1] The Norwegian term typically used is *avhengig*, which may be translated as 'dependent' or 'addicted'. In the psychiatric nomenclature, there are unclear borders between the two concepts; however, in the *Diagnostic and statistical manual of mental disorders (DSM-IV-TR)*, the most widely used nomenclature for research purposes, *dependence* is defined in the following way: 'When an individual persists in use of alcohol or other drugs despite problems related to use of the substance, substance dependence may be diagnosed. Compulsive and repetitive use may result in tolerance to the effect of the drug and withdrawal symptoms when use is reduced or stopped. This, along with Substance Abuse are considered Substance Use Disorders....' (APA, 2000). The related concept of 'drug addiction' has different meanings. Some give it the same meaning as dependence, while others use a narrower meaning, excluding drugs with no evidence of tolerance or withdrawal. In this book, we most often use the term 'dependence', and occasionally the term 'addict', as the concrete noun with the closest appropriate meaning. Even though many researchers in the social sciences are critical of the terms 'dependence' and 'addiction', a number of studies document a cannabis dependence syndrome. It is also operationalised in *DSM-IV-TR* and the *International classification of diseases* (ICD-10; WHO, 1990), and in many Western countries is the most common type of dependence after alcohol and tobacco. Tolerance and withdrawal symptoms (including anxiety, insomnia, appetite disturbance and depression) have been reported, and an increasing number of cannabis users are seeking help (see, for example, Room et al, 2008). However, we would like to point out that the economic and sociocultural dimensions of cannabis dependence – which were of utmost importance in the lives of the young men at The River – are usually not addressed in these diagnostic systems.

[2] Scientific evidence corroborates his view. THC is the main active component of cannabis and a likely cause of sperm and fertility degeneration (Whan et al, 2006).

[3] The exact words were: "But you a blunthead motherfucker 'cause you smoke blunts all day so you ain't no better than me" (Mullins, 2006, p 69). Clearly, he saw the threat as a threat to his masculinity.

[4] Lena Larsen, a Norwegian historian of religion and a practising Muslim, explains how hybridisation and negotiation also have a gender dimension: the Islamic culture is patriarchal. Drugs are a male prerogative. They are taken in male-dominated environments. The Muslim gender discourse is allied to an interpretation that privileges efforts to find flexible solutions to male needs and dilemmas (Lena Larsen, personal communication, 23 June 2006).

[5] Norwegian researchers have witnessed an interesting tendency in recent years: alcohol consumption seems to have declined among adolescents with an ethnic Norwegian background in the eastern parts of Oslo that have an increasing proportion of Islamic immigrants (Amundsen et al, 2005).

[6] There is virtually no scientific literature on drug use based on population data from Muslim countries. Nor have we been able to find studies of a social anthropological nature or within the other social sciences describing local cultural variation in the use of cannabis and alcohol in the countries concerned. We have therefore relied on interviews with *Qur'an* interpreters and with specialists on Islam in Norway, and on various Norwegian surveys of a representative sample of adolescents. This has allowed us to explore consumption patterns by minority ethnic group and by religion.

[7] English translation by Dr T.B. Irving (http://isgkc.org/translat.htm).

[8] Not least Morocco, which has a strong tradition of cannabis use. Whether or not a substance is defined as an illegal intoxicant is subject to cultural variation and different opinions within the Islamic world. As elsewhere, the sanctions brought to bear on the use of drugs also vary.

[9] The connection between religion and cannabis consumption among young men in Norway can be illustrated by the nationally representative dataset known as *Young in Norway 2002* (Ung i Norge, 2002) (N = circa 12,000 aged 13–19). Thirty-one per cent of the boys reported no religious affiliation; 66% were self-perceived Christian; and 3% were self-perceived Muslim. Members of these three groups who had tried cannabis amounted to 20%, 12% and 21% respectively ($\chi 2$ 64.1, df = 2, $p < 0.0001$). The likelihood that self-perceived Muslim boys in Norway will have tried cannabis is almost twice as high as that for self-perceived Christian boys.

[10] The medical term is Flunitrazepan, and in Norway, these pills are sold under the trademarks Rohypnol and Flunipan.

[11] *Tidsskrift for Den norske lægeforening*, 24 November 2003.

[12] In the alcohol area, the classical text is MacAndrew and Edgerton's (1969) *Drunken comportment*. It is an impressive global-scale study of the empirical evidence of how alcohol effects are related to social norms and vary between cultures.

[13] This is not to suggest wilful contrivance. Most of the time during the interviews, we enjoyed very good contact with the young men. They did not see us as representatives of the police or powers of law and order, and they spoke freely, even about serious crimes they had committed. However, there can be little doubt that at a fundamental level, they perceived us as representatives of officialdom. We imagine that some stories about personal drug use sound better in that type of context. Emphasising the *pleasure* of taking drugs

could be problematic if we were perceived to have any official status at all. They had to be careful with stories like that when dealing with the social and health authorities and other welfare authorities and bodies.

[14] Lalander draws an analogy with the backpacker culture. It too allows players to detach themselves from their social and cultural roots. For a few months or years, new identities are created, precisely as backpackers. It can be understood as a theatrical play, but one on which the curtain falls when the players return home.

SIX

Street dealing and drug markets

At The River anyone is a potential customer. Learning to be a street cannabis dealer involves identifying potential buyers among casual passers-by. The more street capital one has however, the less likely one is to escape subjection and marginality.

First-time selling at The River

Selling cannabis is illegal, and its illegality shapes the transactions at The River. In quick succession, an offer must be made, the goods displayed and sampled, a price agreed upon, and money and commodity exchanged. Throughout this process, the participants risk being seen by the police. To survive in the longer term, therefore, dealers need to develop a quick hand and a sharp eye, and to know their way around.

Ebo and Denis learned much about crime as teenagers in their neighbourhood, a multi-ethnic, working-class suburb of Oslo. They stole, sold drugs, and ran errands for an older gang of adolescents in the area that was involved in more serious crime. They earned good money. As they matured, they wondered how they could move on from being 'runners' for the local gang. Setting up an independent operation would increase takings, they imagined.

In Oslo, virtually all adolescents know about The River, even if the bulk of the cannabis distribution takes place in private networks. Ebo and Denis heard stories from young people in their neighbourhood about the cannabis trade at The River. Others learn about it on the streets in the centre of the capital. Some of the refugees said that it was one of the few things that they learned at the asylum centre. So for Ebo and Denis, in their plan to relocate downtown and step into the wider world, The River seemed as likely a prospect as any other. This is how it happened:

> *Denis:* 'You meet people, and they tell you things.'
> *Interviewer:* 'A chance to earn a bit of cash on your own, then?'
> *Ebo:* 'Yeah.'
> *Denis:* 'Yeah, it was, but riskier. There are people out there who'd rip you off, if you don't know who's who....'
> *Ebo:* 'Like, you don't know all these guys. They're all fresh faces as far as you're concerned.'
> *Interviewer:* 'Can you remember the first time you sold cannabis on The River?'
> *Denis:* [laughs] 'It was, it was, it was one boring day, get me? I didn't have a clue, didn't know where to start. Was I supposed to just stand there, like ... [Ebo laughs] you know what I mean. And keep my eyes peeled in case the police showed up ... it was a bit confusing.'
> *Interviewer:* 'So you hadn't actually been there before, like for buying or anything?'
> *Denis:* 'Well, yeah, but that's ....'
> *Ebo:* 'It's not the same.'

The situation at The River was new and confusing to Denis and Ebo. They knew the neighbourhood codes, social spaces, and players back home in the suburb like the back of their hand. They knew the gangs, the opportunities and the dangers. "You don't know who all these people are, downtown," Denis said. However, the biggest risk was the plain-clothes police. Throughout the period of our fieldwork, the police constantly increased surveillance. Rival dealers, theft, dishonest suppliers, problems with buyers, violence – all were part of a normal day at The River. Gradually they were socialised into the street culture. For customers, the transaction is over in no time. They are not interested in unnecessary interaction, nor do they want to be noted by the police or to be seen by relatives or acquaintances. Denis and Ebo insisted that as a buyer, you cannot learn what you need to know to become a dealer.

The River is probably the largest open cannabis drug market in Scandinavia, ever since the famous market in Christiania, Copenhagen was closed down a few years ago. During the last decade, and in particular since the large-scale introduction of the mobile telephone, such open markets have been on the decrease internationally (May and Hough, 2004). In some European countries, such as the Netherlands and the UK, this is also due to increasing domestic production, where the distribution chain typically is very short and linked to private networks (Room et al, 2008. pp 73–4). However, Norway still has relatively little domestic production of cannabis, and this may make the open street markets more important in Norway than they are in some other European countries.

There are several advantages of an open drug market. Customers do not need any introduction to the seller; there is easy access. Another less obvious advantage (which we will return to later) is the fact that customers do not need to interact with the cannabis sellers on a regular basis. Thus, they will not become part of an illegal drug distribution subculture, which could have a number of costs for them. However, the disadvantages of an open drug market are many: such markets are regularly under police surveillance. Customers who want to hide their drug use may be seen by relatives, friends, colleagues and so on. Moreover, closed and network-based cannabis distribution systems are usually not associated with violence, whereas violence and robberies often occur at open drug street markets.[1] Thus, it is easy to understand why private dealing systems, operated on the basis of personal recommendations and by means of mobile telephones, have become more popular. Still, the market at The River was intense and active at times during our fieldwork.

Whyte's (1943) study of Italian youth in Cornerville was novel in that he found order and structure beneath the apparent disorder. He had set out as an anthropologist to identify organisational systems and to reveal their finer structures. A similar challenge confronts youngsters who want to sell drugs at The River. What do you do? What does 'a good price' mean in actual money? Do you just stake out a pitch and start trading? Is there a hierarchy, or a rotation system for the dealers?

Multiple versions of free competition

Denis was used to buying and smoking cannabis. He was apprehensive and shy, but he finally obtained 'a fiver'[2] and went into business. Ebo went through a longer process:

> *Ebo:* 'I didn't start selling at The River immediately. I hung out there, I had mates there, see? I was there intermittently, and I smoked. Selling never occurred to me, you know. I didn't make up my mind, like, overnight.'
> *Interviewer:* 'How long did it take, roughly?'
> *Ebo:* 'Two years.'
> *Interviewer:* 'So you're hanging out there, sort of, and it was OK just being there and …?'

> *Ebo:* 'Yeah, like I said, just hanging out with the crowd, and I got to know them, made starting easier, like.'

Ebo started to frequent The River. Gradually he immersed himself in the ways of The River and the practicalities of dealing. He became a pusher himself but only after a very slow process. As we saw in Chapter Two, some of the youngest boys used The River as a social arena in addition to earning money. This was true for Ebo and Denis as well. Newcomers appear to meet little opposition from the more established dealers at The River. The River is a free zone – there are no wholesalers or 'cartels'. According to international studies, certain players or organisations are frequently powerful enough to control an area or to monopolise a particularly lucrative one (Levitt and Dubner, 2006). This is not the case at The River.

> *Ebo:* 'It's easy to get in if you want to buy or sell, like, you can just stand there. Nobody orders you around or tells you to fuck off, like. The only problem is the police. So anybody can stake a patch, do business, like, and vanish afterwards. Open to all comers, like.'
> *Interviewer:* 'And there's no rivalry between groups?'
> *Ebo:* 'There's always stuff like that. Take the entrance to the underground, like. That's where small kids'll be positioned, easy pickings for the cops. 'Cause they're standing in full view, like, too far forward, you know. Have to stand there because buyers want to get it over with quick, like.'

Established dealers do not prevent new dealers from operating, but they do compete for buyers, and some patches are better than others. One of the underground entrances is a well-known spot, because many people walk by. Dealers positioned here have an advantage over dealers in less conspicuous spots. However, it is a difficult patch in the middle of a large public area. Because it is easy to monitor, business there is risky. Others opt for more secluded patches on small paths leading to the riverside. Some dealers stand clustered together in small groups or pairs; others remain solitary. If a buyer turns up, everybody will move in more or less simultaneously.

There have been occasional attempts to consolidate control of the market and to establish a dealer hierarchy. Ahmed described a system put in place by a person known as Al Capone. He made sure everybody got a chance to sell and no one stole customers. He was a tough character but respected for his experience at The River and his wide connections. He also came across as a fair-minded person, and people were happy with the way he distributed market shares. However, when he was charged and jailed, there was no one to take his place.

Jacobs (1999, pp 50–4) studied crack dealership in St Louis in the US. Although the American ghetto and Norway are not directly comparable, there are similarities. When the young men were on the street, they were not bound by ties of loyalty, duty or solidarity. Selling was disorganised, chaotic and predatory. Jacobs described three forms of group orientation in public drug scenes, or three typical ways to close a deal. The first variant is 'get 'em, got 'em' – the dealer who spots the potential customer first gets to finalise the sale. The second is the 'bum rush', in which dealers descend on the same customer all at once; whoever arrives first gets the sale. The final variant is a rota system for dealers to take turns with customers. Al Capone ran a rota system. It made for a more relaxed situation, with less aggression. We observed all three variants at The River. The rota system was often highlighted as the typical system by interviewees, while the more belligerent bum rushes caused public outrage and anxiety.

Gimme a fiver

After an observation period, we began to interview the young men more systematically. We got to know many of them quite well, and they often laughed and smiled when they realised they were offering us cannabis. After a while, they allowed us to observe transactions. One evening, we had arranged to meet up with Omar for an interview, and we met behind a Church that was one of the sale spots.[3] We realised then that we had so far avoided being in that area at night. We were unprotected, in a dark corner and invisible from the road. By now, though, we felt we were with people we knew.

Soon a muscular ethnic Norwegian in his late twenties turned up. Without hesitating he said, "Gimme a fiver," triggering chaos among the dealers. Nobody seemed to know whose turn it was, and all talked at once. Omar was quicker than the others. He bent down and fished something out from a small pile of dead leaves a couple of feet from where he stood. He pulled out what usually goes under the name of 'a long piece' and handed it over. The buyer, certain he was getting less than his five grams, started arguing. However, he paid 500 NOK and eventually left. Raised voices, bickering and irritation ensued. It was not Omar's turn, some alleged. He defended himself, saying that he was faster than the others. Too fast, was the reply. The buyer could have been a plain-clothes policeman – he looked like one, with broad shoulders and close-cut hair. He could not have been, said Omar, because he did not have an earphone in his ear. Omar wandered off contentedly. Five hundred NOK for five grams was a good transaction – customers seldom want more than a gram or two.

This was typical of the situations we observed during our fieldwork. The young men huddle together, always on the lookout for the next customer. The trick is to get to the customer first. There is a lot at stake and often a lot of competition. Less obvious rules or norms are at play too. For instance, the dealer needs to feel reasonably sure that the customer is not an undercover police officer, and competition among dealers does not extend to prices. In the previous example, if anyone had underbid Omar it would have elicited a strong reaction. There is an unwritten rule against underbidding.

Establishing eye contact with customers and assessing the chances of making a deal are part of the business of dealing. Several interviewees also underlined the importance of persistence. Customers might feel apprehensive and afraid to make the first move. Ahmed described one such incident:

> *Ahmed:* 'We don't go and ask everyone. You have to be a bit careful.'
> *Interviewer:* 'But you know when people are looking at you?'
> *Ahmed:* 'The customer's always going to make eye contact. They'll stare, and they'll come in your direction, they'll keep staring, they don't lose eye contact.'
> *Interviewer:* 'And if people look aside, or at other things?'
> *Ahmed:* 'Yeah, but like, they're really nervous, so they only look straight ahead. Don't say nothing, so we say, like, "Want some dope?", and they say, timid like, 'Yeah.'''
> *Interviewer:* 'What about people who don't want any dope? You ever see people looking anxious?'
> *Ahmed:* 'Well, a lot of people are probably afraid. But that's generally if we're in a group, like, a lot of us. Like when there are six or 10 of us standing on the footpath and sitting on the bench.'

The young men have to learn to interpret customer signals and wishes and create an impression of trustworthiness and composure. Eye contact is the primary means of communication between them. A customer's look can express a desire to engage with the dealer, but sustained glances are as likely to indicate curiosity. In some cases, as we discuss later, undercover police officers will try to provoke an offer. An evasive glance could indicate a lack of interest, but it may signal reticence or apprehension as well. The dealer's task is to interpret the hidden message in these complex signals and, not least, to learn how to put the customer at ease. There is also the setting to think of, with other dealers waiting to move in. It can be a difficult situation for both the buyer and the dealer. It takes time to acquire this competence, a skill that can be conceptualised as street capital.

Fake hash, poor weights

All the dealers smoke cannabis, and they know a good deal about its different qualities. They can tell the difference between Moroccan, Afghan and pollen hash. Differential marking is useful for quality assessment, and the producers often mark their products. "Ox is good hash, and nothing beats hash with the gold stamp. Jew is good too," said Ahmed. Dealing at The River however, was mostly about low-grade cannabis, dishonesty and fake hash. As several people remarked, "at The River, everybody's at it". Wari for example, told us how henna and bark are substituted for the real thing:

> *Interviewer:* 'Do the customers sometimes get stuff that isn't cannabis?'
> *Wari:* 'Like henna. You know what henna is?'

Interviewer: 'I think so.'

Wari: 'Well, like, it's something you dye your hair with. They add a spot of oil and give it a brush, and stick it in a bag.'

Interviewer: [laughs for a second] 'So the effect isn't quite the same, like [laughs].'

Wari: 'And then there are people who sell bark.' [everybody laughs]

Several interviewees told us about henna, and even about tightly packed dry leaves being sold as cannabis. What the customer receives is seldom the amount stated by the dealer: a 'piece' is supposed to weigh a gram, but in reality, the customer often gets only half a gram, and of poorer quality, too. Dealers call it 'dryrock' (*tørrok*), a word that is probably a combination of *moroc* (Moroccan cannabis, the most widespread type in Norway) and *tørr* (dry), the opposite of wet or dank hash. Dryrock, then, is dry, low-grade cannabis, as Rashid explained:

Rashid: 'People from Algeria have taken over, or those from Senegal. They're running the place now.'

Interviewer: 'Do they know each other?'

Rashid: 'No, but they want a slice of the cake before they get chucked out of the country. So that's what they're selling, dryrock.'

Interviewer: 'Selling what?'

Rashid: 'Dryrock.'

Interviewer: 'And what may that be?'

Rashid: 'The cheapest cannabis around. Low grade, no resin. Dry. You don't even get stoned. They're all into it, selling it down there.'

Interviewer: 'And if quality is bad, what …?'

Rashid: 'Well, they pay nothing for it, nearly nothing.'

According to Rashid, refugees awaiting deportation sell most of the dryrock. They take every opportunity to make quick money. Many of the refugee dealers are operating on a highly provisional basis – their main interest is to make as much as possible in the time available. So customers are cheated on quality and quantity. It is a risky business. Ahmed briefed us on an operation that turned sour:

Ahmed: 'I'd done a fast one on a guy, 'cause we were selling henna. So he comes back with three others. I went after them with a knife – got one of them in the leg.'

Interviewer: 'And they cleared off?'

Ahmed: 'No, they didn't, they were still trying to get me, but I had this knife, see, so they couldn't get close up, like. So they disappeared after a bit.'

Interviewer: 'How old were they? Where did they come from?'

Ahmed: 'They were Norwegian. Don't know their ages exactly, around 37 to 40 maybe.'

Interviewer: 'And how much had they bought?'
Ahmed: 'They bought 10 of henna. And henna is just rubbish, you know. When you sell henna, it's a good idea to leave the area pronto. But I still had a bit left, so I couldn't be bothered to go. I didn't expect them to come back.'

The dealers at The River know that buyers will not be calling the police. As Ahmed said, "They can't report it, like, they bought it, didn't they?" During our fieldwork, the police adopted an increasingly tougher policy on buyers. Some were arrested and fined.[4] The dealer–buyer interaction is regulated by those involved, and as neither side wants the authorities interfering, buyers are frequently duped. We will see later how this aversion to police involvement resulted in several robberies going unreported. It also increases the risk of the same happening again, or it initiates a vicious cycle where crime attracts more crime. Mechanisms like these may be much more likely in public settings, where ordinary social control is reduced – places where people are virtual strangers and will probably never meet again.

The River area is difficult to monitor as the lighting is poor during the autumn and winter months. Customers are there for illegal purposes and will avoid reporting hostility or aggressive behaviour. This, in part, explains the area's extremely high robbery rate, and the high robbery rate, in turn, suggests a failure of dealer community norms vis-à-vis their business. It would make more sense for the dealers to step up security and clamp down on aggressive behaviour to protect the market, the deals and their profits. This failure of the market may happen because there are no bosses controlling the business from the sidelines. All the same, the area is not entirely reduced to chaos or divested of internal norms altogether. A fixed-price norm is one example, and in relation to aggressive behaviour, other strong norms are at work as well (see Chapter Seven).

Fixed prices

Dealer rivalry at The River is usually not related to competitive pricing. None of our observations or interviewees indicated that price competition at The River is accepted. It is easy to see why. Lowering the price would increase the pressure from competitors and mean lower income. It could even destroy the market.

One of the more conspicuous features of the cannabis trade in Norway is that the price has remained unchanged more or less since the drug came onto the market in the late 1960s, at approximately 100 NOK per gram. If the price had followed inflation, a gram today would cost more than 700 NOK. In relative terms, cannabis has therefore become cheap. On the other hand, a Norwegian study found that the fall in price of *other* drugs had accelerated from 1993-2004. For example, prices fell approximately 70% for heroin and 60% for amphetamines during this period. Nominally, however, cannabis prices did not change, and the inflation-corrected price fell only slightly (Bretteville-Jensen, 2005). What explains this unusual instance of price stability?

Insufficient research has been done to provide clear answers. What distinguishes the cannabis trade, however, is its scale. The market for cannabis is incomparably greater than that for other illegal drugs. International data confirm the picture. Globally, cannabis production, smuggling and sales are in a different league altogether from opiates or cocaine (UNODC, 2006). Recent population-based data for cannabis use in the adult Norwegian population show that almost 50% of young adults in Oslo have tried cannabis before they reach the age of 30, and 30% of males in their late twenties report having used cannabis during the previous 12 months (Pedersen, 2008). Even if much of this consumption is sporadic, it still suggests a large consumer pool. This fact, together with lower penalties for cannabis smuggling offences relative to other substances, has probably resulted in a steadily tougher competitive climate in all parts of the supply chain since cannabis became available on Norwegian streets.

There is greater heterogeneity in the cannabis supply chain than in those for other substances, and there are many people involved in cannabis distribution. Most of the cannabis consumed in Norway still comes from Morocco. Organised top-level criminals smuggle large consignments, but police and court records also reveal petty smuggling offences by small-time non-professional individuals. Thus, there are many importers, large and small dealers, as well as many users in the cannabis market. Consumption of other illegal substances such as amphetamine or heroin is much lower, there are fewer people involved in production and distribution, and formal and informal sanctions are harsher.

The cannabis market is extensive, with a large consumer pool, high demand, and steady supply lines. Thus, the cannabis market resembles an ordinary, well-working capitalist market. When sales are made by telephone, between dealers and customers who know one another, there is often space to negotiate a price. Discounts can be offered on the basis of either quality or quantity. Dealers will want to hold on to good customers and will tend to offer them good-quality cannabis or a good price. At The River, on the other hand, buyers are not as eager to argue about price. They want to finish the transaction as quickly as possible in order to limit their vulnerability. In any case, cannabis is not an expensive drug to start with, so buyers are less inclined to haggle over price.

Metaphorically, The River is to other cannabis markets what stores like 7–Eleven are to ordinary supermarkets. When we visit the local supermarket, we have an idea of what we want to buy. We buy in bulk, and we keep an eye on quality. However, every now and then we run out of something, which is when we are more likely to visit a 7–Eleven. We can get whatever we need, at any time of the day or night. Items are more expensive, but the store is always open. Customers who ordinarily get their drugs from a familiar contact may find themselves short occasionally. They may have misplaced a mobile telephone number, or a supply channel has run dry or their contact has been arrested. In these situations, they know that cannabis is available at The River. There, because they buy in small quantities – generally one or two grams – the price is not important.

The cops wear hoodies

The young men at The River are in contact with several state welfare institutions (later, we attempt to define the scope and variety of these connections). While they ply their trade, however, the state authority they are most likely to come in contact with is the police. Because police officers try to look like ordinary members of the public, dealers must learn how to tell the difference between innocent buyers and police officers in plain clothes. Amin thought it was easy. He told us what he looked out for:

> *Interviewer:* 'So you know who's a plain-clothes cop?'
> *Amin:* 'Yep! You do. They're a bit bigger round the chest [laughs].'
> *Interviewer:* 'Like you get from weights?'
> *Amin:* 'Yeah, they wear, what d'you call 'em? Vests. You can see 'em, like these short things. If they decide all of a sudden they want to talk to you, and you see them coming, I say, "Sorry, got none," and walk off.'

The police are fit and often patrol the area on bikes. They can also run fast and tend to work in pairs. After eye contact is established, both parties know what comes next. Amin's story is about how he goes about outwitting the police, how he knows exactly what they are up to. The police, on the other hand, being a step behind, are effectively put out of play. The whole thing could be read as an arrangement between relatively equal parties, ruled by a sort of 'gentleman's agreement'. A word is a word, a promise a promise. Some of the young men spoke well of the police. They accepted being occasionally stopped and checked. They said that many officers were highly qualified and professional, but that others had a bad attitude. However, apart from a few isolated cases, police officers usually did not resort to violence.

Still, the dealers stressed that you would not find 'the big fish' at The River, and the police were therefore wasting their time. However, the rationale for policing at The River is not, as some of the dealers believed, to catch 'the big fish'. On the contrary, police activity at The River can be labelled 'low-level drug enforcement', a practice that has been developed in other countries as well (Lee and South, 2003). 'Low level' is taken to mean suppliers and users at the retail level of the market, and police use a number of tactics to inhibit drug transactions. In Oslo, the police have a long tradition of 'disruption patrols' in low-level drug enforcement.

Norwegian criminologist Liv Finstad described what the police are looking for on street patrols (Finstad, 2003, pp 90–5). 'Known individual', 'one of ours' and 'lout' are the three main categories of people. While the first two have partly positive connotations, the third is unequivocally negative. The police are trained to detect 'incongruities'. A lout has certain incongruous features: wrong age and/or sex (young and male), being in the wrong place (downtown), at the wrong time (middle of the night). Black skin colour is another 'lout' attribute (Finstad, 2003, p 93). Finstad's findings echo those of a number of studies on police culture. Chan et al (2003) investigated the socialisation process that police officers go through. 'Dictionary knowledge' refers to categories and labels that police officers gradually develop to make sense of their world. Often an 'us versus them' mentality arises because they meet a number of people who are unfriendly and hostile, such as many minority ethnic groups, poor people and criminals. There are also numerous complaints made against the police (Chan et al, 2003, p 210). The result is that the police officers themselves often admit that their naivety, idealism and tolerance disappear, and they become more realistic and part of 'the street cop culture'.

Such features were also evident in our study. Still, not only are many of the dealers at The River 'known' to the police patrols but also the dealers get to know the officers themselves. In their personal relations with the police, they make efforts to avoid categorisations such as 'lout' in the police officers' dictionary knowledge. To the contrary, many try to develop a position as equal to the officers, a kind of complementary competence.

Wari knew most of the plain-clothes officers by sight but still looked for signs:

> *Interviewer:* 'So how do you spot a customer from a plain-clothes cop?'
> *Wari:* 'They all wear hoodies and stuff. [general laughter] And a telephone plug in their earhole, that's their trademark, like.'
> *Interviewer:* 'And you recognise the faces? The same crowd's patrolling?'
> *Wari:* 'Yeah, man, it's always the same guys.'
> *Interviewer:* 'What if a new one turns up? What makes "police" register in your head?'
> *Wari:* 'You can … if there's a pair of them, like, coming at you at the same time, you can … they look suspicious, you know. They could be ordinary customers, like, and they'll say something. But if they ask for 20 grams straight out…. Then, "OK, man, you're not the fuzz by the way?" first. If he says no, he's not, see? 'Cause the police can't say, "Sorry, mate, I'm not a police officer," can he?'

Wari believed that the police were forbidden by law to deny their official status if asked. Indeed, in practice, the police admit who they are. Rashid, voicing his agreement with Wari, said that he could tell plain-clothes officers by studying the situation. The police, he said, cannot lie if you challenge them, and they are not allowed to "set you up" by provoking a transaction. These constraints create a complex relationship. To press charges, the police need the dealer to make a concrete proposition without provocation. Sting operations are forbidden.

'The police can't ask you for drugs in Norway. So they say, "Allo, can I help you with anything?" There are thousands of ways to get round that little law, the little loophole. They can drop hints like confetti, but they're not saying anything, you know. Hinting and winking, so finally then, he has to say it! "I need some dope man, I want some dope!" If he doesn't say he wants anything, "Qué pasa, babe", chill, chill, s'that simple.'

Usman had been involved in heavy crime and was more dependent on drugs than most of the others. He had a long criminal record. He often used insults like "motherfuckers" when talking about the police. One of them, who apparently looked particularly loathsome to Usman, he called "a skinhead fuckface".

'Yeah, this police guy looked seriously junkified. Masses of scars, dark eyes, like. He looked like he was completely fucked up, like. I'm on my way down and he's standing there, so he says, "Hey, there are cops here; there's the fuzzmobile up above." And then he's standing there, with his badge. He pulls out his ID and, like, wants to frisk me, you know. So I tell him, "Fuck you. I was thinking of buying some shit, but no thank you, you're so bloody thick. You couldn't wait till I asked." Comes down here, and wants to get me. So he pulls me in and tries laying a number on me, but I just say, "Get out of it, fuck you. I ain't signing nothing, no fucking way. What's this evidence you're going on about? Me, haven't the slightest idea about what you're talking about."'

No charges were pressed, and Usman was free to go. This is an example of the carefully orchestrated play that dealers and police put on for each other, one based on clear rules of procedure that the police actually follow. The dealers at The River knew that the police had to keep to the book, and they exploited it. Many of them liked projecting an image of superiority over the police. They kept lapsing into their mother tongue, finding new hiding places for the cannabis and devising new strategies to avoid arrest. We heard innumerable stories about how they tricked the police and got away with large amounts of cannabis. Nevertheless, sometimes a sense of bitterness crept in. The police were also the enemy, as became clear in our interview with Usman:

'But now there are these, like, blacks who are cops. Fuck me. It's a disgrace. I saw a Pakistani who was a cop, and I thought, for Christ's sake, man, what are you trying to prove, you stupid motherfucker.'

The police were tolerated up to a point. However, the idea of minority ethnic police officers clashed with their perceptions of 'us' and 'them'. In a previous study, we saw how downtown minority boys lumped all foreigners together into a single group (Sandberg, 2005). In this way, they could mount a campaign against the 'enemy', which at times appeared to be the ethnic majority. In another study of The River dealers, one of them referred to the police as "the ones who own the country" (Kuvoame, 2005, p 90). Minority ethnic boys saw the police as representatives of the state, to which they were opposed. If members of a minority ethnic group joined the police, not only were they letting their own side down but also they were undermining the validity of the dichotomy. It muddied the distinction between 'us' and 'them, the 'enemy'.

Even though the dealers at The River had some negative experiences with the police, they nevertheless appreciated the officers' 'street capital'. The best among them, they said, were competent, in good physical shape and had a sharp eye for street culture. They could be hard and tough. The state gave them certain powers, and this, paradoxically, carried some weight in the street culture, where might is right. The police were useful because they affirmed and reaffirmed the identities, skills and street capital of The River dealers.

Double or quits

Usman coined a phrase that seems to encapsulate a norm about making money in the drug trade. "It's double or quits," he said. "You have to double your money, every time." International research reports similar sentiments among street-level dealers (Jacobs, 1999, p 46). Normally, dealers should be able to sell for twice as much as they paid. In Norway, if they buy in bulk – a whole kilogram for instance – that would cost around 30 NOK per gram. Successive middlemen will purchase ever-smaller quantities at ever-rising prices. How much the dealers buy depends not least on their financial situation. When business is brisk, a dealer at The River can buy 50 grams – sometimes on credit – for a reasonable price. If business slows down, finding the money for even five grams can be difficult, and profit margins will be squeezed.

Some of the dealers at The River would like us to believe that they made incredible amounts of money. Rashid explained this by way of comparing cannabis with cocaine, heroin and other drugs: "It's a misunderstanding," he said, "that there's more money in cocaine or heroin."

> *Rashid:* 'They'll tell you hash is a waste of time, but I'm telling you, the money fucking rolls in!'
> *Interviewer:* 'How much can you make on a good day?'
> *Rashid:* 'On a good day, like, you can earn, on small rocks, grams like, anything below five for every customer, 100,000 kroner and … no kidding, cross my heart.'
> *Interviewer:* 'One hundred thousand kroner?!'
> *Rashid:* 'Yeah ….'
> *Interviewer:* 'Down here, at The River?'
> *Rashid:* 'You'd have to do it like those characters who sell to the guys who sell. Get in there and sell, for fuck's sake. That lot, they invest

everything they make and buy more. 'Cause the wheel goes round and round. This area is known for it. That's them, those old geezers over there, like sitting round here, I know every one of them.'

Rashid directed attention away from the subject of his own income, first to others' ability to earn money, then to people higher up the supply chain. The big money went to "the guys who sell". We heard many stories about how it was possible to make huge sums of money. What united them was their lack of specificity. It was always someone else who struck gold, not our interviewees. If we asked them to elaborate, we got vague replies. Still, dealers could at times make an unexpectedly good deal. Ahmed called it "hitting the jackpot. A good jackpot is two kings. Or a king – like, you show up empty handed, and you score a king. Or if you've sold like a 10-gram, that's a jackpot too." If a dealer sold 10 grams of cannabis – "a 10-gram" – he could pack up and go home. Jackpots were rare during the week, Ahmed said. "You've got a better chance on the weekend."

Jackpots were exceptions. In the normal course of events, dealers made small trades of one or two grams. Landing two 'kings' – a king is 1,000 NOK – represented a great day's work. This is what the dealer made after deducting his investment. While 2,000 NOK was extremely good, making less than 1,000 for a whole day was considered poor.

Denis was dealing, but he was usually not working all day. He told us how earnings could fluctuate:

> Denis: 'Nah, it's up and down, see. I don't know. You mean, like, did I have good week? Like, you'd make about, 1,000 or 1,500 a day. That's chill man, OK.'
> *Interviewer:* 'It's a lot of money.'
> *Denis:* 'It's OK, like. Kept me happy, but it lasted a couple of months and then they were gone. So you go through a period with people ringing every five minutes. Or you're out all day, with your mates, like. There's a time for everything.'

Denis highlighted the unpredictability of the income. Takings varied, depending on how much effort he put into it, but making between 1,000 and 1,500 NOK was considered respectable. Denis started dealing over the telephone to increase his income and make himself available more hours of the day. Nevertheless, he soon suffered under the pressure – it affected his ability to project an image of coolness, which was important to him, as it was for many of the other young men.

A dealer needs a reliable supplier, one who will sell cannabis at a reasonable price and, if necessary, on credit. Nevertheless, dealers sometimes arrived at The River empty handed. To get started, they needed a small amount of cannabis (called 'startings' in Norwegian), and street-level dealers often borrowed from each other. It served to consolidate relationships and reinforce mutual trust. This is how Ahmed put it:

'If someone comes up to you, and he's out of hash, he says, like, "Hey man, can I borrow startings to get me going?" So you help him out and give him startings. And you say to him, "You can help me next time I'm out," or he'll make it up when he's cash to spare. If you do this, you might start trusting this person, like. If you do it again, and the same happens, you might start hanging out together ... get to know each other.'

The most extensive British study of drug dealing was carried out in four communities (May et al, 2005). The authors described two types of market – structured and fragmented:

> Where the market is structured, a dealer or seller will sell drugs to a 'runner' ... and will have little contact with individuals who buy drugs to consume. Where the market is fragmented, dealers or sellers will, quite frequently, sell directly to a buyer. In each case, dealers/sellers will have an understanding of retail-market operations. However, in a structured market, they are unlikely to have a clear knowledge of supply routes into the market. (May et al, 2005, p 6)

The dealer–runner distinction does not adequately describe the young men at The River. All of them sold on the street, but they viewed the drugs they sold as their own. This was true even when they were selling cannabis they bought on credit or borrowed to get started. The dealers did not appear to know much about the structures further up the supply chain. This included information on the suppliers' ethnicity, income and connections with established criminal networks in Norway. Such information was too sensitive or risky for them to have. They said that some of the information was confidential, but they may have said this simply because they wanted to be taken seriously (see Chapter Eight). They reminded us several times that they did not need to know about the supply chain and that they did not want to know either.

The dealers at The River tried to double their investments. They did this partly by keeping the price at a steady 100 NOK per gram, and partly by shorting the buyers on weight. Dealers also substituted cheaper, lower-grade cannabis, including 'dryrock' (see earlier mention), and fake drugs, like bark or henna. The young men were skilful in these techniques. Dealers with good connections, a broad knowledge of the market and skill in the actual business of selling could earn good money. They could make more than they would in a normal job – that is, if they could actually get a job.

Nevertheless, incomes were much lower than what some dealers wanted us to believe. Studies from other countries show a similar pattern. In his study of the crack economy in New York's Harlem district, Bourgois (2003a) realised how little dealers earned only after several years in the field. He estimated that the hourly wage of the average street-level vendor was about twice the lowest hourly wage in New York at the time, or roughly seven to eight dollars. Obtaining a reliable figure had been difficult because the stories in circulation were about the memorable exceptions, about deals that gave the operator 10 or 20 times as much as usual. The 'runners' of the British study were in an equivalent income bracket, of €660 per week (May et al, 2005). A normal population study from New Zealand revealed that the average yearly income was less than NZ$3,000 (approximately €1,500), and dealers in the top 10% reported an average income of just NZ$25,000 (Wilkins and Sweetsur, 2006). Thus, drug dealers at the middle and retail levels earn less than what many might expect.

Recently, Levitt and Dubner asked: 'Why do drug dealers still live with their moms?' (Levitt and Dubner, 2006). From sociologist Sudhir Venkatesh they obtained the financial records of a crack-dealing gang located in one of Chicago's housing projects (see also Venkatesh 2006, 2008). The gang was organised similarly to McDonald's restaurants, with approximately 100 gangs operating franchise-type businesses that were affiliated with a central organisation. The leader of this particular gang had a college education and reported to a board of directors. Three middle-management figures reported to him. One was in charge of security (enforcer), another of the accounts (treasurer) and the third of moving drugs and money from place to place (runner). Beneath the managers were 'foot soldiers' who peddled the drugs on the streets. The financial records showed how much money the people at the top of the pyramid could make. It was a different story for those at the bottom. A typical foot soldier had an hourly wage of about three dollars. A gigantic gap existed between those at the top and those lower down the hierarchy. Street dealers frequently lived in their mother's homes because other accommodation was beyond their means.

The question arises, therefore: why would the street dealers get involved with drugs in the first place? The answer is: for the same reason that girls leave the backwoods hoping for stardom in Hollywood. They wanted to succeed in a mythologised world. To the young men from the housing projects on Chicago's Southside, selling drugs was a way of achieving a glamorous, stylish way of life. In practical terms, it was often the only way: 'the path to a decent legitimate job was practically invisible' (Levitt and Dubner, 2006, p 105). Most of the youths in the area lived below the poverty line. Three in four lived in single-parent households. They wanted status and money, and getting them by dealing drugs seemed a reasonable proposition. Everybody noticed the gang leaders when they visited the projects, driving Porsches and Mercedes, wearing designer clothing and gold chains. For the jobless person on the corner, the prospect of getting a regular job was practically out of the question.

Bruce Jacobs' (1999) ethnographic study of crack dealers also showed that drug dealing seemed the likeliest means of making a livelihood. People without qualifications, the right type of social skills or seed capital could not earn an income in the legal economy at the level possible from selling drugs. However, Jacobs's findings that selling drugs is not half as lucrative as dealers imply are consistent with those previously cited. Dealers like to boast about the money they are supposedly making, but these stories are myths often extrapolated from single cases of a particularly lucky deal or a series of unusually profitable operations. Most of the lower-level dealers earn little. It is the vision or dream of scoring that 'big kill' that keeps them going and makes their lives bearable. Dealers do not stand much of a chance in the legitimate economy. They do not possess the necessary skills, relevant work experience or cultural capital. At the same time, attributes associated with street capital – coldness, ruthlessness and an ability to look threatening – would count against them in the legitimate economy.

The structure of the cannabis market

Early research on drug markets revealed a multilayer pyramid distribution structure, particularly for 'hard drugs' such as heroin (Preble and Casey, 1969). At the top of the pyramid, we find a small number of drug importers who trade large quantities. The drugs are traded down through the middle and retail levels in progressively smaller weights and by an increasing number of dealers (Caulkins and Reuter, 1998). This has been explained as an effective system, as the increasing number of dealers may result in a high number of potential customers. In addition, it is a good risk-reduction strategy for the top- and middle-level importers because they minimise the number of people they interact with to conduct business (Preble and Casey, 1969; Moore, 1977). In addition, drug markets can be divided into open street-based markets and closed markets (May and Hough, 2004). Open markets are those that are open to any buyer, with no prior introduction to the seller, and few barriers to access. However, such markets are especially vulnerable to police surveillance, and there are few guarantees of quality for the buyers. In closed markets, sellers and buyers will only do business together if they know and trust each other, or if a third party vouches for them. The degree to which markets are closed largely depends on the level of threat posed by the police.

There are few empirical studies on the structure of cannabis markets. However, most of the distribution seems to occur in closed-market social networks. A population-based study in New Zealand revealed high heterogeneity among the customers, as well as among those who purchased rather large quantities of cannabis. Furthermore, a high proportion of people – at all levels of the market – reported receiving cannabis 'for free'. This reflects the social sharing of cannabis during group consumption and non-cash payment in a so-called barter and gift-giving tradition (Wilkins and Sweetsur, 2006). Similarly, a North American study revealed that a large majority of people got cannabis through a friend or relative, and more than half actually got it free the last time they had smoked (Caulkins and Pacula, 2006). Still, in the study from New Zealand (Wilkins and Sweetsur, 2006), a surprisingly high proportion (9%) of those who had used cannabis in the previous 12 months had also purchased cannabis in large enough quantities to qualify as middle-market participants.[5] In this group, seven in 10 had also *sold* cannabis and were therefore classified as 'dealers'. Thus, the cannabis market is characterised by a large number of participants, unclear borders between 'friends' and 'customers', and many people with semi-professional positions in the market.

Most of the cannabis sold in Norway originates in Morocco. As described previously, there are many small importers and dealers in the Norwegian market. However, from interviews with some top-level figures (who were, of course, not dealing at The River) we obtained a picture of the professional import and distribution system.[6] The price of cannabis in Morocco tends to fluctuate around 3–5 NOK per gram (€0.40–0.60). The drug is normally taken in containers by sea and road to Spain. From Spain it is distributed to multiple destinations in Europe, generally via the Netherlands. Norwegian imports are often based on contacts in the Netherlands, where the drug can be bought in large quantities for 8–10 NOK per gram. Deals are based on good connections, high levels of trust and minimum orders of 20–30 kilograms. Most of the time, importers will be looking for consignments of 100 kilograms or more. Given the significant sums involved, most importers find it impossible to pay in cash. Final payment is therefore deferred. Of course, this adds to the cost. Transport between the Netherlands and Oslo costs another 1,000–3,000 NOK per kilogram.

Oslo-based top-level suppliers can usually dispose of 100 kilograms of hash in a month. They sell it to intermediaries at the level below them in units of 5–10 kilograms, at the increased rate of 25–30 NOK per gram. Dealers at the next level usually divide their batch into 200-gram bars, which they sell to the level below for 40–50 NOK per gram. At this level, dealers break the bars into 10–20 gram units, and increase the price before selling to the consumer. While dealers at the lowest level make money by selling the drug for more than they paid for it, they also manipulate quantity and quality, as we have seen. A supply chain thus usually comprises a number of middlemen, and at every step of the way from Morocco to Oslo, each will expect to make money.

Cannabis markets in Oslo

The dealers we interviewed hung out at The River. They did not have the vantage point of an outsider's perspective. However, we also did a series of interviews with young cannabis users – who did not sell – and asked their opinions about the cannabis supply channels in Oslo (Sandberg et al, 2007). The majority of interviewees said that The River was not their main supply source but offered a useful alternative. Joakim, aged 27, put it like this: "Like, you want a fizzy drink when you're at the supermarket shopping, in the same way you have The River, like, where you can go and get it, you know." Nevertheless, they had little respect for this market: "The hash sucks and costs the earth. The deals stink." "You get less than you paid for, or get incense, liquorice, or bark, see." They also said that people were stressed out, they argued over prices and there was a lot of aggression. However, The River did have the advantage of always being open, of being the cannabis market's answer to 7-Eleven, as described previously.

Those who smoke regularly commonly buy cannabis from dealers who operate out of their apartments. An advantage of this source is the lack of police surveillance. Furthermore, customers are less likely to be cheated. Economic sociologists emphasise that uncertainty about products leads people to prefer sellers with whom they have non-commercial ties – people who buy and sell with friends and relatives report greater satisfaction, especially for risk-laden exchanges (DiMaggio and Louch, 1998). Thus, *trust* has been described as an important mechanism in economic transactions (Granovetter, 2005). This is, of course, particularly important when it comes to illegal products.

The River is vulnerable to police surveillance. In addition, it lacks quality control mechanisms. It is also a milieu that most ethnic Norwegian dealers prefer not to know. They feel superior to the immigrant River dealers and see selling from an apartment as more sophisticated and 'honourable'. From their apartments, they sell to friends and acquaintances with whom they more readily identify. On the other hand, the bonds that are established in these contexts may also turn out to be a problem for the customers. As the buyer knows the dealer, or both are acquainted with an intermediary, a close relationship may develop. Transactions often take a long time, inviting a great deal of social interaction: "You can drop in on this guy, like, and you get yakking and killing the hours, like, you know." The customers must maintain good relations with the dealer, and they may end up buying more than they originally intended. The two will often smoke cannabis together. If the customer cannot stay, this risks hurting the dealer's feelings:

> 'What can you say, you feel like you've behaved badly, not sitting down and lighting up with him, when he starts rolling a joint. It's all natural like, and there's this hash waiting and you're supposed to act polite, like, like this ain't too bad, it's OK, and like, it's what you're expected you do, take it easy and smoke that joint together. It's not on, saying, like, "Sorry, mate, I didn't really come round to smoke and stuff." I prefer to get my hash on the street.'

Because deals at The River are not perceived as anything other than a purely economic transaction; cannabis can be bought without the social rituals of apartment-based deals. Intriguingly, some people clearly prefer buying at The River to avoid these social duties. They do not want dealers as friends, and at The River, friendship and relations of a more personal nature are neither sought nor required.

In Oslo, there is also a third supply channel, a semi-open scene. On the south side of Grünerløkka, close to The River, there are a number of what are colloquially known as 'brown pubs' – restaurants where cigarette smoke has literally yellowed the walls. Some have been in business for decades, and this area has always had its fair share of downmarket 'watering holes'. Cannabis is also available in these places, sometimes the staff sold it, and sometimes dealers conducted business in the pub. As these are public places, care is required. Dealers avoid handling cannabis in bulk, and there is always the risk of being discovered by staff members or plain-clothes police officers.

At The River, and in the dealer's apartments, it is obvious to the buyer who the seller is. At a restaurant, the seller must be identified, which can involve much time-consuming chatter. When trust is established, the dealer describes the hash and a deal is concluded, with money and drugs passing discreetly from one to the other under the table. There might be a social obligation here as well, insofar as the parties are sometimes expected to 'fix a joint' and smoke together, on the street outside.

Comparing these three transaction sites, it is easy to see why The River is the preferred choice on some occasions, despite its drawbacks. An apartment or restaurant sale is likely to take more time – business presupposes an investment in a social relationship. At a restaurant, reading ambiguous signals can be fraught with difficulty. At The River, the transaction is simply a means to an end, involving no further social commitments. Furthermore, people without connections in the drug economy can resort to The River. The market is never closed and is eager to please all customers – teenagers, party smokers and impulse buyers. The River is a constant temptation but also a way of avoiding deeper ties to the drug establishment.

Economy, subculture and dependence

Many of the young men at The River thought about saving up for a place to live, to get an education or to buy a car. Most dreamed of starting a family. They told us about money put aside for building a home in Somalia or Pakistan.[7] In reality, the odds are stacked against them and their dreams. Jacobs (1999) found the same thing in his study. Rather than putting money aside, dealers directed it into conspicuous consumption – that is, consumption in line with prevailing street standards (Katz, 1988; Wright and Decker, 1997). It gave them an air of 'cool transcendence', raising them above the everyday concerns of ordinary people. The young men at The River seldom invested in symbols and articles that would ease their way into mainstream society (see also Bucerius 2007). This is a pattern often observed. There is a connection between the way the money is earned and how it is spent. People working long hours in low-paid jobs spend it more slowly, more intermittently and on different things than those to whom money comes easily from illegal activity.

Some of the young men found it hard to get up in the morning to go to work. Taking orders was difficult as well. For those who had never been seriously socialised into the mainstream economy, obtaining what would probably turn out to be a monotonous and strenuous job in the transport, retail or service sector was not easy. Jacobs (1999) describes how street culture norms encourage people to evade control and subservience. The macho ideals of street culture require autonomy and independence. No one would dare push a real man around. Drug dealing may also be emblematic of a more relaxed set of norms. At best, it provides a livelihood and a choice of where and when to work. A normal job calls for subservience, sobriety and punctuality. Socialising with friends and acquaintances is out of bounds. So a key attribute of the players in the drug economy is the need for a specific type of autonomy.

Several of our respondents had largely similar profiles to others with substance use problems. Nevertheless, our data suggest a particular characteristic of the type of drug dependence found among the young men at The River. It seems to have escaped usual diagnostic dependence measures. Their daily life, income, lifestyle and language were formed early on by membership of a criminal subculture and an economy located on the fringes of mainstream society. Membership of a minority ethnic group had relegated them to a marginal position, and membership in the criminal subculture served to consolidate what had been achieved through ethnic marginalisation.

A Norwegian team of researchers used a similar approach in their study of a group of ethnic Norwegian illegal drug users (Smith-Solbakken and Tungland, 1997). They found that the relationships formed within the black economy increased dependency, not only on alcohol or drugs but also on a whole way of life. Culture, economy and identity were associated with a so-called 'culture-economy'. This is why breaking out was so difficult. In the black economy, illegal drug users were 'experts', whereas in a white economy they were 'clients'. In the white economy, illegal drug users were suspicious interlopers whose behaviour left much to be desired. They had dropped out of school, had no occupational qualifications and came with a dismal record. Their chances of successfully changing their way of life for the better were equally bad. In the illegal drug economy, however, they were considered experienced, skilled players. They fitted in and they were reliable. They could be excellent pushers, or good at forging prescriptions. Within the black, criminal economy, they enjoyed a high creditworthiness, notwithstanding the fact that banks would never give them a loan.

The term 'cultural-economic dependency' in this study may perhaps be read as a total subjugation of illegal drug users to external forces beyond their control. Such a definition could be criticised for consolidating the 'victim narrative' it is trying to abandon. In light of our previous discussion (see Chapter Three), we suggest to conceptualise this as street capital instead. It would allow us to approach the tight cultural-economic bonds described as forms of street capital and social capital within a street culture. The problems involved in breaking free may be understood as related to embodied street habitus.

In Chapter Four, we described how the young men at The River experienced racism and – as a result – a sense of alienation or estrangement in relation to Norwegian society. Their counter strategy involved cultivating the identity of a dangerous, but accomplished, stylish individual. In this chapter, we have shown how they set themselves up within an economy that, for all intents and purposes, runs alongside the normal white economy. They learned how the black, illegal economy operates, and developed skills and abilities needed to survive in a marginal, despised and denigrated corner of society. Confronted by a community that in their view does not value them, they banded together to form a different, alternative community. In this community street culture dominated interaction, with its own rules and norms, rewards and sanctions.

However, what The River dealers know about supply chains and finding their way in the drug market, about assessing drug quality and price setting, about spotting plain-clothes police officers, is only relevant within the street culture. Street capital is not convertible. In fact, the more of it one has, the less likely one is to escape subjection and marginality.

Notes

[1] It is often argued that cannabis markets are associated with little violence (see, for example, Room et al, 2008, p 74). However, there is much to indicate that this is a simplification. Open drug scenes – including those associated with dealing cannabis – are often associated with 'systematic and opportunistic violence' (May and Hough, 2004, p 551), whereas closed networks, at least in the upmarket cannabis distribution system, usually seem to lack these characteristics.

[2] *En femmer* – five grams of cannabis.

[3] Field observation, Sveinung Sandberg, December 2005. See picture of church in Chapter Nine.

[4] The media published several articles on this topic in February and March 2006; see, for instance, *Aftenposten Aften*, 27 February, 'Jailed for buying cannabis'. According to the newspaper *VG* on 20 June, the police had made 408 arrests, 39% of which were for purchasing offences.

[5] In this study, those who reported purchasing half or full ounces (28 grams) of cannabis were defined as middle-market participants, while those who purchased smaller weights were defined as retail-level participants.

[6] This section is based mainly on information from interviews with two prison inmates serving lengthy sentences for drug offences. The interviews took place on 10 May 2006. Further information was kindly supplied by Paul Larsson, a researcher at the Norwegian Police University College (interviewed 17 March 2006), and Kåre Stølen, Grønland Police Station (interviewed 20 March 2006).

[7] We discuss in Chapter Eight why certain narratives and forms of knowledge seem easier to produce than others in an interview setting. A quiet life, family, children and a job are leading values in society. Perhaps we should not have been surprised to hear them extolled by our interviewees.

SEVEN

Violence and street culture

There is a fine mixture of renovation and decay in this part of town. For decades, the run-down buildings around The River have made it an area for marginalised groups, and violence and muggings are common. Having a potential for violence is at the core of what we coin 'street capital'.

Violent drug markets

We were sitting one night in a pub with John, one of the cannabis dealers. He had just completed his last trade for the day. We drank coffee, warmed ourselves and talked about how to avoid the perils of drug debt. John saw something through the window and remarked drily:

> *John:* 'They're gonna fight. D'you see?'
> *Interviewer:* 'How do you know?'
> *John:* 'I know them, they're dealers too.'
> *Interviewer:* 'Ah. But how do you know they're going to fight?'
> *John:* 'Because there's a bunch of them. If you go around in twos or threes, you're dealing. If there's a crowd all of a sudden, eight like, it means a fight's brewing.'

A gang was assembling, ready to set off in search of someone they wanted for some reason. If they found him, he would have been in deep trouble. The account resembles many of the stories about fights in downtown Oslo. An insult or remark often triggers a conflict. Opposing groups send out calls to friends and acquaintances to strengthen their numbers. Muggings and fights are staples of everyday life at The River. Most of our research participants had been involved in serious fights, and several had convictions for acts of violence. Moreover, knowing how to fight and to inspire fear was an important asset in their street capital, their most conspicuous resource.

John was unhappy. He had been mixed up in too much trouble, he felt. He dreamed of a few months he spent in northern Norway as a 15-year-old. Everything had been better then. We asked him:

> *Interviewer:* 'So what d'you think about all this fighting?'
> *John:* 'Nobody wins. They only get hurt and stuff. They don't get nothing out of it. Hurt ourselves ... after. Injuries and a night in the lock-up. The River's a hellhole, y'know. It's a hard life.'

There are several reasons for violence at The River. The boys had grown up fighting and had kept on fighting. However, aggressive behaviour can also be linked to the drug economy and street culture. As emphasised in the previous chapter, the dealers sometimes tried to increase takings by cheating customers. That could obviously lead to trouble. 'Pulling a fast one' and borrowing often increased the likelihood of brute force. Ahmed told this story:

> 'I sat on the grass, opposite the tube. So I'd downed some pills, then this guy shows up, so I, like, wave him over, and he says he wants to buy a gram of hash. So I give him a bit short, to con him. But he wants more, and he starts making a racket and pushing me around. So I punch him, first, then me mate turns up and gets hold of a stick and we give him a real going over.... Us two, we stood there punching and kicking the guy.'

Afterwards, Ahmed stated proudly, "The guy pushed off – we never do. Only if the cops turn up, we'll run." Never giving in is a deeply rooted sentiment in the violent street culture and an important part of gangster discourse.

Although violence was an integral part of life at The River, its occurrence is often overstated when it comes to closed and network-based illicit drug markets (Adler, 1985; Zaitch, 2005). In open markets however, there is a clear tendency for 'systematic' and 'opportunistic' violence to emerge (May and Hough, 2004). Systematic violence often emerges as conflict resolution in the absence of other authorities (Topalli et al, 2002), and opportunistic violence is common because both buyers and sellers are unlikely to call the police (Jacobs, 2000; Jacobs et al, 2000).

Several of the dealers said that they avoided problems by paying cash for their cannabis and never borrowing money. If they did happen to lose any money, at least it was their own, and they avoided getting into trouble with figures higher up in the criminal networks. Violence and dealing cannabis at The River was intricately interwoven, not least because of the hustling. Daniel recounted what happened when he tried to con a much older customer:

> 'So he burned it [the cannabis], and then he said, "Why you trying to pull one on me?" I said, "OK, I'm not bullshitting you mate, just give me back my kif." He threw it away. So I thought, OK. So when he walked past me and called me a kid, like, I said, "Don't you go calling me a fucking kid, like," and he lunged at me, so I landed one on him. He was with a couple of his brethren, and I was alone, like. I hit back, and they said, "Don't hit me". I was on my own, and they needed to be two.'

The story tells how the fight started with an insult, not the fact that the drug was low grade. The customer could tolerate being swindled as far as it went, and Daniel could tolerate the customer tossing the cannabis onto the ground. What he would not accept was being called a 'kid'. Sensitivity to insults is often linked to street masculinity (Mullins, 2006) or protest masculinity (Connell, 1995). It is also linked to the accumulation of street capital. The larger picture reveals a pattern of dealers and drug users at The River creating a potentially combustible mixture. However, the violence at The River, as in other illegal drug markets, was not so much because of the drug market itself but a consequence of the violent street culture in which the market operated (Coomber, 2006).

Fights with friends and strangers

One winter night during our fieldwork, we witnessed a big fight.[1] It started when a young man broke a bottle on another young man's head. Suddenly there were 20–30 youths fighting in the street. We could not decide who was fighting whom, but it was clearly organised. Some tried to calm the others down, but most were involved in the fighting. From a nearby street, young men came running to assist the fighters, probably alerted by mobile telephone calls. Close to us, four men in their early twenties were bashing another young man. He was backed up against a car, protecting his face and taking a lot of hits to his body. The attack with the bottle was obviously vicious, an example of brutal violence. The fighting at the car, however, seemed to be another story. Thinking about the event in retrospect, it struck us that the victim could have escaped if he wanted to. The attackers could also have hurt him more severely. They seemed to hold back their punches. Maybe by taking the hits the victim showed that he could take beatings and was not a sissy running away. That may be why the attackers pulled their punches, because they respected his courage.

Fights occurred most often among the young men themselves. Trivial arguments could provoke a fight, and drugs were frequently involved. They were sometimes at a loss to explain how the fight had started in the first place. However, although feelings got bruised, fights between friends and acquaintances seldom led to longlasting enmity. One interviewee compared fights with people he knew to fights with strangers: "When we fight amongst ourselves, it's not, it's like, someone takes a swipe at you, like, and we push each other around a bit. Then we make up and we're mates again." Friends often fought and made up afterwards. There is a parallel here to the so-called initiation rites of established gangs, where a ritual beating is a prerequisite for admission (Vigil, 1996). Respect can be gained on the street not only by giving a beating but also by taking one.

Fights could be motivated by boredom, to test the group's internal hierarchies, or even just to let off steam. Whatever the reason, there were rules in place to prevent things from getting out of hand. The regulatory mechanisms included friendship and a shared past. There were rules too against using weapons and hitting people when they were down. Fights between friends and acquaintances were often over girls. The following is a typical story:

> 'So one of them told him to stop sending messages to his girlfriend all the while, like. And this guy says, "Dunno what you're talking about," so he starting shoving him, y'know, so we told 'em to cool it, man, leave him alone. So they jumped on us, so we started defending ourselves. We won, and they cleared off in a hurry, the pair of them. So off we went to Byporten [shopping mall], when a gang suddenly appeared, might have been 16 of 'em altogether. We walk on like, OK, so they're making like they're gonna get us, so we jumped on them, and got in a few hits, like, but some security guards came running, like. So we move on, and then they come back, even more of them this time, y'know. They walk into Oslo City [another shopping mall] and tell us to go with them to the tube, like. Like, there's no cameras there, so you can fight in peace.'

This gangster discourse image of fearless, proud masculinity shapes the story. It seems as if the young men were ready to do whatever it took to protect their reputation. Beneath the surface, however, was a consensus to keep fights within certain limits. No one was afraid of being beaten to a pulp, so the most important thing was to find a place where they could "fight in peace". They were not friends, but they knew each other and had a shared definition of the situation.

Several of the interviewees had been involved in serious violent incidents with significant repercussions. These more dangerous fights were often with outsiders. In these conflicts, it seemed as if other rules applied. Several of them spoke about unmotivated aggression. Weapons were allowed in these fights, and it was in these incidents that people sustained the gravest injuries.

Confrontations often began with hostile stares. In Vigil's (2002) study of Mexican Americans, this was called 'mad dogging'. One of The River dealers described such stares as seeming as if the other "wanted to eat you". When this occurred, they were *allowed* to go up to the other person, saying, "What are you looking at? Why are you staring at us in this way?" He further explained: "If someone walks in the street staring meanly at you, what's that about? I don't get it. He doesn't know me, is he trying to be tough?" The necessary response to a hostile stare is to show no fear of physical confrontation. When challenged or harassed, it is important to retaliate, "otherwise it would only be more and more pressure". For the young men at The River, it was always important to project an image of a potentially violent individual, especially so in conflicts with other groups. In street culture, a reputation for violence is an important asset. Legends of past hostilities, public shows of strength and aggression, and sensitivity to insults make up an important part of people's street capital.

Rational irrationality

Violence was an important part of street life, not because the young men were fighting all the time but because violence organised social hierarchies and fed mythology. When Daniel and Mattar were 16–17, they were involved in a brawl with another group of minority ethnic boys. They had beaten up a couple of boys, and then the elder brothers of the boys had come and given them a thrashing. They quickly realised that they were out of their league against the older men. Daniel remarked, "You don't play tough, like, with that lot. You hit them, they hit you. Get it?" They retreated, one with a serious injury. Two years passed before they saw the other boys again.

According to Daniel and Mattar, this rival group now assumed they could mess with them: "They thought, like, 'Yeah, we did 'em once, and they never came back. We can play games with 'em again if we want.'" But this time, Daniel, Mattar and their friends were in no mind to leave without a fight. They decided to make a stand. It was a tough fight. One of the rival gang members got an injury he will never recover from. When we interviewed Daniel and Mattar, they still lived in constant fear of retribution: "Doesn't matter if it takes 10 or 20 years, they'll never forget 'cause their mate was fucked up real bad. For nothing." However, they did not want to move to a safer place in the city. When we asked them why, they said simultaneously, "Nah, that'd be chickening out."

This incident highlights some street culture mechanisms. Disputes can escalate when the implicated parties feel compelled to act by their sense of self-respect and honour – and, not least, to avoid trouble further down the line. Analysed as a narrative, the moral of the story is clear. If you do not retaliate, the problems will come back to haunt you, and with added force. Chris, whom we introduced in Chapter One, said that he always hit back, even after a real beating. "If you don't," he said, "it just gets worse and worse." This rationale is well known from studies of violent cultures (see, for example, Wolfgang and Ferracuti, 1967; Luckenbill and

Doyle, 1989; Anderson, 1999; Vigil, 2002, 2003; Bourgois, 2003a). If others fear the consequences of a confrontation, they will be less likely to start trouble.

These statements and observations in our data are similar to Bourgois's (2003a) description of the psychiatric patient Caesar, who gained status as a drug dealer from his reputation for being out of control or crazy. They also bear resemblances to Vigil's (1987) descriptions of the 'locuro' attitude (from the Spanish *loco*, meaning mad) among Mexican Americans, and Anderson's account of the respect that street people acquire by developing a reputation and self-image based on 'juice' (Anderson, 1999, p 33). If a street dweller ensures that people know his potential for violence, they will be careful around him. Running away from a confrontation will likely shatter an individual's self-esteem and invite further disrespect (Anderson, 1999, p 76). Thus, building a violent reputation, or building street capital, not only commands respect but also serves to deter future assaults. Mette, one of the few girls at The River, played the same game. She often dramatised herself as an aggressive, violent character and had one of the most consistent gangster discourse self-presentations.

> *Mette:* 'Nah, you just play him around for a bit, he'll soon realise that he can't shit with us, like. We kick him and punch him for a few minutes before we leave off. Then we kick him one last time before we go. That one usually lands in his face.... You can cause a lot of damage in a bloke's face, y'know, if you put your boot in....'
> *Interviewer:* 'You're not worried about putting them out of commission altogether?'
> *Mette:* 'Don't think anybody cares much about that down at The River; I don't give it a second thought, me, like.'

She continued: "You can't let them see you're afraid of fighting. If you do, you sink and sink so low you can't believe it. Nobody's going to respect you any longer. They'll just use you. It's totally crazy man!" Street capital is gendered and closely linked to street masculinity (Mullins, 2006). Mette, therefore, always had a lot more to prove, and her story can be read in that light. Despite her gender and small size, she wanted people to respect her and fear her for being ruthlessly violent.

One of the more brutal episodes we heard about was about a buyer who was mugged by seven of The River dealers after buying some pills. They stabbed him in the back twice and he sustained multiple bodily injuries. Why they attacked the boy remained unclear, even after they told the story repeatedly. Were they mesmerised by a form of mass suggestion? They said that they had been high on pills and it was difficult to remember exactly what happened. Another explanation could be that they wanted to boost their reputation as irrationally violent, in the same way as Mette, mentioned previously. It was still rational, however, in one sense. By choosing a solitary, intoxicated victim, they were unlikely to get hurt themselves, and by choosing someone who had come to The River to buy drugs, they were unlikely to be reported to the police. In this way, they built a reputation for violence in their dealings with other youths. Katz (1988) describes this as the rational use of seemingly irrational violence.

The seduction of crime

Acts of violence can be seen as practical, rational attempts to accumulate street capital. At the same time, because behaving aggressively is inherently exciting, often inducing a sense empowerment or invincibility, it cannot be reduced to simple practicality or rationality. Usman gave the following animated account:

> 'But you know, when you're young, you like that feeling, "Ah! ... victory". It's like being in the ring, innit. "Whack!" And you survive, y'know. Gives you a kick, like. Like in a hefty car crash. Unbelievable, raw, like. That adrenalin spike, like.'

The metaphors derive from boxing and car crashes. Usman compared defeating an assailant to winning in the boxing ring. It was as exciting as being in a car accident: the rush of adrenalin, and he felt alive.

Katz (1988) criticises the prevailing view of crime among social scientists. Crime, he contends, has been reduced to three main explanations. First, crime has been described as a rational strategy to achieve an end, the most important being money. Bourdieu's concept of practical rationality is one such explanation, even though it is more sophisticated than most rational economic approaches. The second explanation is different. Crime is viewed as an expression of mental imbalance. Criminals have no understanding of their actions; they are ill. The final explanation links crime to variables like age, sex, ethnicity and socioeconomic status. The last of these explanations is often linked to marginalisation approaches, as in Vigil's (2002, 2003) and Wacquant's (2008) work. In Katz's view, the 'seduction of crime' is also necessary to understand violent behaviour and other crimes. The attraction, seduction and compulsion to commit crime have intrinsic values, and these are easy to forget when researchers emphasise marginalisation or economic and rational analysis.[2]

Muggings

Unlike members of the drug scene and the criminal milieu, ordinary people are seldom mugged in Norway.[3] At The River, however, robberies or muggings were widespread.[4] As with fighting, the dealers on the scene were themselves the main targets. They could be robbed if they were too intoxicated to put up any defence. According to some of the boys, robberies sometimes occurred in connection with fights. If a fight was in progress, somebody might seize the moment to steal a mobile telephone or cash. Two of our research participants recounted:

'They're his mates, but let's say you pick a fight with him, like, and, y'know, "Give us me money back," the others see a chance, "Maybe he's got a mobile, maybe a wallet with money …" [laughs]. So they pile into the fight, as well.'

It is often easier to rob other members of the street culture, because the victims are unlikely to report the matter to the authorities. Many also carry drugs and money, precisely what the robbers are after. As Jacobs (1999) points out, robbery is also the ultimate humiliation and therefore a useful instrument of revenge. Robbery results in both physical and economic injury.

When the dealers robbed strangers, the victim was usually an inebriated male making his way home and looking to buy some cannabis on the way. Mette was one of the few who spoke candidly and in detail about mugging people from outside the street culture.[5] This incident happened one evening as a couple of dealers were hanging out under a bridge at The River. They were short of cash, when a woman approached:

> *Mette:* 'And then … yeah, then you know … need cash, like, and then … we see this woman with a bag and we say, like, "She'll do". So it's, like, spontaneous, you know.…'
> *Interviewer:* 'So what did you do, did you hit her first or …?'
> *Mette:* 'Nah, it was, like, I came up from behind with a knife, like this [gestures demonstratively]. And he came from the front with a knife, like this.'
> *Interviewer:* 'So you both held knives to her throat?'
> *Mette:* 'Mmm. She got real scared, and backs away behind us, then she bumps into that wall, you know, like. So me mate, he throws my knife at her face and he nearly hits her here. So then she drops her bag.… So he was only inches away from her mug. So she drops her bag, but I don't notice it. And I dunno what happens to me mate. So then she grabs her bag, and runs off, like.'

The woman ran off, dropping her mobile telephone and purse as she made her escape. The dealers took both. Possibly the most intriguing thing about this episode is what happened in the seconds leading up to the dealers' decision to commit the robbery. They responded spontaneously; the robbery was not planned. Nothing about it seemed based on rational calculation, not the choice of victim, the crime scene or the risk of capture. The situation was chaotic, and both Mette and her friend were high. However, they were more familiar with this chaos than the victim and got more or less what they were after in the end.

Wright and Decker (1994, 1997) have written about burglars and robbers based on interviews with active criminals. There are similarities between these criminals and the young men at The River. They often needed money in a hurry, and robbery was the quickest way to get cash. Selling drugs took longer. Nevertheless,

Wright and Decker did not see the muggings or robberies they heard about as rational or calculated behaviours, which is the position of classical criminology and the mindset promoted by routine activities theory.[6] Among other things, most of the burglaries and muggings were committed in close proximity to the perpetrators' usual haunts and often under the influence of drugs. Moreover, street muggings do not, as a rule, produce significant profits. Mette on one occasion made only 30 Euro cents. Thinking of it brought a smile to her face. She was trying to steer clear of that sort of thing nowadays, she said, digressing from gangster discourse for a minute and presenting a self-narrative more in line with neutralisation theory.

Talking in a more general sense about her modus operandi for muggings along The River, Mette said:

> *Mette:* 'If they're carrying a bag, we just take the bag, and then we run like hell. But if they're not carrying a bag, then what happens is … we block their path, then we threaten them. Then we say, like, "Give us everything you've got." If they don't give us what they've got, they get punched in the face. Then we check their wallet … take everything they've got.'
>
> *Interviewer:* 'So you threaten them: "If you don't hand over … we'll knock you down," like?'
>
> *Mette:* 'Nah, that's not what we say, we just say, "Give us what you've got, money, mobile – the lot." And if they don't, we just hit them, like. And once they're flat on their face, they'll probably get kicked as well.'

The initial interaction between perpetrator and victim shifts the balance of power to the former. In Mette's story, the use of force – punching and kicking – makes the power structure even more apparent. The robbers want their victim to realise that they mean business.

We have already noted the connection between violence and excitement or a sense of power. The same connection helps explain muggings. Anderson (1999) points out that a sense of controlling the actions of others can motivate robberies. The robber wants the person 'with something' to acknowledge the power of the perpetrator. The wise victim will understand this and defer to the attacker. Similarly, one of the robbers interviewed by Wright and Decker said: "I make happen whatever I want to happen." Another described it as a "control thing" and boasted about the power he felt when his victims realised he could kill them if he wanted to (Wright and Decker, 1997, p 56). The muggers knew they were at the bottom of both criminal and conventional hierarchies, but by brandishing a knife, they reversed the power balance.

Katz (1988) describes that muggings differ significantly from other criminal behaviour because they take time. The victim and perpetrator interact over a considerable period of time, reinforcing the sense of power and control the mugger feels. The robbery can be seen as a way of getting a kick, demonstrating power by ridiculing or humiliating the victim. The perpetrator shows demonstratively that he has no fear of losing anything – a central tenet of street culture.

Socioeconomic marginalisation can only partially explain these occasionally brutal muggings and use of force. Muggings were not a lucrative means of securing income by any means, and the robbers sometimes behaved with unnecessary ferocity. Muggings were about getting hold of ready cash when the dealers lacked the money to buy cannabis or did not have the time to hang out and deal. However, the muggings were also about control and excitement. Although violent behaviour can be a source of street capital, giving its owner a privileged position on the street, it also carries a certain fascination and excitement. In this way, street culture balances between calculation and practical rationality on the one hand and the 'seduction of crime' on the other. There are different motivations for violence, and for analytical purposes, they can be treated separately. In practice, however, it is harder to define what exactly sets it in motion. As we have seen, the dramatisation of irrationality can itself be highly rational.

The smart gangster

Up to this point, the focus has been on the violence and muggings that take place along The River. This is a well-known story from the international literature on street culture. Even though the North American ghetto and the Scandinavian welfare state are worlds apart, there are similarities in the cultural processes that groups of marginalised youths develop. Street culture is not necessarily violent, however. In some cases, violence at The River was stopped or at least limited. Many of the dealers did not carry a knife because that would cause trouble if the police were to search them. They also knew that violence (more than drug dealing) attracted police attention and was bad for business. This rationale sometimes came up during interviews.[7]

Smiling broadly, Rashid described a recent incident. Two young men were selling cannabis. One was a refugee, new to The River scene. "All those new guys, they think they own the place," he commented resignedly. The second was an old-timer. Just as Rashid walked past them, a customer stopped and asked them for five grams of hash – an unusually large quantity. The two dealers started arguing over which of them should make the deal. As they fought, they rolled down a flight of steps. One of them suddenly produced a knife. While all this was going on, Rashid, in his own words, "tiptoed" over to the customer and told him to "come with me". The story had a very clear moral.

> 'I said to them both, "You are so fucking stupid!" I said it, right there, "You're pulling each other's frigging hair out, and the customer's standing right in front of your noses." I know I shouldn't have done it, but I did it, whatever. Just to teach them a lesson. "While you two were knocking the shit out of each other, I was selling hash. Wanna

know how much I got?" So I pull out the 500 [NOK] note, and do like this [waves a 'note' in the air]. They were extremely not pleased, I can tell you. So they turned all that hatred and aggression on me instead.'

There is no way of telling whether the story is true. Another dealer recounted the same story. It may be an urban legend. Anyway, its moral is important enough: fighting can imperil a sale. The story also shows how the gangster persona involves different, sometimes conflicting images. One is the dangerous, violent person, a trait that earns you respect. The other is also important: it is about mastering the role of the smart gangster. A real gangster needs to create a sense of fear, but he needs to be smart as well. Mullins (2006) reveals a similar contradiction. Wearing a mask during a robbery, for example, could be seen as both 'punk' and street smart. A combination of a reputation for violence and quick-wittedness is best. We will return to this in the final chapter.

Ethnicity, violence and street culture

There are many parallels between the young men at The River and the youths who have been rioting in France during the last couple of years: they are male, many are from minority ethnic cultures and many are Muslims. The religious aspect is easy to misinterpret. The French social scientist Olivier Roy (2004) claims that there are two typical ways of dealing with minority ethnic groups – multiculturalism and assimilation. The first is widespread in Northern Europe, the second in France. However, the paradox is that both strategies are failures, and for the same reason. Both assume an inherent relationship between culture and religion. It would be more useful, he suggests, seeing cultural disintegration as leading rather to new forms of religiosity. French minority ethnic youth groups are increasingly abandoning Arabic as a spoken language, but at the same time, they are growing increasingly religious and 'inventing a new Islam'. They construct a new urban subculture, where they mix in Western clothes, music, fast food and petty crime.

Towards the end of 2005, tensions exploded in the suburbs of Paris and other French cities. Cars and homes were torched, and minority ethnic youths were the driving force. According to Roy (2006), the protagonists were young people aged 12–25. Adults stayed inside. The riots unfolded in disadvantaged, run-down areas known colloquially as *quartiers difficiles* or *les banlieues* (ghettos) and long since acknowledged as high-risk zones. The rioters were gangs of young men numbering between 20 and 200, mostly second-generation immigrants of different ethnicities. Their main characteristic was their area identity, not their Muslim identity. Most importantly, they belonged to an excluded, ignored social group. The French manufacturing sector, which used to give jobs to their fathers, had disappeared. It was replaced by a service sector that is inaccessible to most of the young men. As with The River dealers, the French rioters had connections with hard-core criminals involved in drug crime. The gangs protected their territories against all interlopers – police, press, social workers and rival gangs. Street or protest masculinity, based on violence, and gang fights were the basic ingredients of social order.

The development of criminal and deviant subcultures is often associated with new immigrant groups; for example, Whyte's (1943) Italians. At other times, it is associated with established minority ethnic groups, such as Anderson's (1999)African Americans, Vigil's (2002) Mexican Americans, Bourgois's (2003a) Puerto Ricans or the French rioters. This has sometimes led researchers to emphasise 'honour' and 'respect' deriving from a feudal mindset as explanations for the formation of gangs (Lien, 2001), important parts of street masculinity (Bourgois, 2003a)[8] or important cultural influences on drug dealing (Bucerius, 2007).

In our study, however, we found it hard to find a direct link between so-called 'traditional honour cultures' and violence. Moreover, apart from the strict ban on alcohol in Islam, which may weaken relative barriers to using and dealing cannabis (and making contacts with criminal networks), we did not find religion important either. First, as other studies confirm, the young men and their parents and grandparents entertained very different notions of what honour means (Larsen, 1992). Also, most of the them felt estranged not only from mainstream Norwegian society but also from their minority ethnic cultures – and most had broken or fragile ties to their families. Second, The River dealers mainly used the cultural influences of gangsta rap and gangster movies, not Islam, when mythologising or neutralising their crimes.

Honour and respect have always been important in street culture, but that importance has little to do with the cultures of the Middle East or South East Asia. The dynamics of street culture are a better place to look for rationales for the violence we observed at The River. The dealers' concepts of respect and honour are predominantly associated with a criminal subculture for which the accumulation of street capital is important. As described by the Chicago and Birmingham Schools, street culture is an arena where stigmatised and marginalised groups can win respect. Street understandings of honour and respect are crucial narratives in these efforts, and living by them accumulates street capital.

Cahill (2000) describes the special skills needed by young people to negotiate life on the street – street literacy. There are three methods of self-protection, the first being to mind your own business.[9] Another strategy is cognitive mapping, an exercise in establishing categories of places, times and people that are safe or dangerous. If seen as gendered, these two strategies are female, even though they are the most widely used for both sexes.

The third method is masculine and can be a source of real power. Researchers have described how youths in both New York (Cahill, 2000) and London (Alexander, 2000) protect themselves by behaving and dressing aggressively. They 'pose as gangsters' to avoid trouble. Being from a minority ethnic group or newly arrived refugees encourages particular strategies and gives particular advantages in these efforts. In this way, ethnicity becomes important, but it has more to do with skin colour, particular experiences, and socioeconomic marginalisation than with a traditional honour culture. The River dealers, for example, played on the image of the 'dangerous foreigner' or translated experiences from war zones into street capital. Situated at the bottom of social space hierarchies, they responded at a micro level to the socioeconomic marginalisation processes we described in Chapter Four. This opposition is less politicised than the Paris rebellions, but it can still be seen as a form of protest.

Posing as 'dangerous foreigners'

One strategy for protection in public spaces is to acquire a reputation for violent behaviour. This may be done by aggressive stares and manners, or through association with feared symbolic figures.

In the US, there are several indications that the majority seem to associate criminality with particular ethnic groups (see, for example, Covington and Taylor, 1991; St John and Heald Moore, 1995; Chiricos et al, 1997, 2001; Peterson et al, 2006).[10] In the UK, Back (1996) has pointed out that black people are associated with aggressiveness and sexual potency. Webster (1996, 1997, 2007) has similarly emphasised how, from 1988 to 1995, Asian youth changed from being categorised as law abiding to being associated with criminality, drugs, violence and disorder. Similar tendencies are seen in Norway.[11] The public visibility of small groups of minority ethnic juveniles involved in crime may have increased stereotyping. By hanging out in conspicuous places in downtown Oslo, they make easier pickings for the authorities and news media (Prieur, 2001).

Stereotypical images of minority ethnic groups are reflected on the street. Norwegians or white people are seen as easy prey to rob, physically challenge and harass. Several of dealers from The River stated that ethnic Norwegian boys could not, or would not, defend themselves, and that they did not have friends to support them. A minority ethnic 17-year-old we interviewed for a similar study of street culture in Oslo (Sandberg and Pedersen, 2008) stated that:

> 'It is safer to be a foreigner than Norwegian in Norway, see. A Kurdish boy has 0.1% chance of being attacked. Nobody would go after him. But there's a big chance a Norwegian kid will be mugged and have everything he's got stolen from him. It is really terrible.... I'm glad I don't look Norwegian.'

He had lived his entire life in Norway with his Norwegian mother. His Latin-American father also lived in Norway. While he had only twice been back to his father's home country and did not speak Spanish, he presented himself as a foreigner and even spoke in a manner characteristic of individuals with a foreign first language. Maybe such a self-presentation made life in the city centre easier. In the context of his story about assaults on ethnic Norwegians, this is a feasible interpretation. Other young minority ethnic men interviewed for that study told similar stories, stressing the advantages for themselves as 'foreigners':

> 'It's fun when white guys go by just to take the piss. If you try that on a Pakki, innit, he'll just get hold of masses of cousins, and they'll come and back him up. So, you shouldn't mess with them. But whites, you know, they don't have the back-up, like.'

Sometimes ethnic Norwegian boys confirmed these types of stories. A 15-year-old told stories about gangs of Pakistanis who came to bash him and his friends when they were skating in a particular area downtown. Another ethnic Norwegian feared gangs of immigrants because "they don't know that we have rules in Norway", and one of the older ethnic Norwegians who was involved in serious gang crime in the 1990s stated that you "have to prove yourself a little more when you are the only white". In the street culture of Oslo, he felt he had to display violent potential more frequently because he was ethnic Norwegian and white.

Some of The River dealers said it more indirectly. "In Oslo, you see everything, you can even have Norwegian kids going around with knives, see." The implied message here is that 'white kids' usually did not carry knifes; it was the exception. These statements may indicate a particular social capital that is specific for minority ethnic groups. They may actually have had more relatives to support them. However, the statements are also illustrative of a symbolic association among minority ethnic men.

Stereotyping is generally a problem for minority ethnic groups. However, stereotypes can also be used strategically. For young men on the street, it may serve as a resource when posing as gangsters and creating a dangerous appearance. When the young men emphasised that they were foreigners, it could be seen as pride in cultural difference or as a black trend in popular culture, or could be attributed to identity. It is difficult to escape the social meanings carried by the body through skin colour (Andersson, 2005). At the same time, it is possible that young minority ethnic men used signs of minority ethnic status to protect themselves and to advance in street hierarchies. Similar observations have been made in other ethnographic studies of criminal minority ethnic men in Oslo (Vestel, 2004; Andersson, 2005; Moshuus, 2005a). In this way, racism is turned on its head, and black becomes a symbol of strength (Andersson, 2005).

Most stereotypes have a double character, and stigmas can be rewarding if they are transformed into something positive (Lemert, 1967). In street culture, mainstream society's negative stereotypes can provide protection and status. In the theoretical framework developed in this book, symbolic signs associated with the category 'foreigner' can be conceptualised as a form of *embodied* street capital or street habitus. The River dealers and other minority ethnic men devoted to street culture may have been strategically posing as 'dangerous foreigners' to advance in the social hierarchies of the street. Unfortunately, this increases the original stigmatisation from mainstream society and binds the young men to street culture.

Embodied symbolic capital is generally inert and difficult to change. Habitus is 'social necessity made second nature, turned into muscular patterns and bodily automatism' (Bourdieu, 1984, p 474). When it includes symbolic associations with skin colour, it becomes even harder to transform.

Socialisation to the street

To develop a street habitus takes time. Several of our interviewees told us about growing up in violent families. Usman, whom we introduced in Chapter Two, was from Pakistan, and he had been involved in serious gang crime even as a child. Mohamed, from Somalia, had been taught to wrestle by his grandfather. He became so adept, he managed to beat one of his uncles, three years his senior. Many of the dealers told us that they were expected to know how to fight from a young age.

Experiencing violence in childhood can stunt the development of basic trust and the ability to empathise. It wreaks untold havoc on the child. However, in a street culture setting, this deficit can be turned into an asset. Middle- and upper-class people, says Bourdieu (1984), acquire and form their cultural capital and habitus during childhood. Similarly, children from violent homes may develop a tolerance for violence that can become a form of empowerment and street capital.

Some of The River dealers described what it was like to grow up in abusive homes and how it acclimatised them to violence as young teenagers. "When I was 15, obviously we were fighting every day," one of them told us. "I used to go downtown, go from club to club, like, and make trouble," another said. Partying at friends' places and trips downtown often culminated in fights. Usman described a culture of irrational violence into which drugs and alcohol had recently found a channel:

> 'Friday night, Saturday night, we got drunk, or you're on some type of ecstasy. You just beat the shit out of someone. You do whatever you want on the spur of the moment, and you're not afraid of anything. You can't feel fear anymore. It's hard the first time, but when you've done it a few times, it gets like normal.'

Because habitus integrates past experiences, it endows an ability to tackle unforeseen situations (Bourdieu, 1977, 1990). A street habitus takes time to mature, and it resists change. Usman's account shows how inhibitions against violent behaviour gradually erode. The first time, acting aggressively is difficult. However, with practice, it gets easier, until it gets to the point where you do not give it a second thought.

Most of the dealers at The River were involved in innocent fights from an early age. Many also started mugging other children. Rashid describes how these muggings started:

'Y'know, it wasn't like you go round planning muggings, like. They were talking about this concert that was supposed to be so great, like, and people went round Majorstua and Frogner [areas in the affluent Oslo west]. If you wanted something you had to take it. If your family, like, bought clothes, they'd be so out of fashion you wouldn't be seen dead in them. So we sort of found out we could help those rich kids get rid of theirs. So it started, like, cool, calm and easy, like. The kids handed over their tickets and said, "Fuck you! Now we've gotta go and ask mummy for more money to buy tickets," like.'

It was a light-hearted story, told with a smile on Rashid's face. Stealing from rich kids was also easy to justify, because they had more money, and they could get more from their parents anyway. Despite the light-hearted tone, in the background, we heard another story: the boys were marginalised in many different ways. They belonged to minority ethnic groups, some had grown up with violence, they had less money and they did not do as well at school as their ethnic Norwegian counterparts. However, they had something other children and youths lacked. They knew how to fight, and they were not afraid of taking a beating. Mugging children and teenagers gave them concert tickets, clothes and mobile telephones, but it also gave them an intoxicating feeling of control and power. Street capital acts like power does in other settings. It is a key to material rewards but also to self-confidence and a sense of belonging.

Converting war experiences into street capital

Most of the non-Western immigrants in Norway come from war-inflicted areas (except for the Pakistanis). We met many who had experienced war, either as participants or as civilians. Most of them were from Somalia, the newest group of immigrants. One revealed about his childhood, "I've seen a lot of people die in Somalia. A lot of children, women, every day. Every day." Both his parents were dead, and he had witnessed carjackings and shootouts. Several of the refugees had trouble sleeping because they remembered traumatising incidents from their past. A Somali told us, "I was six when the war started. Fighting was common." Comparing Somalia to juvenile gangs in Oslo, he continued. In Somalia, "when they start fighting, hundreds die. So I'm not afraid when those people fight." Referring to fighting and conflicts at The River, another asked rhetorically, "Is this trouble?" Then he stated laconically, "I've seen trouble."

Many of the refugees at The River had not been soldiers or involved in violence themselves, but they had seen it and experienced it and were used to it — at least, more so than youths who had grown up in Norway. Some refugees had been more directly involved in war and violence. Hassan, whom we introduced in Chapter Two, told a story about an innocent game of football that escalated into a pitched battle. He was shot, sought to avenge himself and had to flee the country as a consequence. Another refugee, Mohamed, mentioned the movie *Black*

Hawk Down when describing the atmosphere in the Somali capital (Mogadishu) during the civil war. He had had a job as a security guard and was carrying arms as a 12-year-old. Mohamed knew a great deal about weapons and was able to describe the various makes of gun in detail. Once, while their security squad was interviewing a thief, Mohamed's gun accidentally went off. The thief started talking, giving Mohamed's reputation a chance boost. "So I earned a few points that day. I got a star." Asked if he was afraid, he said:

> 'No, never. Never gave it a thought. Never, when you're a kid, you don't think about dying. Didn't know much about what was going on, but I'm glad as hell I didn't kill anyone, and nobody was hurt, on my shift, like. And we used to work during the daytime, but the worst stuff happened at night. That's when some of the big boys did the dirty work.'

It would be hard to imagine a young boy on the verge of adolescence not feeling fear in circumstances like these. By stressing the violence and absence of fear during childhood, Mohamed set himself at the centre of a gangster discourse, making him harder and tougher than others.[12] There are real underlying differences as well, however.

Traumatic experiences such as Mohamed's had happened to some of the other refugees along The River. The traumas explained what the refugees described as "more than enough problems already", and why they wanted to avoid getting into trouble in Norway. "We didn't come to Norway to sell dope on the street," they said repeatedly. They had survived hardship and dreamed of getting a job and starting a new life. However, they still ended up at The River, in the midst of a violent street culture. Most had been involved in violent disputes, some in serious crime and heavier drugs.

In public spaces, 'posing as a gangster' (Cahill, 2000) is possible using signs associated with the 'dangerous foreigner'. The young Somali men may have been using their background as a symbol in such an enactment. However, their stories also indicate real differences in embodied experiences. In a fight, winning will depend on embodied street capital or habitus. When the young men glare at each other in anticipation of a brawl, the absence of fear needs to be embodied. In one way or another, they have to be familiar with the situation.

The literature on street culture contains numerous examples of how kids are socialised into a street way of behaviour. To survive, they are taught to protect themselves and instructed in various forms of criminal activity. Experiences from violent communities can be seen as historical relations deposited in individual bodies, or habitus. In one way or another, most of the Somalian refugees were more used to violence and weapons, and less frightened by death, than are young people growing up in Norway. In a street culture where violence is thought to be the single most critical resource for achieving status (Wilkinson, 2001), and young inner-city males often characterise their neighbourhood as a war zone

(Fagan and Wilkinson, 1998), habitus formed in an actual war zone can be an advantage.

Many of the men raised in Norway were from dysfunctional and violent families. Some had also been involved early in criminal activity within the larger family network. A young man stated that he learned to fight by being bashed, another that you really got to know people by fighting them. Such an upbringing may have facilitated a street habitus favourable in street culture. Nevertheless, in Oslo, the capital of a wealthy welfare state, the equivalent of experience from war-inflicted countries is hard to find. Thus, refugees with wartime experience have an uncommon habitus that translates into status and money in the particular social context found at The River.

Street capital versus cultural capital

Most minority ethnic youths in the same socioeconomic circumstances as our dealers manage to steer clear of crime and to have enough money for their needs. Street capital nevertheless has to be weighed against the chances of success in society. Using Bourdieu's terminology, it needs to be seen in relation to other forms of capital. Activating war experiences and violent upbringings and enacting stereotypes only have meaning if they are seen as a form of currency in the absence of economic and cultural capital.

The absence of economic capital is the first thing that springs to mind, the most obvious need. When young men from destitute families need money, they rely on resources they possess already. They can convert their street capital quickly and easily into cash by selling drugs and mugging people. All the same, except for the non-returnable refugees, there was not much evidence of serious financial distress. They used money from drug dealing and muggings for conspicuous consumption, or to create the look of 'cool transcendence' required to maintain their image as street 'aristocracy' (Wright and Decker, 1997, p 40). The younger dealers, especially, spent more on conspicuous consumption, such as expensive designer clothes or playing the 'big shot' out on the town. They wanted to create the impression that they were *worth* something, and they wanted to be noticed. In this way, the lack of cultural capital possibly counted more than the lack of economic capital.

Notes
[1] Field observation by Sveinung Sandberg accompanied by two members of the Oslo Outreach Service team, January 2006.

[2] For an elaborated critique of economic and rational analysis, see Bucerius (2007).

[3] Muggings are still popular media fodder, victims are more willing to speak publicly and offenders tend to be reported more frequently (Pedersen, 2001).

[4] In 2005, for instance, 47 robberies were committed in the area around The River; 35 were classified as 'brutal'. However, this is only the tip of the iceberg. When customers are robbed, they usually do not report it to the police; nor do dealers who have been robbed by other dealers.

[5] Maybe she did so because this was an extreme version of a gangster image shaped by gangster discourse, which she exaggerated to prove that she was one of the tough men.

[6] Theories of *routine activities* and *lifestyles* in relation to violence gained popularity in the 1970s, expanding on theories of violent subcultures. The hypothesis is that the coincidence of time and place, of suitable victim and perpetrator, combined with absence of control, is the key to understanding violence. Violence in this reading cannot be construed as blind but as a function of numerous easily observable parameters.

[7] These narratives were not consistent throughout the interviews, however, and in the next second, the young men could return to more well-known stories of how they always struck back and were extremely violent. This is what we describe as interdiscursivity in Chapter Eight.

[8] Bourgois (2003) argued that the masculinity constructs he found on the streets of El Barrio were imported mainly from 'the *jibaro* hillsides' in Puerto Rico (see also Jensen, 2007). However, he emphasised that the material basis of the *respeto* that males could expect there was unattainable in post-industrial New York (Bourgois, 2003, p 222).

[9] These strategies for avoiding trouble will, paradoxically, increase the risk of trouble by reducing more general social control mechanisms. Witnesses will, for example, prefer not to talk to the police.

[10] Some even propose that criminality is seen as a black phenomenon (Chiricos et al, 2004).

[11] Whether minority ethnic youth are more prone to commit criminal offences *in actual fact* is a complicated question. The prosecution rate among minority ethnic groups is higher than among ethnic Norwegians (Skardhamar, 2006). At the same time, there seems to be a covariance with the poorer living standards of minority ethnic groups in Norway. Low educational achievements, high jobless rates and low income levels all play a role. In an all-else-being-equal scenario, overrepresentation would persist, but the margin would not be particularly wide. There is also the fact that the young men are more conspicuous than other groups and therefore attract police attention (Finstad, 2003). They also tend to gather in places that enhance visibility. According to self-reported data, however, minority ethnic juveniles are more likely to be law abiding than other groups (Torgersen, 2001). The population of minority ethnic youth seems to be divided into two distinct groups. The majority are well adapted, but a small minority of young men account for the overrepresentation of criminal activity and violence.

[12] Even though this is balanced with the statement that he was glad that he did not kill anyone. For these complex narrative formations balancing conventional discourse and gangster discourse, see Chapter Eight and Sandberg (2009b, 2009c).

EIGHT

Between the street and the welfare state

The neighbourhood where the street market ends houses four large welfare organisations. They are run by the city council or private charities, financially supported by the government. The omnipresent Nordic welfare state probably contributed to the development of victim narratives.

I know how the system works

We met up with Johs one autumn afternoon. He was one of the dealers with a long criminal record. It was raining, and we had already been at The River for several hours.[1] Two dealers suddenly crossed the road, obviously eyeing an opportunity to make a sale. We said "no thanks" but told them about the book we were writing. One of them, Johs, was immediately intrigued – his friend, he told us, did not speak Norwegian. If we wanted to do an interview, it would have to be with him. Putting an arm around our shoulders, he said he would "tell us everything". We suggested a local bar as a likely interview setting, but Johs had some unfinished business with the owner. We found a table at another nearby pub instead. He ordered a beer, and we ordered tea. After the interview, he bought us a beer and we stayed on to talk for hours. Johs liked talking and he became one of our best sources of information. That evening, he told us about his childhood, the local youth gang, and relations with the social services.

> 'There were a lot of people out there helping me. Child welfare people, different organisations who wanted to help us. So we had no excuse for what we did. We knew it was wrong, but we were treated fucking leniently.... The trouble didn't have any negative consequences, in fact, if anything, it helped, got more attention, got more help. Those guys in the child protection agency and the police, they really listened to us.'

He also stressed the support offered by various parts of the welfare state system. They took him seriously and tried to help. His experience clashes with what one tends to read and hear in the media and from the welfare establishment. Johs elaborated:

> 'We had three options when we were teenagers. An independent organisation and two programmes run by the authorities. 'Cause if you were in contact with them and they were on your side, the child welfare agency wouldn't be called in. They could talk them out of it. Vouch for you, sort of. So it helped to use the right people, like. Some of us chose the independent organisation and some the government programmes.'

In the media, the charities and welfare state establishment often complain about the lack of services for adolescents and young adults with problems. The government and city council are accused of not doing enough, so that teenagers are left to fend for themselves. However, according to Johs and several other young men, a bundle of organisations and agencies virtually queue up to deliver assistance, particularly to youngsters under the age of 18.

During fieldwork, we also observed that the number of representatives for charity and welfare organisations at The River could be quite concentrated at times. Johs laughed when he said he could "live a life of luxury at the expense of the social services". He had spent most of his childhood in Norway and felt that he knew his way around the public services. This was unlike other young men hanging out at The River, not least some of the refugees who were relatively helpless in this respect. Johs's story prompted several new questions. What sort of relations did the dealers enjoy with the welfare organisations at The River? Did they learn different ways of acting and talking? If they did, was this an aspect of street capital, the contours of which (by then) were becoming apparent to us? The youth gang Johs was a member of became notorious when he was a teenager. This pressed politicians into a corner, which resulted in some funding for welfare organisations. Johs described relations between his gang and welfare organisations as a symbiosis: "They got something out of it, we got something out of it." The boys perceived the services as useful. They went on trips organised by welfare groups, and they got tickets to the cinema and sports gear. In return, the welfare organisations were perceived as having the gang in "their portfolio". Johs explained: "It means they get more money, and more prestige." Media coverage brought the youth gang to public attention. For public and charity organisations working with the gang, the public purse strings were suddenly a lot looser.

In a study of intravenous heroin users in Oslo, we found something similar (Sandberg and Pedersen, 2008). An 'open drug scene' was frequently featured in the print and broadcast media. Our study suggested that welfare organisations, private and public, had a lot to gain from working in this particular area, with these particular people. Working for a specific well-known group in a visible and public area gave them easy access to publicity, added legitimacy, and helped boost financial support. By contrast, it was harder to get public funding when working with less visible social problems.

Substance abuse, social marginality and discrimination are real problems. However, they are also, paradoxically, 'resources' for welfare-dispensing organisations and agencies. The welfare machinery is there precisely to get welfare to people who need it. Defining who needs it most, or which problems require the most urgent attention, is not always self-evident. This may encourage welfare recipients to develop particular rationales to acquire services. It is also possible that such processes are especially prevalent in benevolent welfare states, where there are more economic resources available for poor people and there is more interaction between social workers and different groups of clients. This tendency was uncovered in another Norwegian study of non-institutionalised drug users:

> It was not hard to tell that most of the substance abusers were used
> to talking about themselves to psychologists, social workers, doctors,
> police officers etc. In these conversations, they were the patients,
> clients, needy or criminals, and their disadvantaged state became
> an advantage, a ticket to prescription drugs, to treatment, to money.
> (Smith-Solbakken and Tungland, 1997, p 26, our translation)

As we will discuss later such observations are well known from 'neutralization' literature elsewhere, a literature that mainly emerges from interviews in an institutionalised context (for example in prisons and drug rehabilitations centres). The difference is that in Norway drug users and offenders *on the street* seems to speak in the same way as institutionalised offenders and drug users elsewhere.

Johs had frequent dealings with the welfare system. This was how he came to understand how the system worked. He said, "We live on a small planet. Everything's connected in a way, you just have to find where they connect. I'm one of the people who do just that. I know how the system works." By pulling the right strings and contacting the right bodies, he believed it was possible to get support amounting to several million NOK. Johs's claims concerning his knowledge of the system were of course exaggerated. Nevertheless, his story highlighted the difference between living on the street in a Scandinavian welfare state and in a North American ghetto – the birthplace of much of the literature on street culture. There are similarities such as violence and drug dealing, but in a welfare state aid is never far away. Street capital thus also comes in distinct versions and can be used in different ways.

Sympathetic, useful, nerds

As with the open drug scene near the central station and on Oslo's main street, The River has attracted attention because what goes on there is visible to the public eye. During our fieldwork, the media were full of stories about the drug dealing there. We also counted nine different organisations that were targeting The River at various times. They included public agencies, minority ethnic organisations, religious charities and other third-sector initiatives. Time invested in the milieu varied, especially among the smaller organisations, but they were often keen to make their presence publicly known. The big public and private charity organisations, however, were there on a more permanent basis. A public outreach agency patrol was in action almost daily, and most of the youngsters were aware of them. One particular project, designed expressly with the dealers at The River in mind, was considered helpful. Here is what one of our interviewees said:

> 'Things pile up, stupid things, things that need to be changed. That's why the outreach people were brought in. They tried to help us and give us somewhere to talk about problems and get us a break from all that other shit.'

This project was hailed a success. The young men were equally appreciative of help they received from other organisations. However, they did question the social workers' motives sometimes. Johs was a veteran of The River; he had seen organisations and workers come and go. Many disappeared almost as quickly as they appeared. They were not much help.

> 'So there's a bunch of people working for teens, they're in it for themselves. It's not like they really want to help people. If they get a chance, they may approach a couple of the lads. "You oughtn't to use drugs, you know...." To them it's a one-off thing, or a couple of times, no big deal.... A guy would have to say a lot about himself before you'd get the slightest idea about his problems.'

According to Johs social workers need to be involved over the longer term. It takes time to identify the problems and develop trust. Nevertheless, our research participants had a generally positive attitude towards charity and public organisations, and they described social workers as helpful and kind, even useful.

As mentioned previously, Johs got trips, tickets and sports equipment. Others had obtained legal aid, and appointments with the job centre and welfare authorities had been set up. Some of the dealers from The River had even persuaded one of the organisations to help them get time in a studio to record hip-hop music.

Welfare organisations and street capital

While social workers were both useful and sympathetic, there were still important differences between them and the young men. Usman explained the differences between the police and welfare organisations: "The police, they're in good shape, physically. So they're good. You can see they've got muscles, run fast and all that." Social workers, by contrast, were "totally fucking nerds". The police could be tolerated, at a pinch; they had a kind of street capital based on their potential to use violence. According to Bourgois (2003a, p 35), the police and criminals both adhere to a 'culture of terror'. While this probably is more pertinent in the US than in Nordic countries, it is still interesting to note the degree to which police powers resemble those encapsulated by street culture. Ultimately, police officers' powers reside in their ability to use physical force.

Welfare organisations were something else entirely. They had a limited stock of what we have conceptualised as street capital. The River men assumed that the social workers led relatively boring lives. They were not tough, and as far as they were concerned, their knowledge of drugs was poor. Thus, given the type of street identity the dealers had, it was difficult for them to relate to social workers. Social workers were able to overcome these barriers, however, if they worked with them for an extended period.

Former gang members founded one of the private organisations. Their experience of life on the street helped to close the gap between the dealers' culture and that of the organisation. As one of The River dealers put it, "knowing what they've been through, like, they know what they're talking about. It's easier for them." They could mediate between the young men and the established criminal networks, or help them with problems stemming from debt. The street capital the organisation's leaders had acquired helped them to design workable preventive measures. Their social capital (social networks) made it possible to intervene and communicate in ways that were beyond the capabilities of other organisations. In this way, it became easier to gain the respect of the men at The River.

However, a person's street background must come with credibility and integrity, and several problems arise in building a career based on one's former street capital. Former gang members risk being accused of having "lost your capital", of "never having had any", or of having "sold out". There is a similar problem when former drug users adopt new roles as guardians or caregivers intent on intercepting and addressing problems – precisely by virtue of having 'been there'. It might promote prospects for a career in certain areas of the welfare system, but it makes it difficult to be accepted elsewhere. With a lot of street capital, it is difficult to integrate into mainstream society and to accumulate mainstream cultural and social capital.

The language on the street

As described in Chapter One, we spent a great deal of time at The River, but the men only intermittently allowed us to spend time with them or join them when they were dealing. Therefore, much of our analysis relies on interviews. These took place in cafes and pubs or in our research participants' homes. We met up with many of them several times and got to know them – but not so much in situations where they were actually dealing. Our data are comprehensive and contain many vivid stories that are helpful for an understanding of The River and its dealers. However, as with most of the other data in this field of research, they were for the most part actively produced and shaped by the research participants themselves. This is typical of the social sciences more generally as well: it interprets material already interpreted by the actors in the field.

Data emerging from interviews should therefore be read not only as an objective report of practice but also as an expression of vivid narratives and strategic self-presentations within a particular social context.

Narratives can be seen as an expression of the prevailing language or *discourse* in a field, and as strategic self-presentations. The following example illustrates the point. In Chapter Five, we discussed the problems we ran into whenever we tried to elicit comments on the pleasures of heavy drug use. Because the young men sometimes saw us as representatives of the 'system', it was more natural for them to talk about suffering and problems caused by substance abuse than about the pleasures of drugs. The former were the narratives that circulated within the welfare sector itself. Narratives of the pleasures of drug use were more predominant on the street.

Taking drugs is clearly both pleasurable and problematic. Both observations are 'true'. The different stories of taking drugs, however, are anchored in different settings, and they are drawn from various institutions. The setting will therefore often decide which stories are told. This influence of the setting will often present a problem insofar as we are looking for the 'truth' of drug taking. Nevertheless, understanding the different ways people present themselves assists an understanding of their circumstances and the wider social setting.

As Chapter Three points out, it is important to see the possibility of action residing in and dependent on already existing structures. While Wacquant (2008) accentuates the limitations imposed on actors by *economic* structures, a discourse analysis explores instead how *discursive* structures affect people. Identifying the narratives that the young men at The River live by may help us understand the way they live. Narratives are embedded in larger cultural discourse and these discourses affect, or define, existence on the street. In the same way, street life generates particular discourses.

Of discourses circulating among the dealers at The River, two stand out in particular. One is what we call an oppression discourse, the other a gangster discourse. The meetings with Ali and Chris can illustrate them. Both discourses reveal something of interest about living on the street in a benevolent welfare state.

Oppression discourse

We were doing an interview with Ali, but establishing a bond was difficult. He was conscious of the interview setting and seemed to be using us as his personal microphone, and he was lying. For example, he lied about his name (which we had not asked for), age and country of origin. Later on, when we knew each other better, he corrected some of these early misrepresentations. Our fieldwork revealed others. Despite the lies, the interview was interesting. To Ali, we were envoys of the welfare system. We were white, well educated and members of the Norwegian establishment. He wanted to establish his own version of his situation vis-à-vis the system.

The interview started with him describing how he ended up in bad company as a teenager, dropped out of school and ran into more problems. "But," he assured us, "I'm not into breaking the law and that sort of crap. That's not how I am." We tend not to ask about illegal activity until well into the interview, so we tried drawing him out on topics related to family and girlfriends, but Ali zoomed in on what he believed we really wanted to hear.

> *Interviewer:* 'D'you have a girlfriend?'
> *Ali:* 'I've got a girl I like very much … and I work hard … getting a job, permanent job and that … good pay. But it's hard, sometimes, very hard. Not many understand that about The River. You're out of work, got no wages coming in. And if you don't have money, 'cause everything you do in Norway costs money, innit. Wanna eat, gotta have cash. Pay your rent, gotta have cash. It's not like everybody you see there wants to be there, like, you know. It's like when you haven't got a chance anywhere else, 'cause the kids you see there, like, they think it's better than stealing, innit.'

Ali refers to "the kids you see there", but he is also talking about himself. He clearly feels under some pressure. He expected that we wanted him to talk about The River (which we did), and that we would try to persuade him to change his ways (as social workers do).

This interview demonstrated a way of justifying one's presence at The River to social workers and other representatives of mainstream society. Ali told us that he had a very good reason for being there. First, he had to make money. "You need money," that's something everybody knows. Later in the interview, he talked about the difficulty of getting a job with a foreign-sounding name. Thus, the only chance of obtaining money was The River. Second, it was better to sell cannabis than to steal and commit other crimes in order to get money. This utilitarian argument has featured in a similar media debate about public begging, and the same rationale is rehearsed in arguments about the desirability of selling cannabis over heavier drugs. As demonstrated in Chapter Five, the young men at The River did not consider cannabis particularly dangerous. Ali maintained, for instance, that alcohol was riskier than cannabis because it was more addictive. Cannabis may even have a positive effect, he argued. The kids at The River, Ali conceded, were in trouble, but not because they used drugs or alcohol. Their main problem was the lack of a steady job:

> *Ali:* 'But in my opinion, the system in Norway is ultimately to blame for what goes on at The River 'cause they can help those kids more than just letting them…. You know, they can do something for the kids down at The River. There's no help in just leaving them to…. It would be much better if they did something, that's what I think. If I was the government, like….'
> *Interviewer:* 'What can they do?'
> *Ali:* 'Whatever they want. Get them into public schemes.'

Carrying on an interview with Ali was not easy. He was high on drugs, he lied and he was always on the defensive. After the interview, we wondered if it had been worth the effort, but looking at the transcript later, we found a relatively coherent defence tale. Ali had probably told the same tale several times before the interview – to welfare officers in public offices and social workers out in the field. At any rate, it came unprompted and was very detailed. Ali, it seemed, *knew* the story.

The types of street capital we have discussed so far revolve around crime or violence. Another kind of street capital is the ability to present oneself as a victim to private and public welfare organisations, and to speak the language of the system. Most of the young men had this ability not just to present a coherent narrative but also to season it with the correct terminology and jargon. Ali's use of the word 'scheme' is an example. It is not part of the normal street vernacular. It is learned in contact with officials and agencies. Ali had assimilated it and brought it out whenever he felt circumstances suggested it would be useful to speak the language of the welfare system. It made it easier to obtain various types of assistance from public and charity organisations. Moreover, Ali attempted to establish *parity* in his relations with these agencies, by adopting their jargon.

A closer examination of the interview with Ali revealed how a larger construction of sameness ran through all the stories he told us. Generally, his message was that the young men at The River were not very different from mainstream society. They needed a job, and when work failed to materialise, The River was the only way out. They put in a full day's work, and what they earned there provided their means of support. By comparing cannabis and alcohol use, the difference diminished further. In Ali's view, smoking cannabis was not much different from the drinking habits of the majority population, and the effects no more harmful. "Many 'straight' people smoke cannabis," he added, asking us by way of clinching the argument if we had tried cannabis. When we confirmed, he laughed contentedly and concluded, "Yep, like I say, the hashish people aren't that different after all."

We have already commented on reports on the pleasures of cannabis use; opinions about amphetamines, cocaine and pills were more mixed. This can probably be interpreted within the same framework. Because cannabis is widely used, there is room for establishing a position of equity. Other, less widespread substances naturally bring out differences between the dealers at The River and mainstream society. In the same way, the men often told us that they really wanted to live a quiet life, raise a family and have a job. Values like these rank high in our society and help bridge the gap between them and us.

The emphasis on sameness can also be seen in relation to violence and fighting. Ali believed that anybody in a similar situation would react in the same way:

> *Interviewer:* 'So, on the street, like, who's fighting who?'
> *Ali:* 'Everybody can fight normally. Like, you can't just poke me in the face and walk off. I've got to defend myself. Like, if I was mooching around on the street and came up to you and whacked you, like, for no reason, and walked off, you wouldn't like it.'

Ali asked us to compare our lives with his. We needed a job, we drank and had smoked cannabis, and we respond in the same way to aggressive behaviour. By establishing a position of parity, Ali dismantled some of the barriers related to ethnicity, education and lifestyle between him and us. This made it easier for us to put ourselves in his shoes and thus to identify and sympathise with him.

In an early work, the Norwegian criminologist Nils Christie (1972) described how those Russian prisoners of war who successfully made their Norwegian guards see them as fellow human beings were treated better. These were the prisoners who, for example, brought out pictures of their families for the guards to see and had learned a few Norwegian words and phrases. The guards saw themselves in their image and found their inhumane treatment increasingly difficult to justify. In a similar vein, by adopting the jargon and conceptual approach of the welfare system, the young men at The River appeared less different and less dangerous. This stirred up sentiments of identification and commiseration. People often sympathise more with people who are similar to them. By appearing less as the Other, the young men at The River more easily achieved recognition as 'worthy' and 'needy' persons.

Within a framework of discourse analysis, accounts of discrimination and marginalisation – such as those in Ali's story above or in Chapter Four – can be seen as a common narrative in an 'oppression discourse'. Typical narratives include the following:

- stories about discrimination and hardship in labour markets, education and housing markets. A common example was problems for people with foreign-sounding names obtaining employment;
- stories about racism – both severe/violent racist attacks and everyday racism. Many of the dealers tended to call people that they disliked 'racists';
- stories about psychosocial problems, often caused by, or at least not alleviated by, government institutions;
- narratives about meagre government support.

The points highlighted in an oppression discourse are, of course, important in their own right. We have already described the structural challenges facing the young men. They are discriminated against in school and employment, and as refugees and immigrants many of them have to deal with severe problems. However, such accounts can also be seen as narratives embedded in, and made possible by, an oppression discourse emphasising the structural or societal causes of crime. In such a discourse, subjects such as violence, selling and using drugs are relegated to the sidelines by psychosocial problems, combined with a government and city council that are unwilling to help. The moral of the tale is that everybody would act in a similar fashion under similar circumstances.

We can shed light on the oppression discourse by means of neutralisation theory. Sykes and Matza's (1957) maintained that offenders and delinquents are aware of conventional values. They understand that their offending is wrong, and they mitigate the anticipated shame and guilt associated with violating societal norms. Thus, delinquents do not reject mainstream moral values but neutralise them so that they are able to commit delinquent actions. They *drift* between criminal and conventional action (Matza, 1964). In Matza's view, the ideology of neutralization is reinforced by the juvenile court, which declares that juveniles are not responsible for their actions.

Similar to Sykes and Matza's techniques of neutralisation, oppression discourse served to neutralise drug dealing at The River. The young men often combined it with another more recently conceptualised neutralisation technique – for example 'techniques of risk denial' (Peretti-Watel, 2003). Risk denial appeared mainly as assurances of the relative harmlessness of cannabis in comparison with alcohol. Oppression discourse and risk denial seemed to be associated with meetings with the welfare system. Nevertheless, they were also important in the young men's attempts to understand their own situation.

Johs's story, which we recapitulated at the beginning of this chapter, demonstrates how oppression discourse can be part of a deliberate strategy for dealing with welfare organisations.[2] Most of the time, however, such discursive strategies exemplify what Bourdieu (1990) calls practical sense or habitus: they are learned, strategic, but used without reflection – much akin to tennis players using their strokes during a game.

The victim as subject position

The welfare state apparatus was not the only cultural influence on The River, however, not even the most important. The clearest contrast with the oppression discourse is what we term the gangster discourse, which we return to later. However, even one of the dealers, in whose interviews the gangster discourse was most clearly present, exclaimed, "I just want a fucking job, get it?" The lack of work featured at the top of the young men's expressed list of problems. This compares well with oppression discourse as described previously, as well as the findings of other Norwegian refugee and minority ethnic studies (Berg, 2003; Fangen, 2006). Along The River, work and the job market are prevalent topics, as both problem definitions and solutions. The expression 'just get me a job' was symptomatic of a left-wing-biased welfare machinery, which attributed social problems to economic structures.[3] As opposed to a psychodynamic therapeutic approach often found in drug treatment, it had appeal to The River men because it could easily be combined with cultural narratives of maleness/masculinity.

Projecting the image of an oppressed individual can be a dignity-promoting project. Shifting the blame to external causes removes some of one's own responsibility. However, the oppression discourse comes with a definite dilemma: the young men had to see themselves as 'victims'. Borrowing Laclau and Mouffe's (1985) conceptualisation, being a victim is the only possible subject position for them in such a discourse. The position of victimhood will therefore restrict what they can say and do if they perceive themselves only through the lens of an oppression discourse.

It is difficult for oppressed groups to conceive of themselves *solely* as the result of oppressive processes. Most people must accept some measure of subjectivity to maintain a minimum of self-respect. Seeing themselves as victims was especially difficult for The River men. They were devoted to street and protest masculinity, and in contemporary society, the victim is a predominantly feminine role. Thus, the young men tended to combine the oppression discourse with other discourses to allow for higher levels of agency in their lives. Although the oppression discourse featured regularly in the interviews, we were surprised by how often the men themselves emphasised having a choice. Mattar, almost pleading with us, said: "there's a word, it's 'choice', it's important. If you want to get anywhere, it's your choice, see?" Because his father had never had a job, he never had any money. It was tempting to steal, he said, but "I'm not putting the blame on him. I can put the blame on myself." Amin said something along the same lines: "You can try; it doesn't take long to apply for a job. Write on the computer, write a CV and go and hand it in. I've done it before and got a job, see." Most of the young men criticised themselves in this manner.

Johs conducted the same self-examination. He had been thinking about moving somewhere and leaving all his problems behind:

'I don't say I'm thinking of doing a vanishing act, just trying to change my life. Trying other options. Trying other doors. When I've gone through them, God knows what's on the other side. I'm a fucking good worker, bright, got the papers to show it, but still, I can't find a single fucking job. I don't do as much as I could to get myself a job either. If a criminal chance turns up though, I'm telling you I'll climb down the chimney. A door and a chimney [laughs], see what I mean, I never think twice. So what's stopping me, then?'

The doors were open to a job in the mainstream economy, but he preferred the complicated approach – climbing the roof and climbing back down through the chimney. In the extract, Johs laughed, pleased with his elegant metaphor. Later in the interview, he was desperate to know what was stopping him. Sometimes he used religious terminology and described it as a "taste for sin"; other times, as a "need for excitement". His account of his childhood was illustrative of the same attitude. "There was no excuse for what we did," he pleads, adding later, "there's a difference between us and the apes. We have the option of making a choice. Free will. Animals don't have that. That's why we're over them."

The way Johs read his situation is not uncommon, either in our own material or in other studies. Bourgois (1998, pp 59–60) described how substance abusers he met in a shooting gallery rejected out of hand his political/economic construction of their situation as the result of migration, racism and unemployment. Doc, the gang leader, first sang the praises of Malcolm X before telling Bourgois that they used to attend his meetings to steal wallets. Bourgois could not get his theories confirmed and sanctioned by the people they concerned.

Johs's account makes it easier to understand the men's apparent unwillingness to accept socioeconomic explanation of their drug use and criminal activity. If people thought him incapable of making autonomous decisions, he would be no more than an animal. If this capacity were removed, his humanity and masculinity would be undermined. In an indirect way, most of the young men were sensitive to such reasoning. When they accentuated their free will, therefore, we can see how it contrasts with the role of the victim supplied by a well-meaning welfare system. By taking responsibility for their own lives, the men became *individuals*, not products of predefined processes or economic structures.

In frameworks that privilege economic structures, such as Wacquant's (2008), the dealers' self-conception will be taken as an expression of false consciousness. Bourgois sometimes presents similar views. Summing up his impressions of Doc, he writes: 'His oppression is fully internalised and, almost like a neo–liberal ideologue, he takes full responsibility for his poverty, illiteracy and homelessness' (Bourgois, 1998, p 60). It is possible similarly to imagine the dealers along The River lulled into what ultimately is an illusory feeling of empowerment. However, we can also take what they say at face value, in fact, public statistics come to their support. Marginalisation processes are much more severe in the North American ghetto than in the Norwegian welfare state, but even there, most people are working and committed to work ethic (Newman, 1999). Many also move between work 'off the books' and legitimate economies (Venkatesh 2008). From a perspective that privileges economic structures, voluntaristic narratives can only be read as symptoms of a false consciousness, or an expression of individualistic or neoliberal ideology. Under perspectives that give greater credence to active agents, the same narratives may be taken as absolute 'truth'. Exaggerating either position will benefit neither of them. Agents, after all, retain and practice agency constrained by their structural position – economic, social and discursive.

Jimerson and Oware (2006) observed a similar dilemma in a discussion of Anderson's (1999) concept of the 'code of the street' and the relationship between ethnography and ethnomethodology.[4] They suggested 'ethnomethodological ethnography' as a compromise. In short, codes of conduct serve as cognitive maps as well as conversational tools. Thus, participants' accounts can be valid, but they can also be self-serving, and they must be interpreted in situ. The approach we use in this study is somewhat similar. Even though The River men were exaggerating and giving us self-serving accounts, listening to and analysing their stories can tell us something important about life on the street in a welfare state.

The gangster discourse

The oppression discourse may have negative effects. If the only subject position is that of the victim, this can prevent marginalised and stigmatised people from searching for counter-narratives in which they are masters of their own destinies, and not least, 'real men'. The gangster discourse is one such gendered resource. In this discourse, the dealers' subject positions are tough and capable gangsters. It may strengthen self-confidence and make the daily, unavoidable dose of humiliation at the bottom of social space easier to bear.

It is difficult to survive on the street if one is limited to presenting or perceiving oneself only as a victim. In this respect, Chris (whom we met first in Chapter One) was Ali's antithesis. Even though he touched on oppression discourse, he mainly portrayed himself as a successful, violent and dangerous criminal. In this way, he claimed a gangster subject position, made available by a gangster discourse and a mix of street and popular culture. He boasted, for instance, about the money he had made and how he fooled the police:

> 'If I'd been a cop, I could've fucking nailed every crook in the city. I know every single motherfucking one of them. I know where they stash dope and money. And those guys, what they get up to.'

The subject of fighting was broached as well. Typical statements included "I tell ya, no motherfucker gets in my face, because if they do, my mates would go and fuck his mother, like." Chris was interested in weapons too: "You sleep better at nights with a piece." If anybody was out to get him, "I stand there with that pistol, like, loaded, goes without saying. Rounds like those armour-piercing bullets, go through anything." It was almost like an action movie, with Chris scripting a role for himself. Nobody dared touch him, and if they were that stupid, they would regret it. He also claimed to be more intelligent than other criminals. "No one's fucked me up yet," he informed us proudly. His stories spun a romantic, fascinating narrative about a solitary, invincible, tough-skinned and smart gangster. Chris brought his story to its culmination with a detailed account of how he smuggled large quantities of cannabis from Sweden using advanced techniques:

> 'I used to bring it over from Sweden. We had this dual car system. One of them had to look awesome, got up so as to look conspicuous, loud music, fucking suspicious. And the other had to be a fucking queer fanny car.... So you tune up two BMWs, premium styling in red lacquer for the top, and suspicious in the extreme. Loads of foreigners inside.... So you give customs something to keep them busy and you drive a little Opel Corsa, with 100 kilo right behind. They think, "Hang on, there's a couple of sports cars there filled with youngsters. That means trouble." So they flag them down – never fails. And behind there's you sitting driving a little Opel Corsa with 100 kilo weed up your arse. And you just drive on, right into Norway. They do it every day.'

We do not know if Chris had been involved in large-scale trafficking – in the final sentence, a 'we' gets turned into a 'they'. In the main, though, Chris talked about dealing at The River in small quantities. His story of how cannabis is smuggled into Norway from Sweden may in fact be part of an urban myth doing the rounds, a particularly vivid, exciting gangster narrative. It highlights their intelligence, pulling off a customs scam. Chapter Six describes how competent the young men were when they were dealing. Such accounts can be seen as valid descriptions of interactions between police and dealers at The River. However, it is also interesting to see how some of the narratives from Chapter Five, Six and Seven can be read as elements of a gangster discourse aimed at demonstrating toughness, superiority and competence.

The gangster discourse featured in most of the interviews, even though it was not always as explicit as it was with Chris. Its typical narratives included the following:

- stories about how the young men were thick skinned and not afraid. They posed as gangsters to avoid confrontation in an environment laced with aggression;
- accounts about how life on the street was hard and operated under different rules from the rest of society;
- stories about how easy it was to make a lot of money quickly, an ability they included with acquired skills and knowledge;

- stories about how sexually promiscuous the men were: they have had lots of sex, and girls find them attractive.

The gangster discourse bears clear resemblances to Anderson's (1999) 'code of the street'. However, while the code is a set of informal rules governing interpersonal behaviour, using the concept of discourse highlights that oppression and gangster discourses are also conversational tools used to justify behaviour retrospectively. Jimerson and Oware (2006) describe it as 'telling the code of the street' and argue that it is as interesting as using codes to explain conduct. Topalli (2005) describes it as 'neutralising being good'. As in Sykes and Matza (1957), his argument is that active criminals neutralise to support their offending. However, in contrast to the offenders Sykes and Matza studied, Topalli's hard-core offenders strive to protect a self-image consistent with a code of the street rather than a conventional one. They identify with the code of the street more than the code of decency, and neutralise being good rather than being bad (Topalli, 2005).

Gangster discourse is a similar tool. By using gangster discourse, the young men wanted to be smart, and occasionally irrational and impenetrable. When Mette told us that the last kick should go to the person's head because kicking people in the face does the most damage, she wanted to demonstrate her ruthlessness. Similarly, stories about positive experiences with drugs and brutal, seemingly irrational aggression surfaced when the dealers were in gangster discourse mode.

As opposed to oppression discourse, gangster discourse emphasises *difference* between the young men and mainstream society. Gangster discourse is about a construction of Otherness. In this way, the young men want to be seen as smart, brutal and sexually attractive. Such a construction of difference helps bolster self-respect and garner respect from others. The young men become active capable individuals in their own, alternative universe.

Between the street and the welfare state

The River dealers used the oppression discourse mostly in dealings with the welfare system. It is a discourse that privileges structural problems, such as difficulties getting a job, an education and finding accommodation. Marginalisation and discrimination are typically highlighted. Oppression discourse also privileges shared features rather than differences as the dominant mode of representing marginalised groups. Emphasising sameness can be seen as a strategy for winning sympathy and support by playing down what separates the young men from members of mainstream society. It is a strategy that marginalised groups often use in meetings with the public agencies and charity organisations.

Minority ethnic groups may have particular resources in oppression discourse, which may also bind them to such a self-understanding. They do, for example, fit the stereotype of the 'victim', and they can use experiences with war, racism and ethnic discrimination as discursive 'resources'.

Goffman (1961) argues that individuals take measures to adjust their behaviour to manage the impression they leave on others. In the early stages of an interaction, the onlooker's ability to influence the definition process will be greater than that of the actors. They are the authors of meaning. In oppression discourse, privileging parity makes it easier to identify with welfare clients and criminals. In this way, the storytellers get sympathy and compassionate understanding.

As pointed out previously, the problem raised by the oppression discourse is marginalised groups' limited choice of subject position – there is only one choice, that of the victim. This can cause a sense of disempowerment. Gangster discourse counteracts oppression discourse. It gives prominence to sexual conquest, sophisticated illegal activity and fighting. It lends one an aura of superiority, intelligence and proficiency. The River men used the discourse to distance themselves from conventional society. The Otherness cultivated by the discourse granted independence and served both to frighten and to fascinate people in their immediate environment. As with oppression discourse, black and minority ethnic people have distinct 'resources' in such a discourse; for example, the stereotype of the 'dangerous foreigner', the symbolic value of black masculinity and the linguistic resources of African–American English, which is used more authentically by young black men than by white.

Katz (1988, p 122) discusses the difference between deviant middle-class youth culture and deviant working-class youth culture. According to Katz, street culture is not particularly anti-police or anti-establishment, unlike middle-class youth intent on rebellion. Instead, street people 'act as if they live in a country that is foreign to and independent of the one the police represent'. Gangster discourse is the language in such a street country. Only the street guys know what it is like living on the street. Outsiders, such as social workers or other youths, are treated as people looking in, whether with fascination or alarm. The young men realise they would never win a staged battle with the majority, so they withdraw and use gangster discourse to construct a deviant subculture. In Oslo, The River became a spatial symbol of this Otherness.

Many of The River dealers felt excluded from mainstream society. Discrimination and racism were constant companions, even when they were selling cannabis. Moreover, because they were 'foreigners', they felt branded as 'criminals' from the outset. In this way, allegiance to a gangster discourse became a self-fulfilling prophecy.

Institutionalised discourses

Often, what is understood as identity or self depends on given systems of signification, words, conceptualisations and even grammar. They are all organised by discourses. Throughout his career, Foucault stressed how society shapes these discourses. Together they constitute what Foucault first termed the 'archive' (Foucault, 1972a) and later 'the order of discourse' (Foucault, 1978), which makes production of meaning possible. In his critique of social institutions such as prisons, hospitals and mental asylums, Foucault proposed that social institutions were the primary carriers of society's available discourses (see, for example, Foucault, 1965, 1970, 1977, 1978). Social institutions have the resources to produce, the power to enforce and the machinery to maintain certain forms of knowledge. At The River, the police and welfare organisations were the most important public institutions.

Oppression discourse is produced, enforced and maintained by welfare organisations. We have already discussed how closely linked the oppression discourse is with the welfare system's mode of thinking, shaped as it is by its tendency to see the causes of problems in socioeconomic structures. Moreover, in the same way that the young men must emphasise sameness to obtain sympathy from social workers and others, welfare organisations must emphasise parity to justify the redistribution of public funds via welfare. Oppression discourse gets the public and authorities to see marginalised groups as worthy recipients of support. By constructing public sympathy and compassion for their clientele, welfare organisations are more likely to receive support for their particular projects. They therefore have a common interest with their clients and leftist political parties in publicly framing marginalised groups and their problems in oppression discourse.

While the connection between oppression discourse and welfare organisations is relatively obvious, it is more surprising to find links between right-wing political parties, the police and the gangster discourse of The River dealers. Police authority depends ultimately on its physical force. When the need arises to justify such force publicly, people on the receiving end need to be described as different from ordinary people. This has often been described as the construction of 'folk devils' in the Birmingham School tradition (Cohen, 1972). If alleged criminals are not demonised, members of the public may come to see themselves as likely targets of the penal system's prerogative to use physical force.

Something similar was going on, for instance, when the police speculated that cannabis distribution at The River was managed by well-organised criminal networks,[5] or when a well-known conservative politician alleged that the dealers "virtually forced people to buy drugs".[6] Unlike the welfare system, the police have little to gain from accentuating parity between offenders and the general public. It would undermine their authority. The police are therefore willing to support narratives emerging from gangster discourse; for example, that the young men are tough and violent, have large supplies of money and commit clever and well-organised crimes. People with right-wing political views behave similarly, with their 'law and order' rhetoric, to justify longer prison sentences and less 'mollycoddling'. Paradoxically and unwittingly, therefore, they help create and sustain discursive resources and narratives that criminals can use in their gangster discourse.

Discourses sustained and/or generated by the welfare system and police may have unintended consequences. The welfare system's oppression discourse is useful and necessary as a means of justifying welfare services. At the same time, its effect on the clients' everyday lives can be questioned. The oppression discourse turns them into victims and does not encourage a sense of self-confidence. The young men therefore reject it as an instrument of self-understanding. Paradoxically, in their search for other workable discourses on which to build their self-understanding, the picture presented by the police is more attractive. A gangster discourse that draws on popular culture, the men's own life stories and the police's reality claims do, after all, make them tough, occasionally smart, and (not least) responsible for their own lives.

The content of gangster discourse is strikingly similar to what Anderson (1999) conceptualises as the code of the street and what the main North American literature in the field describes as street culture. Thus, even though the socioeconomic contexts are poles apart, individuals dealing drugs on the street in Norway seem to share certain ways of thinking and speaking with their counterparts in the North American ghetto.

We might however ask if oppression discourse and strategies of constructing sameness in conversations is unique to life on the streets in a Scandinavian welfare state or whether it is a common feature of street life. Based on this study, it is difficult to come up with definite answers. Our guess is that oppression discourse will be more prevalent in contexts with a high density of welfare organisations and in states with a socialist or social-democratic history. Emphasising parity between a speaker and an 'audience', however, is probably a strategy for producing sympathy across national borders and street contexts.[7]

Being oppressed without being a victim

There are uncovered fundamental problems with discourses generated by both police and welfare agencies. They steer the young men into gangster and victim subject positions, respectively. Popular culture, on the other hand, may give rise to other more dynamic and attractive subject positions. Hip-hop and gangsta rap not only facilitate a gangster position but also engage ethnic pride, and pride in one's socioeconomic background. Hip-hop in general, and gangsta rap in particular, were the first forms of popular culture to celebrate life in the ghetto (Perry, 2004, p 89). The poem 'The rose that grew from concrete', written by Tupac when he was 19 years old illustrates the point:

> Did u hear about the rose that grew from a crack
> in the concrete
> Proving nature's laws wrong it learned 2 walk
> without having feet
> Funny it seems but by keeping its dreams
> it learned 2 breathe fresh air.
> Long live the rose that grew from concrete
> when no one else even cared!
> (Shakur, 1999, p. 3)

Instead of saying, 'Look what we've been through – you should feel sorry for us!', in oppression discourse mode, the poem says, 'We've been through a lot, and it made us strong!'. Thus, in hip-hop culture, negative connotations of a difficult childhood, marginalisation and exclusion undergo subtle redefinitions and re-emerge as valuable resources.

Hip-hop can be seen as a hybrid or mixture of oppression and gangster discourses. In the rap-lyrics they merge into one and the same narrative. Thus, hip-hop culture facilitates the production of powerful amalgams featuring, for instance, combinations of the oppression discourse with more attractive subject positions from gangster discourse. As elements of a person's self-image, this is doubtless important, but as a means of effecting change in how the young men live, it may be even more important. A self-understanding as active, smart and responsible for one's own actions is, after all, a better starting point than one based on structural determinism.

Codes of the street

The dominant discourse on the street is the gangster discourse, and the young men used the oppression discourse in dealings with the welfare system. So far, Chris and Ali have exemplified the two discourses, respectively. Both were firmly devoted to their subject positions as gangster and victim. Most of the other dealers had a wider repertory of self-presentations, making it harder to pin down their active discourses. It often depended on our own responses during interviews. The gangster discourse was more likely to surface when we interviewed two dealers at the same time. The interviewees were probably behaving more like they did with friends on the street. They would, for example, be more likely to mention sexual conquests, fights and success as cannabis dealers. In a setting that involved two interviewers and only one interviewee, however, talk about such topics was more often downplayed. Nevertheless, the most striking feature of the interviews was how the research participants switched between discourses as the interview progressed. The ability to read the situation and activate the most appropriate narrative was a fascinating aspect of the young men's repertory.

Anderson (1999) writes in a similar vein about how some of his informants appeared able to switch between a 'code of decency' and a 'code of the street'. In contrast to Anderson, however, we also noted oppression discourse, which possibly can be seen as a variant of the code of decency, when the young men justified their crimes. Moreover, as opposed to Anderson's code switching, the changes between codes or discourses were often done in the same interviews, changing from one minute to the other (see also Sandberg, 2009b, 2009c). The River dealers sometimes tried to justify their criminal behaviour by using oppression discourse to appear as decent victims without any other choice than drug dealing. In the next minute, however, they could use gangster discourse to protect a self-image consistent with the code of the street. In discourse analysis terms, this is known as interdiscursivity, a term influenced by Bakhtin's intertextuality (Fairclough,

1995a). When people speak or write, numerous discourses can be brought into play, often in the same text or conversation. Individuals borrow, consciously or unconsciously, to create meaning in different immediate settings.

Such observations challenge the dichotomisation of ghetto residents into good or bad, for which Anderson has been criticised (see Wacquant, 2002, Venkatesh 2006). It also complicates the picture of both Sykes and Matza's (1957) techniques of neutralisation and Topalli's (2005) expansion of the theory. In the first case, offenders are committed to conventional values, while in the latter, 'being good is bad'. In our conceptualisation, two discourses replace good and bad people. They partly speak for the subject, but they are also used in self-understandings and as strategic conversational tools for people living on the street.

The ability to negotiate both an oppression discourse and a gangster discourse should be seen as a form of street capital. Just as the men need to be gangster-like to survive on the street, they need to *know* the welfare state to obtain the help made available by the state and charities. To survive on the street in a Scandinavian welfare state, one must master both oppression and gangster discourses. It is easy to imagine the interviewees adopting a tough external mask while giving precedence to the 'real me' when talk turns to personal problems. Or to see them as bad criminals, who only manipulate welfare organisations and others that try to help them. However, such a search for the 'real self' is starting in the wrong end.

When the men described the pleasures of taking drugs, and the sensation of power derived from having money and acting aggressively, they were talking about real, important aspects of their lives. Just as importantly, however, the young men were vulnerable and largely marginalised by mainstream society. As members of minority ethnic groups and/or refugees, they enjoyed fewer options than most. One discourse is not 'true' and the others 'false'. It is more useful to see the interdiscursivity as a reflection of the social context and complex reality in which the men live.

Abilities to negotiate both oppression discourse and street discourse interdiscursively can be seen as being at odds with Bourdieu's concept of habitus. Habitus is characterised by being embodied and difficult to change. The two insights can nevertheless be combined. For example, the dealers at The River were proficient when it came to switching roles, but some of them sometimes found it difficult to break free from an embodied gangster discourse. For example, social workers reported that a gangster habitus and gangster discourse occasionally slip into situations when the young men are trying to get jobs or accommodations, reducing, of course, their chances of success.

Notes

[1] Field observation, Sveinung Sandberg, November 2005.

[2] Another interviewee showed even more clearly how the interview could be used to launch a strategic presentation of self. A senior figure in one of Oslo's most notorious minority ethnic gangs organised his narrative exclusively around the irrational interest

of the police in his gang, which could only be understood as an expression of racism against his friends who were nothing if not law-abiding folk who ran convenience stores, garages and small businesses, and whose expensive cars and other luxury accoutrements were the result of regular saving habits.

[3] The same could be said of much of the welfare system committed to addressing the then-new drug problems of the 1970s. It emerged as a response to conventional alcohol care and treatment and was politically underpinned by a rather relentless radicalism. It is a platform shared by therapeutic communities such as Tyrili (see, for instance, Tjersland et al, 1998, p 80), and Oslo city's outreach programme (see Berntsen, 1981, p 79).

[4] They argue that ethnography uses codes to explain behaviour (see, for example, Anderson, 1999), while ethnomethodology uses behaviour to explain codes (see, for example, Wieder, 1974). Anderson contends that a code caused slum dwellers to behave stereotypically, whereas Wieder claims that addicts cited a code to justify their actions, no matter how they acted (Jimerson and Oware, 2006, p 26).

[5] *VG*, 20 June 2006.

[6] City Councillor Margaret Eckbo at a council meeting, 22 June 2005.

[7] In Anderson's study, for example, the interviewees may have anticipated what he wanted to hear and thus presented the code of decency to construct sameness.

NINE

Conclusion

In the process of growing up most of the young men eventually quit their dealing and left The River. Devoted social workers and empowerment ideology was helpful. The dilemma of social work however, is that the social identities the welfare apparatus offer does not appeal to proud young men.

A street drug market

The River is probably the largest street cannabis market in the Nordic countries. Day and night, all through the year, a handful of young men sell cannabis – in all kinds of weather. The market shares many parallels with the 7-Eleven in the legal economy: the prices are high, the quality is low and customers therefore tend to buy small quantities. The advantages are that the market is easy to find and always 'open'. The River is constantly fuelled by a large pool of customers from the gentrified white middle-class area around the market. Despite increasing pressure from property owners and constant police surveillance, that is the main reason why the dealers are still there.

When we first came to The River, it was hard to differentiate one dealer from another. The social structure was also highly confusing. We saw the same tendency in the public and the media: the dealers appeared as a homogeneous group of young black men in a chaotic setting. After more than a year of fieldwork, however, we had uncovered a complex social system based on what we coin street capital.

The street drug market had a social structure with its own rules and norms, and the young men constantly redeveloped the skills of the trade. We also uncovered rather heterogeneous lifecourses among the young men.

Trapped at The River

There were three main trajectories to The River. One was typical for some of the younger dealers we met. They were seeking excitement and social identities. The River offered networks, membership in a hidden subculture and easy money. A second trajectory was typical for some of the older dealers. They had usually been involved in serious crime. An escalating drug habit and lack of success had excluded them from the established criminal gangs of Oslo, and they had been left without street credibility or a social network. For them, dealing at The River was not a first choice, but it offered an acceptable income, and not least, the opportunity to take up old leadership roles. A final trajectory to The River was the refugees' path. The non-returnable asylum seekers were officially barred from the labour market in Norway, and they were not allowed to go to secondary school or college. Many of them needed food and a place to stay. Dealing drugs covered some of their basic living expenses.

All the young men started dealing because of the money. The street market was also a place where they could pursue status and respect and experience excitement and thrills. All had felt what Katz (1988) has conceptualised as 'the seduction of crime'. Marginalisation processes also had started early. Experiences in the family, the neighbourhood and the school system had been embodied in the young men's habitus. In their late teenage years, most had also experienced discrimination in the labour and housing markets, and many of them had experienced incidences of direct racism. A feeling of not belonging, or rather, of belonging outside of mainstream white society, was typical. However, the most striking marginalisation process involved the political treatment the non-returnable asylum seekers received. It can be no surprise that people left without any legal opportunities to work – in a society that also that lacks a 'legitimate' underground economy – end up committing petty crimes. The trajectories to The River were heterogeneous. Still, they illustrate how starting to deal drugs can be the result of a marginalised habitus meeting a particular social context. Few end up dealing drugs on the street simply by chance.

Ethnic minority men and crime

We have often been asked what kind of policy is needed to address the particular problems that people from minority ethnic groups have, problems that seem to lead some of them into marginalisation and a violent street culture. The most important tool for making a change is to understand the present situation. We hope that this book has contributed something to an understanding of deviant subcultures, drug dealing and marginalisation processes. We also hope that readers will see that the differences between minority ethnic youths and at-risk youths in the majority population are not as great as they are often described. A 'feudal honour culture' is less important than the mechanisms that have been described in studies of Western deviant subcultures since Whyte's (1943) *Street corner society*.

Moreover, the differences between different minority ethnic groups are great, and this calls for very different policy solutions. In our study, the youngest dealers born or raised in Norway could most easily be reached by the welfare organisations that were already were working in the area. The older dealers often struggled with their drug habits, were socialised for years into criminal networks and knew little of the world outside. They found few sources of respect outside the drug culture. Their marginalisation had developed over years and had become embodied in a way that made it hard to change. To socialise this group back into mainstream society is a hard task. We must deal with their deep involvement in crime and their drug problems, as well as their lack of social networks and cultural capital suited for the ordinary job market. The problems for the non-returnable refugees, on the other hand, can only be solved at a political level. They had no rights in the welfare state and therefore received no protection from it. To deal with their problems, immigration policy and the way 'problem cases' are solved have to be changed. Otherwise, non-returnable refugees and illegal refugees will always represent a recruitment pool for street-level crime.

Quitting dealing

We have so far emphasised trajectories to street drug dealing, but there were also ways out of it. A few of the younger dealers we met had been deeply involved in dealing, but they changed their ways. One told us that he was proud of not hanging out there anymore. It did not do any good and he felt that he had brought shame to his family. He had also quit smoking cannabis, more or less. The reason was that cannabis "made him crazy". He wanted to get in shape and start to play football again. He used to be a good footballer, he told us. Another got a new girlfriend who disapproved of his drug dealing. She had friends who had ended up as prostitutes or drug addicts. When we asked if she was looking after him, he answered, "It is not so much looking after as a 'zero tolerance' thing." She would break up with him if he started again, and he loved her too much to risk that. She still accepted that he smoked once in a while. He also wanted to become more serious with his hip-hop music, and he realised that it would be difficult to combine a music career with the lifestyle at The River.

Some former dealers also talked about the insight they got when one of the main dealers in their network became a father at young age. Realising that he could not "hang around here when I have kids and stuff", he quit. This inspired several of his friends as well. Feeling the need to grow up, and already having lost several years on what they later would describe as "nothing" or "just nonsense", made them take up school again or try to get a job. Being in a group of friends who did this together made it easier.

In this process, they also got help from one of the welfare organisations that targeted youths at The River.[1] There were probably several reasons why this organisation managed to establish contact with the dealers in a way many of the other organisations did not. One important reason was that some of the leaders had a minority ethnic background, and the young men identified more easily with them. Another reason was that a whole group of dealers was targeted instead of one individual at the time. This strengthened the 'growing up' processes mentioned previously, which were already in play. Most importantly, however, this social work was based on an empowerment ideology, wherein the young men were in charge of much of the activity themselves. They decided both the kinds of activities to do and how to do them – and they decided which rules applied for members. In this way, they avoided the subject position of the passive recipient and victim, which characterised many of the other interventions from the welfare state apparatus.

Today, this group of young men still smoke cannabis now and then to relax, but for most of them the days of heavy daily smoking are over – as is their dealing. As a group, they have activated identities other than those related to drug dealing. Hip-hop and sports have again become important. Some of them have oriented themselves towards the ordinary job market. This group's way out of The River context can serve as a reminder for all kinds of marginalisation approaches, which tend to exaggerate social reproduction. After all, in the process of growing up, sooner or later, most people leave deviant subcultures.

Still, not all have managed to change their ways. Even in this group of friends who decided that enough was enough, a couple of them have continued to deal cannabis and gradually also become involved in more serious crimes and heavy drug use. They may have been more disposed to drug dependence, but in the background, we can also see the importance of family strain, psychosocial problems shaped by early upbringing, and a lack of cultural capital. The complex and many-faceted processes of marginalisation are, in other words, still important even among those out at the margins. Even among the young men at The River, some are much more vulnerable than others.

Cannabis policy

Legalisation has regularly been proposed as a solution to a wide range of problems with cannabis. People argue that such a common behaviour should not be criminalised – that cannabis is a 'soft drug', less harmful than cigarettes or alcohol, for example.[2] Another argument is that, by legalising cannabis, we would get rid of a large illegal economy and split the market between softer and harder drugs. For many of The River dealers, for example, the fact that cannabis was illegal and penalised increased their social marginalisation. It triggered and fuelled the development of deviant subcultural identities and gave them connections in the illegal economy. Many were socialised into criminal networks in this way.

Still, the issue is more complex than these arguments suppose. The River men's early initiation into cannabis use had been an important *rite de passage* into adulthood, and they gradually learned to enjoy the psychoactive effects of the substance. Their daily life, habits, rituals and small talk with friends were to a large degree centred on cannabis. After many years of smoking, many had developed what they themselves labelled as 'cannabis dependence'. Several had great problems quitting, using cannabis at school or at work, resulting in poorer performance. Moreover, the substance had become their most important source of income and the glue that made social gatherings easy and pleasant. All these ritual, social and economic bindings, which are still typically underdescribed in the literature on cannabis dependence, is probably more serious than the 'psychological dependence' that usually is described. Some of these problems may be reduced by legalisation, but most of them will not.

Obviously, cannabis may be a dangerous substance, especially for groups and individuals that are already at the outskirts of society or are disposed to mental health problems. At the same time, the fact that the substance is now illegal and outside the reach of societal regulations reduces the probability of a rational policy approach. In regard to tobacco and alcohol, the authorities have a large set of tools to regulate consumption patterns related to, for example, availability and prices. In the cannabis field, no such instruments are available (Room et al, 2008).

The Norwegian cannabis regime has been increasingly 'softened' during the last decade.[3] There are no easy solutions in this area at the moment.[4] However, our study will probably support further development in this direction: with minimal enforcement of cannabis legislation the young men would probably have been less marginalised and less involved in harder drugs. Without the illegal status of cannabis, there would have been no reason for our research participants to hang out at The River at all.

Street capital and gangster discourse

Studying marginalised drug dealers in a street culture raises the dilemma of the relationship between individual responsibility and social structural constraints – a dilemma embedded in the irresolvable debate of structure versus agency. The concepts of habitus and capital are Bourdieu's (1990) contribution to this debate. The habitus concept can be criticised for being too structural (King, 2000), and the concept of cultural capital can be criticised for not acknowledging the everyday resistance in autonomous fields and popular culture (Thornton, 1995). However, the two concepts still capture an important tension between structural limitations and the practical rationality of social life. Our empirical study in a Nordic welfare state makes this particularly evident. Without the ghettos and the deprived neighbourhoods often described in the dominant North American literature, theoretical conceptualisations that include agency and strategic actors become even more important.

In this book, competence and skills that had previously been conceptualised as 'streetwise' or knowing the 'code of the street' (Anderson, 1990, 1999) have been reconceptualised as street capital. The River dealers were positioned at the bottom of the hierarchies of society, and street capital became a way to gain both self-respect and respect from others. By using the concept of street capital the embodied character of this knowledge is emphasised. This concept also points to the importance of early socialisation and the practical rationality involved when young men start dealing illegal drugs. Street capital refers to the knowledge, competence, skills and objects that are given value in a street culture. It is masculine in its essence, and values violence, retaliation, fashionable clothes and the attraction of females. Most importantly, street capital is a form of legitimate power that is relational and has the capacity to generate profit.

The River dealers' street capital can be seen in their technical and mythological knowledge of illegal drugs and dealing. This includes argot and smoking techniques, narratives about learning to use cannabis and ways to resist dependence. It also includes knowing about cannabis types and qualities, the ability to identify plain-clothes police and avoid arrests, and ways to deal illegal drugs. Moreover, the young men's street capital could also be seen in their readiness to use violence and in their self-presentation as gangsters. As with cultural capital, street capital can be converted to economic capital, and it is closely linked to the social capital of its possessors. As opposed to cultural capital, however, it is difficult to transfer to other social arenas.

Street capital is the most important symbolic capital in street culture, and it is upheld by and embedded in gangster discourse, which is the street culture's dominant linguistic practice. Gangster discourse adds a social constructivist dimension to the concept of street capital. The appeal of gangster discourse is that individuals in street cultures have more exciting and rewarding lives than individuals in conventional society. Gangster discourse thus creates fascination and fear by constructing Otherness, and the dealers at The River used it to gain self-respect and respect from others.

Street capital in a welfare state

In a Nordic context, with a high density of welfare state institutions and private welfare organisations out in the streets, presenting oneself as a victim is also an important part of what we conceptualise as street capital. Oppression discourse includes personal narratives of unemployment, racism and psychosocial problems, often combined with stories about the government and city council being unwilling to help. Drug dealers at The River used the oppression discourse to justify drug dealing and violence, both in self-understandings and in meetings with welfare agents.

The social context of a benevolent welfare state is easy to misinterpret. Most importantly, marginalisation takes place in this context as well. The dealers at The River came from families at the bottom of the social hierarchy. Even in a social-democratic welfare state, social class and social marginality are reproduced over generations. Ethnic minority background further increases obstacles to educational and professional success. The realities of malignant experiences in the school system and in the job sector are harsh. Most of our research participants had also experienced incidences of direct racism. The more subtle experience of Otherness – or not belonging – in everyday interactions was, however, more important. The 'whiteness' of the welfare state apparatus may have increased feelings of estrangements. The overwhelming majority of the employees are white, ethnic Norwegians. The young men's meetings with this system reproduced an ethnic hierarchical system: they were black, the welfare state system overwhelmingly white.

The Nordic context also demonstrates that to understand street culture, we need more than marginalisation theory. Street culture is not only about poverty, discrimination or other socioeconomic processes. The benevolent welfare state provided most of The River dealers with solid economic support and help. Still, groups are left out, and they seek alternative arenas for identity development. One reason is that the main social identity or subject position the welfare state offers marginalised youths is that of the victim. Many proud youths will not consider such a position attractive, and they may seek out other social arenas that are rewarding in more empowering ways. In other words, no matter how much money is put into prevention efforts and welfare programmes, these efforts will fail unless there are some attractive identities offered to youths as well.

Notes

[1] The group was organised by Uteseksjonen, a local municipal organisation.

[2] A study by Nutt et al (2007) has been important in the recent debate on cannabis. On a global harm score for 20 substances, cannabis was placed well behind both alcohol and tobacco.

[3] You may now, for example, carry up to 15 grams of cannabis and only get a fine. The police will usually not invest much energy in pursuing ordinary cannabis users. In a series of interviews we conducted with rather regular cannabis users, fears of police and prosecution were surprisingly absent.

[4] First, Norway is tied up by international conventions that give it little room to manoeuvre. Moreover, the Dutch position of de facto legalisation, which is often recommended, has increasingly turned out to be problematic. The Netherlands has a huge 'back-door problem'; that is, a large and destructive illegal economy behind the more regulated coffee shops.

Bibliography

Aden, A. (2008) *Se oss*, Oslo: Aschehoug.

Adler, A. (1992) *Understanding human nature*, Oxford: Oneworld.

Adler, P.A. (1985) *Wheeling and dealing: An ethnography of an upper-level drug dealing and smuggling community*, New York, NY: Columbia University Press.

Adler, P.A. and Adler, P. (1983) 'Shifts and oscillations in deviant careers: the case of upper-level drug dealers and smugglers', *Social Problems*, vol 31, pp 195–207.

Alexander, C. E. (2000) *The asian gang: Ethnicity, identity, masculinity*. Oxford: Berg.

Alpheis, H. (1996) 'Hamburg: handling an open drug scene', in N. Dorn, J. Jepsen and E. Savona (eds) *European drug policies and enforcement*, Basingstoke: Macmillan.

Amundsen, E. J., Rossow, I. and Skurtveit, S. (2005) 'Drinking pattern among adolescents with immigrant and Norwegian backgrounds: a two-way influence?', *Addiction*, vol 100, no 10, pp 1453–63.

Anderson, E. (1990) *Street wise*, Chicago, IL: University of Chicago Press.

Anderson, E. (1999) *Code of the street: Decency, violence, and the moral life of the inner city*, New York, NY: W. W. Norton.

Anderson, T. L. and Mott, J. A. (1998) 'Drug-related identity change: theoretical development and empirical assessment', *Journal of Drug Issues*, vol 28, no 2, pp 299–328.

Andersson, M. (2003) 'Immigrant youth and the dynamics of marginalization', *Young Nordic Journal of Youth Research*, vol 11, no 1, pp 74–89.

Andersson, M. (2005) *Urban multi-culture in Norway*, Lewiston, NY: Edwin Mellen.

APA (American Psychiatric Association) (2000) *Diagnostic and statistical manual of mental disorders: DSM-IV-TR*, Washington, DC: APA.

Atkinson, P. (1990) *The ethnographic imagination: The textual construction of reality*, London: Routledge.

Atkinson, P. and Coffey, A. (2003) 'Revisiting the relationship between participant observation and interviewing', in J. F. Gubrium and J. A. Holstein (eds) *Postmodern interviewing*, London: Sage Publications.

Back, L. (1996) *New ethnicities and urban culture: Racism and multiculture in young lives*, London: Routledge.

Bakhtin, M. (1981). *The Dialogic Imagination*, Austin: University of Texas Press.

Bakken, A. (2003) *Minoritetsspråklig ungdom i skolen: Reproduksjon av ulikhet eller sosial mobilitet?*, Oslo: NOVA.

Baldwin, P. (1990) *The politics of social solidarity*, New York, NY: Cambridge University Press.

Barthes, R. (1972) *Mythologies*, London: Paladin.

Baudrillard, J. (1983) *Simulations*, New York, NY: Semiotext(e).

Bauman, Z. (1997) 'Dominant and demonic discourses of culture: their relevance to multi-ethnic alliances', in P. Werbner and T. Modood (eds) *Debating cultural hybridity*, London: Zed Books.

Becker, H. (1953) 'Becoming a marihuana user', *American Journal of Sociology*, vol 59, pp 235–42.

Becker, H. (1963) *Outsiders: Studies in the sociology of deviance*, New York, NY: Free Press.

Becker, H. (1967) 'History, culture and subjective experience: an exploration of the social bases of drug-induced experiences', *Journal of Health and Social Behavior*, vol 8, pp 163–76.

Bell, D. (1973) *The coming of post-industrial society*, New York: Basic Books.

Bennett, A. (1999) 'Subcultures or neo-tribes? Rethinking the relationship between youth, style and musical taste', *Sociology*, vol 33, no 3, pp 599–617.

Bennett, A. and Kahn-Harris, K. (eds) (2004) *After subculture: Critical studies in contemporary youth culture*, London: Palgrave Macmillan.

Berg, E. (2003) *Samhandlingens monolog: En studie av interaksjon mellom klienter med innvandrerbakgrunn og ansatte i tiltaksapparatet for rusmiddelbrukere*, Oslo: SIRUS.

Berger, P. L. and Luckmann, T. (1967) *The social construction of reality*, New York, NY: Doubleday.

Berntsen, H. F. (1981) *Stoffmisbruk: Myter og virkelighet*, Oslo: Aschehoug.

Bjørgo, T., Carlsson, Y. and Haaland, T. (2001) *Generaliserte hat – polariserte fellesskap*, Oslo: NIBR.

Blackman, S. (2004) *Chilling out: The cultural politics of substance consumption, youth and drug policy*, Maidenhead: Open University Press.

Booth, M. (2003) *Cannabis: A history*, London: Bantam Books.

Bourdieu, P. (1973) 'The Berber house', in M. Douglas (ed) *Rules and meanings: The anthropology of everyday knowledge*, Harmondsworth: Penguin.

Bourdieu, P. (1977) *Outline of a theory of practice*, Cambridge: Cambridge University Press.

Bourdieu, P. (1984) *Distinction: A social critique of the judgment of taste*, London: Routledge.

Bourdieu, P. (1985) 'The genesis of the concepts of habitus and field', *Sociocriticism*, vol 2, pp 11–24.

Bourdieu, P. (1986) 'The forms of capital', in J. G. Richardson (ed) *Handbook of theory and research for the sociology of education*, New York, NY: Greenwood.

Bourdieu, P. (1988) *Homo academicus*, Cambridge: Polity Press.

Bourdieu, P. (1990) *The logic of practice*, Stanford, CA: Stanford University Press.

Bourdieu, P. (1991) *Language & symbolic power*, Cambridge: Polity Press.

Bourdieu, P. (1993) *The field of cultural production*, Cambridge: Polity Press.

Bourdieu, P. (1998) *Practical reason*, Cambridge: Polity Press.

Bourdieu, P. (2001) *Masculine domination*, Stanford, CA: Stanford University Press.

Bourdieu, P. and Wacquant, L. J. D. (1992) *An invitation to reflexive sociology*, Cambridge: Polity Press.

Bourgois, P. (1998) 'Just another night in a shooting gallery', *Theory, Culture & Society*, vol 15, no 2, pp 37–66.

Bourgois, P. (2003a) *In search of respect: Selling crack in El Barrio*, Cambridge: Cambridge University Press.

Bourgois, P. (2003b) 'Crack and the political economy of social suffering', *Addiction Research and Theory*, vol 11, no 1, pp 31–7.

Bradby, H. (2007) 'Watch out for the aunties! Young British Asians' accounts of identity and substance use', *Sociology of Health & Illness*, vol 29, no 5, pp 656–72.

Bramness, J., Skurtveit, S. and Mørland, J. (2006) 'Flunitrazepam: psychomotor impairment, agitation and paradoxical reactions', *Forensic Science International*, vol 159, no 2–3, pp 83–91.

Bråthen, M., Djuve, A., Dølvig, T., Hagen, K., Hernes, G., and Nielsen R. (2007) *Levekår på vandring*, Oslo: Fafo.

Brekke, J. P. (2008) *Making the unreturnable return: The role of the welfare state in promoting return for rejected asylum seekers in Norway*, Oslo: Institute for Social Research.

Bretteville-Jensen, A. L. (2005) *Økonomiske aspekter ved sprøytemisbrukeres forbruk av rusmidler*, Oslo: SIRUS.

Brotherton, D. C. (2008) 'Beyond social reproduction: bringing resistance back in gang theory', *Theoretical Criminology*, vol 12, no 1, pp 55–77.

Bucerius, S. M. (2007) '"What else should I do?": cultural influences on the drug trade of migrants in Germany', *Journal of Drug Issues*, vol 37, no 3, pp 673–97.

Cahill, C. (2000) 'Street literacy: urban teenagers' strategies for negotiating their neighbourhood', *Journal of Youth Studies*, vol 3, no 3, pp 251–77.

Carpentier, C., Meacham, M. and Griffiths, P. (2008) 'Monitoring cannabis availability in Europe: issues, trends and challenges', in S. Sznitman, B. Olsson and R. Room (eds) *A cannabis reader: Global issues and local experiences*, Lisbon: EMCDDA.

Caulkins, J. P. and Pacula, R. (2006) 'Marijuana markets: inferences from reports by the household population', *Journal of Drug Issues*, vol 36, no 1, pp 173–201.

Caulkins, J. P. and Reuter, P. (1998) 'What price data tell us about drug markets', *Journal of Drug Issues*, vol 28, no 3, pp 593–612.

Chan, J. B. L., Devery, C. and Doran, S. (2003) *Fair cop: Learning the art of policing*, Toronto: Toronto University Press.

Chiricos, T., Hogan, M. and Gertz, M. (1997) 'Racial composition of neighborhood and fear of crime', *Criminology*, vol 35, no 1, pp 107–31.

Chiricos, T., McEntire, R. and Gertz, M. (2001) 'Perceived racial and ethnic composition of neighborhood and perceived risk of crime', *Social Problems*, vol 48, no 3, pp 322–40.

Chiricos, T., Welch, K. and Gertz, M. (2004) 'Racial typification of crime and support for punitive measures', *Criminology*, vol 42, no 2, pp 359–89.

Chouliaraki, L. and Fairclough, N. (1999) *Discourse in late modernity: Rethinking CDA*, Edinburgh: Edinburgh University Press.

Chouliaraki, L. and Fairclough, N. (2000) 'Language and power in Bourdieu: on Hasan's "the disempowerment game"', *Linguistics and Education*, vol 10, no 4, pp 399–409.

Christie, N. (1972) *Fangevoktere i konsentrasjonsleire: En sosiologisk undersøkelse av norske fangevoktere i "serberleirene" i Nord-Norge i 1942-43*, Oslo: Pax.

Cloward, R. and Ohlin, L. (1960) *Delinquency and opportunity*, New York, NY: Free Press.

Cohen, A. (1955) *Delinquent boys*, New York, NY: Free Press.

Cohen, P. (2005) 'Subcultural conflict and working-class community', in K. Gelder (ed) *The subcultures reader*, London: Routledge.

Cohen, S. (1972) *Folk devils and moral panics: The creation of mods and rockers*, London: Granada.

Coleman, J. W. (1998) *Criminal elite: Understanding white collar crime*, New York, NY: St. Martin's Press.

Connell, R. (1995) *Masculinities*, Cambridge: Polity Press.

Connell, R. (2002) *Gender*, Cambridge: Polity.

Coomber, R. (2006) *Pusher myths: Re-situating the drug dealer*, London: Free Association Books.

Courtwright, D. (1998) *Dark paradise: A history of opiate addiction in America*, Cambridge, MA: Harvard University Press.

Covington, J. and Taylor, R. B. (1991) 'Fear of crime in urban residential neighborhoods: implications of between- and within-neighborhood sources for current models', *Sociological Quarterly*, vol 32, no 2, pp 231–49.

Cromwell, P. and Thurman, Q. (2003) 'The devil made me do it: use of neutralization by shoplifters', *Deviant Behavior*, vol 24, pp 535–50.

Cross, M. and Waldinger, R. (1997) *Key issues for research and policy on migrants in cities*, Utrecht, The Netherlands: ERCOMER Publication Office.

Dahl, E., Fløtten, T. and Lorentzen T. (2008) 'Poverty dynamics and social exclusion: an analysis of Norwegian panel data', *Journal of Social Policy*, vol 37, no 2, pp 231–49.

Davis, J. E. (2005) 'Victim narratives and victim selves: false memory syndrome and the power of accounts', *Social Problems*, vol 52, no 4, pp 529–48.

Dawson, D. (2000) 'The link between family history and early onset alcoholism: earlier initiation of drinking or more rapid development of dependence?', *Journal of Studies on Alcohol*, vol 61, no 5, pp 634–46.

Denton, B. and O'Malley, P. (1999) 'Gender trust and business: women drug dealers in the illicit economy', *British Journal of Criminology*, vol 39, no 4, pp 513–30.

Denzin, N. K. and Lincoln, Y. S. (eds) (2005) *The Sage handbook of qualitative research*, London: Sage Publications.

DiMaggio, P. and Louch, H. (1998) 'Socially embedded consumer transactions: for what kinds of purchases do people most often use networks?', *American Sociological Review*, vol 63, no 5, pp 619–37.

Duncan, G., Hill, M. S. and Hoffman, S. D. (1988) 'Welfare dependence within and across generations', *Science*, vol 239, no 4839, pp 467–71.

Dyson, M. E. (2001) *Holler if you hear me: Searching for Tupac Shakur*, New York, NY: Basic Civitas Books.

EMCDDA (European Monitoring Centre for Drugs and Drugs Addiction) (2006) *Annual report*, Lisbon: EMCDDA, http://ar2006.emcdda.europa.eu/en/page022-en.html

Epland, J. (2005) *Veier inn i og ut av fattigdom: Inntektsmobilitet blant lavinntektshushold*, Oslo: Statistics Norway.

Esping-Andersen, G. (1990) *The three worlds of welfare capitalism*, Cambridge: Polity Press.

Fagan, J. and Wilkinson, D. (1998) 'Guns, youth violence, and social identity in inner cities', *Crime and Justice*, vol 24, pp 105–88.

Fairclough, N. (1992) *Discourse and social change*, Cambridge: Polity Press.

Fairclough, N. (1995a) *Media discourse*, London: Arnold.

Fairclough, N. (1995b) *Critical discourse analysis*, London: Longman.

Fangen, K. (2006) 'Humiliation as experienced by Somalis in Norway', *Journal of Refugee Studies*, vol 19, no 1, pp 69–93.

Fangen, K. (2008) *Identitet og praksis – Etnisitet, klasse og kjønn blant somaliere i Norge,* Oslo: Gyldendal.

Fekjær, S. N. (2006) 'Utdanning hos annengenerasjons etniske minoriteter i Norge', *Tidsskrift for samfunnsforskning*, vol 1, pp 57–96.

Felson, M. (1987) 'Routine activities and crime prevention in the developing metropolis', *Criminology*, vol 25, no 4, pp 911–31.

Finstad, L. (2003) *Politiblikket*, Oslo: Pax.

Foucault, M. (1965) *Madness and civilization*, New York, NY: Pantheon.

Foucault, M. (1970) *The order of things*, New York, NY: Pantheon.

Foucault, M. (1972a) *The archaeology of knowledge*, New York, NY: Pantheon.

Foucault, M. (1972b) 'The discourse on language', Appendix, in M. Foucault (ed) *The archaeology of knowledge*, New York, NY: Pantheon.

Foucault, M. (1977) *Discipline and punishment*, New York, NY: Pantheon.

Foucault, M. (1978) *The history of sexuality*, vol 1, New York, NY: Pantheon.

Fritsche, I. (2005) 'Predicting deviant behaviour by neutralization: myths and findings', *Deviant Behavior*, vol 26, no 5, pp 483–510.

Gamella, J. F. and Rodrigo, M. L. (2008) 'Multinational export–import ventures: Moroccan hashish into Europe through Spain', in S. Sznitman, B. Olsson and R. Room (eds) *A cannabis reader: Global issues and local experiences*, Lisbon: EMCDDA.

Garfinkel, H. (1967) *Studies in ethnomethodology*, Englewood Cliffs, NJ: Prentice Hall.

Gelder, K. (ed) (2005) *The subcultures reader*, London: Routledge.

Goffman, E. (1959) *The presentation of self in everyday life*, New York, NY: Doubleday.

Goffman, E. (1961) *Asylums: Essays on the social situation of mental patients and other inmates*, London: Pelican Books.

Goffman, E. (1963) *Stigma*, Englewood Cliffs, NJ: Prentice Hall.

Goode, E. and Ben-Yehuda, N. (1994) *Moral panics: The social construction of deviance*, Cambridge: Blackwell.

Gramsci, A. (1992) *Prison notebooks*, New York, NY: Colombia University Press.

Granovetter, M. (2005) 'The impact of social structure on economic outcomes', *Journal of Economic Perspectives*, vol 19, no 1, pp 33–50.

Gubrium, J. F. and Holstein, J. A. (eds) (2001) *Handbook of interview research*, London: Sage Publications.

Gubrium, J. F. and Holstein, J. A. (eds) (2003a) *Postmodern interviewing*, London: Sage Publications.

Gubrium, J. F. and Holstein, J. A. (2003b) 'From the individual interview to the interview society', in J. F. Gubrium and J. A. Holstein (eds) *Postmodern interviewing*, London: Sage Publications.

Gullestad, M. (2006) *Plausible prejudice*, Oslo: Universitetsforlaget.

Gundel, J. (2002) 'The migration–development nexus: Somalia case study', *International Migration*, vol 40, no 5, pp 255–81.

Haasen, C. and Prinzleve, M. (2004) 'Cocaine use in Europe – a multi-centre study', *European Addiction Research*, vol 10, no 4, pp 139–46.

Hall, S. (1972) 'The determination of news photographs', *Working Papers in Cultural Studies*, vol 3, pp 53–89.

Hall, S. (1973) 'Encoding and decoding in the television discourse', Paper for the Council of Europe Colloquy 'Training in the critical reading of televisual language', organised by the Council and the Centre for Mass Communication research, University of Leicester.

Hall, S. (1992) 'The capitals of culture: a nonholistic approach to status situations, class, gender, and ethnicity', in M. Lamont and M. Fournier (eds) *Cultivating differences: Symbolic boundaries and the making of inequality*, Chicago, IL: University of Chicago Press.

Hall, S. and Jefferson, T. (eds) (1976) *Resistance through rituals: Youth subcultures in post-war Britain*, London: Hutchinson.

Hall, S., Critcher, C., Jefferson, T., Clarke, J. and Roberts, B. (1978) *Policing the crisis: Mugging, the state and law and order*, London: Macmillan.

Hall, W. D. (2006) 'Cannabis use and the mental health of young people', *Australian and New Zealand Journal of Psychiatry*, vol 40, no 2, pp 105–13.

Halleröd, B. (2004) 'What I need and what the poor deserve', *Social Forces*, vol 83, no 1, pp 35–59.

Halvorsen, K. and Stjernø, S. (2008) *Work, oil and welfare*, Oslo: Universitetsforlaget.

Hanks, W. F. (2005) 'Pierre Bourdieu and the practices of language', *The Annual Review of Anthropology*, vol 34, pp 67–83.

Hansen, H. (2008) 'The dynamics of social assistance recipiency: empirical evidence from Norway', *European Sociological Review*, in press (Advance Access published 19 July: doi:10.1093/esr/jcn040).

Hansen, M. N. (2006) *Fluctuations in intergenerational mobility in economic status in Norway*, Memorandum no 6, Oslo: Department of Sociology and Human Geography, University of Oslo.

Hansen, M. N. (2007) 'Valgfrihet og styring i skolen', *Søkelys på arbeidsmarkedet*, vol 24, pp 337–49.

Harvey Brown, R. (1987) *Society as text: Essays on rhetoric, reason, and reality*, Chicago, IL: University of Chicago Press.

Hasan, R. (1999) 'The disempowerment game: Bourdieu and language in literacy', *Linguistics and Education*, vol 10, no 1, pp 25–87.

Hauge, R. (1970) *Gjengkriminalitet og ungdomskulturer*, Oslo: Universitetsforlaget.

Heath, A. and McMahon, D. (1997) 'Education and occupational attainment: the impact of ethnic origins', in V. Karn (ed) *Education, employment and housing among ethnic minorities in Britain*, London: HMSO, pp 91–113.

Heath, A., Rothon, C. and Kilpi, E. (2008) 'The second generation in Western Europe: education, unemployment, and occupational attainment', *Annual Review of Sociology*, vol 34, no 1, pp 211–35.

Hebdige, D. (1979) *Subculture: The meaning of style*, London: Routledge.

Hernes, G. (1978) *Makt og avmakt: En begrepsanalyse*, Bergen: Universitetsforlaget.

Hier, S. P. (2008) 'Thinking beyond moral panic – risk, responsibility, and the politics of moralization', *Theoretical Criminology*, vol 12, no 2, pp 173–90.

Hoffer, L. D. (2006) *Junkie business: The evolution and operation of a heroin dealing network*, Belmont: Thompson Wadsworth.

Holsten, J.A. and Gubrium, J.F. (2000) *The self we live by. Narrative identity in a postmodern world*, New York: Oxford University Press.

Horowitz, R. B. (1983) *Honor and the American dream*, New Brunswick, NY: Rutgers University Press.

Irwin, J. (1977) *Scenes*, Beverly Hills, CA: Sage Publications.

Jacobs, B., Topalli, V. and Wright, R. (2000) 'Managing retaliation: drug robbery and informal social control', *Criminology*, vol 38, no 1, 171–98.

Jacobs, B. A. (1996) 'Crack dealers and restrictive deterrence: identifying narcs', *Criminology*, vol 34, no 3, pp 409–31.

Jacobs, B. A. (1999) *Dealing crack: The social world of streetcorner selling*, Boston, MA: Northeastern University Press.

Jacobs, B. A. (2000) *Robbing drug dealers: Violence beyond the law*, New York, NY: Aldine de Gruyter.

Jaworski, A. and Couplan, N. (1999) *The discourse reader*, London: Routledge.

Jenkins, R. (1983) *Lads, citizens and ordinary kids: Working class youth lifestyles in Belfast*, London: Routledge & Kegan Paul.

Jenkins, R. (2006) *Cannabis and young people*, London: Jessica Kingsley Publishers.

Jensen, S. Q. (2006) 'Rethinking subcultural capital', *Young*, vol 14, no 3, pp 257–76.

Jensen, S. Q. (2007) 'Fremmed, farlig og fræk: unge mænd og etnisk/racial andenhed – mellem modstand og stilisering', PhD thesis, FREIA, University of Aalborg.

Jimerson, J. B. and Oware, M. K. (2006) 'Telling the code of the street', *Journal of Contemporary Ethnography*, vol 35, no 1, pp 24–50.

Johnson, B. and Natarajan, M. (1995) 'Strategies to avoid arrests: crack sellers' response to intensified policing', *American Journal of Police*, vol 14, no 3-4, pp 49–69.

Johnson, B. D., Goldstein, P. J., Preble, E., Schmeidler, J., Lipton, D. S., Spunt, B. and Miller, T. (1985) *Taking care of business: The economics of crime by heroin abusers*, Lexington, MA: Lexington Books.

Jørgensen, M. and Phillips, L. (2002) *Discourse analysis as theory and method*, London: Sage Publications.

Kangas, O and Palme, J. (eds) (2005) *Social policy and economic development in the Nordic countries*, Basingstoke: Palgrave Macmillan.

Kangas, O. and Ritakallio, V.-M. (2007) 'Relative to what? Cross-national picture of European poverty', *European Societies*, vol 9, no 2, pp 119–45.

Kao, G., and Thompson, J.S. (2003) 'Racial and ethnic stratification in educational achievement and attainment', Annual Review of Sociology, vol 29, pp 417-442.

Katz, J. (1988) *Seductions of crime*, Oxford: Basic Books.

Keire, M. L. (1998) 'Dope fiends and degenerates: the gendering of addiction in the early twentieth century', *Journal of Social History*, vol 31, no 4, pp 809–22.

Keiser, R. L. (1969) *The vice lords: Warriors of the streets*, New York, NY: Holt, Rinehart & Winston.

Keyes, C. L. (2004) *Rap music and street consciousness*, Chicago, IL: University of Illinois Press.

King, A. (2000) 'Thinking with Bourdieu against Bourdieu: a "practical" critique of the habitus', *Sociological Theory*, vol 18, no 3, pp 417–33.

Klein, D. C. (1991) 'The humiliation dynamic: an overview', *Journal of Primary Prevention*, special issue, part I, vol 12, no 2. pp 93-121.

Klockars, C. B. (1974) *The professional fence*, New York, NY: Free Press.

Krims, A. (2000) *Rap music and the poetics of identity*, Cambridge: Cambridge University Press.

KRIPOS (2006) 'Narkotikastatistikk 2005', http://www.politi.no/portal/, retrieved 6 March 2006.

Kubrin, C. E. (2005) 'Gangstas, thugs, and hustlas: identity and the code of the street in rap music', *Social Problems*, vol 52, no 3, pp 360–78.

Kuvoame, M. B. (2005) *Eikaguttene*, Oslo: Rusmiddeletaten.

Kvale, S. (1996) *Interviews: An introduction to qualitative research interviewing*, London: Sage Publications.

Laclau, E. and Mouffe, C. (1985) *Hegemony and socialist strategy*, London: Verso.

Lalander, P. (2003) *Hooked on heroin*, Oxford: Berg.

Lalander, P. (2005) 'Loading the street: the creation of the Callejero lifestyle', in P. Lalander and M. Salasuo (eds) *Drugs and youth cultures: Global and local expressions*, Helsinki: NAD.

Larsen, C. J. and Pedersen, W. (2005) *Bytte, kjærlighet, overgrep: Seksualitet blant ungdom i randsonen*, Research Report 10/05, Oslo: NOVA.

Larsen, G. (1992) *Brødre*, Oslo: Pax forlag.

Lee, M. and South, N. (2003) 'Drugs policing', in T. Newburn (ed) *Handbook of policing*, Cullompton: Willan Publishing.

Leggett, T. and Pietschmann, T. (2008) 'Global cannabis cultivation and trafficking', in S. Sznitman, B. Olsson and R. Room (eds) *A cannabis reader: Global issues and local experiences*, Lisbon: EMCDDA.

Lemert, E. M. (1967) *Human deviance, social problems and social control*, Englewood Cliffs, NJ: Prentice Hall.

Levitt, S. D. and Dubner, S. J. (2006) *Freakonomics*, London: Penguin.

Lewis, O. (1968) *La vida: A Puerto Rican family in the culture of poverty*, San Juan and New York, NY: Vintage.

Lien, I. (2001) 'The concept of honor, conflict and violent behaviour among youth in Oslo', in M. W. Klein, H-J. Kerner, C.M. Maxson and E.G.M. Weitekamp (eds) *The Eurogang paradox*, Dordrecht: Kluwer Academic Press.

Lien, I. (2002) 'Ære, vold og kulturell endring i Oslo indre by', *Nytt Norsk Tidsskrift*, vol 19, no 1, pp 27–41.

Light, A. (1996) *Tupac Shakur*, New York: Crown.

Lilleaas, U. B. (1987) *Stoff som ressurs: Om legeprofesjones bruk av narkotiske stoffer i forrige århundre*, Oslo: Universitetet i Oslo.

Lindner, E. G. (2000) 'The psychology of humiliation: Somalia, Rwanda/Burundi, and Hitler's Germany', PhD thesis, Department of Psychology, University of Oslo.

Lindner, R. (1996) *The reportage of urban culture: Robert Park and the Chicago school*, Cambridge: Cambridge University Press.

Lorentzen, T. (2006) *Social assistance dynamics in Norway*, Oslo: FAFO.

Luckenbill, D. F. and Doyle, D. P. (1989) 'Structural position and violence: developing a cultural explanation', *Criminology*, vol 27, no 3, pp 419–35.

Luling, V. (2006) 'Genealogy as theory, genealogy as tool: aspects of Somali "clanship"', *Social Identities*, vol 12, no 4, pp 471–85.

Lyotard, J.-F. (1984) *The postmodern condition: A report on knowledge*, Minneapolis, MN: University of Minnesota Press.

MacAndrew, C. and Edgerton, R. B. (1969) *Drunken comportment: A social explanation*, New York, NY: Aldine.

McAuley, R. (2007) *Out of sight: Crime youth and exclusion in modern Britain*, Cullompton: Willan Publishing.

McIntosh, J., MacDonald, F. and McKeganey, N. P. (2003) 'Knowledge and perceptions of illegal drugs in a sample of pre-teenage children', *Drugs: Education, Prevention and Policy*, vol 10, no 2, pp 331–44.

Maffesoli, M. (1996) *The time of the tribes: The decline of individualism in mass society*, London: Sage Publications.

Marcus, G. E. (1986) 'Contemporary problems of ethnography in the modern world system', in J. Clifford and G. E. Marcus (eds) *Writing culture: The poetics and politics of ethnography*, Berkeley, CA: University of California Press.

Marks, G. (2005) 'Accounting for immigrant nonimmigrant differences in reading and mathematics in twenty countries', *Ethnic and Racial Studies*, vol 28, no 5, pp 925–46.

Massey, D. and Denton, N. (2003) *American apartheid: Segregation and the making of the underclass*, Cambridge, MA: Harvard University Press.

Matza, D. (1964) *Delinquency and drift*, New York, NY: Wiley.

May, T. and Hough, M. (2004) 'Drug markets and distributions systems', *Addiction Research and Theory*, vol 12, no 6, pp 549–63.

May, T., Duffy, M., Few, B. and Hough, M. (2005) *Understanding drug selling in communities*, York: Joseph Rowntree Foundation.

Merton, R. K. (1938) 'Social structure and anomi', *American Sociological Review*, vol 3, no 5, pp 672–82.

Merton, R. (1959) *Social theory and social structure*, Glencoe, IL: Free Press.

Mieczkowski, T. (1990) 'Crack distribution in Detroit', *Contemporary Drug Problems*, vol 17, no 1, pp 9–30.

Miles, S. (2000) *Youth lifestyles in a changing world*, Buckingham: Open University Press.

Miller, J. (2001) *One of the guys: Girls, gangs and gender*, New York, NY: Oxford University Press.

Miller, W. (1973) 'The molls', *Society*, vol 11, no 1, pp 32–5.

Miller, W. (1975) *Violence by youth gangs and youth groups as a crime problem in major American cities*, Washington, DC: US Department of Justice.

Miller, W. B. (1958) 'Lower class culture as a generating milieu of gang delinquency', *Journal of Social Issues*, vol 14, no 3, pp 5–19.

Minor, W. T. (1981) 'Techniques of neutralization: a reconceptualization and empirical examination', *Journal of Research in Crime and Delinquency*, vol 18, no 2, pp 295–318.

Moore, J. W. (1978) *Homeboys*, Philadelphia, PA: Temple University Press.

Moore, J. W. (1991) *Going down to the barrio: Homeboys and homegirls in change*, Philadelphia, PA: Temple University Press.

Moore, M. (1977) *Buy and bust*, Lexington: D.C. Heath.

Morgan, P. and Joe, K. (1996) 'Citizens and outlaws: the private lives and public lifestyle of women in the illicit drug economy', *Journal of Drug Issues*, vol 26, no 1, pp 125–41.

Morris, K. (1998) 'Seeking ways to crack cocaine addiction', *Lancet*, vol 352, no 9136, p 1290.

Moshuus, G. (2005a) 'Young immigrants on heroin: an ethnography of Oslo's street worlds', PhD Thesis, Department of Anthropology, University of Oslo.

Moshuus, G. H. (2005b) 'The gangster as a hero: ethnic identity management on the streets of Oslo', in P. Lalander and M. Salasuo (eds) *Globalization, youth cultures and drugs*, Kalmar: Nordic Council for Alcohol and Drug Research.

Muggleton, D. and Weinzierl, R. (eds) (2003) *The post-subcultures reader*, Oxford: Berg.

Mullins, C. W. (2006) *Holding your square: Masculinities, streetlife and violence*, Cullompton: Willan Publishing.

Murray, C. (1984) *Losing ground: American social policy 1950–1980*, New York, NY: Basic Books.

Nelson, C. B., Rehm, J., Ustun, T. B., Grant, B. and Chatterji, S. (1999) 'Factor structures for DSM-IV substance disorder criteria endorsed by alcohol, cannabis, cocaine and opiate users: results from the WHO reliability and validity study', *Addiction*, vol 94, no 6, pp 843–55.

Newman, K. (1999) *No shame in my game: The working poor in the inner city*, New York, NY: Russell Sage Foundation and Knopf.

Nietzsche, F. (1968) *The will to power*, New York, NY: Vintage Books.

Norderhaug, E. (2004) *Saynab – min historie*, Oslo: Aschehoug.

Nutt, D., King, L., Saulsbury, W. and Blakemore, C. (2007) 'Development of a rational scale to assess the harm of drugs of potential misuse', *Lancet*, vol 369, no 9566, pp 1047–53.

Palme, J. (2005) 'Coming late – catching up: the formation of a "Nordic model"', in O. Kangas and J. Palme (eds) *social policy and economic development in the Nordic countries*, Basingstoke: Palgrave Macmillan.

Pape, H. and Rossow, I. (2004) '"Ordinary" people with "normal" lives? A longitudinal study of ecstasy and other drug use among Norwegian youth', *Journal of Drug Issues*, vol 34, pp 389–418.

Park, R. E., Burgess, E. W. and McKenzie, R. D. (1925) *The city*, Chicago, IL: University of Chicago Press.

Parker, H., Measham, F. and Aldridge, J. (1998) *Illicit leisure: The normalization of adolescent recreational drug use*, London: Routledge.

Pavis, S. and Cunningham-Burley, S. (1999) 'Male youth street culture: understanding the context of health-related behaviours', *Health Education Research*, vol 14, no 5, pp 583–96.

Pearson, G. and Shiler, M. (2002) 'Rethinking the generation gap: attitudes to illicit drugs among young people and adults', *Criminal Justice*, vol 2, no 1, pp 71–86.

Pedersen, W. (1994) 'Oh doctor shoot me quick', in W. Pedersen, *Ungdom er bare et ord: Samfunnsvitenskapelige essays*, Oslo: Norwegian University Press.

Pedersen, W. (2001) 'Victims of violence in a welfare state: sociodemography, ethnicity and risk behaviors', *British Journal of Criminology*, vol 41, no 1, pp 1–21.

Pedersen, W. (2005) *Nye seksualiteter*, Oslo: Norwegian University Press.

Pedersen, W. (2008) 'Hasjbruk hos unge voksne', *Tidsskrift for Den Norske Lægeforening*, vol 128, pp 1825–8.

Pedersen, W. (2009) 'Cannabis use: subcultural opposiation or social marginality? A population-based longitudinal study', *Acta Sociologica*, vol 52, pp 135–48.

Peretti-Watel, P. (2003) 'Neutralization theory and the denial of risk: some evidence from cannabis use among French adolescents', *British Journal of Sociology*, vol 54, no 1, pp 21–42.

Perkonigg, A., Lieb, R. Hofler, M., Schuster, P., Sonntag, H. and Wittchen H-U. (1999) 'Patterns of cannabis use, abuse and dependence over time', *Addiction Research and Theory*, vol 94, pp 1663–78.

Perry, I. (2004) *Prophets of the hood: Politics and poetics in hip hop*, Durham and London: Duke University Press.

Peterson, R. D., Krivo, L. J. and Hagan, J. (2006) *The many colors of crime: Inequalities of race, ethnicity and crime in America*, New York, NY: New York University Press.

Plummer, K. (1997) *The Chicago school*, vol 1–4, London: Routledge.

Polhemus, T. (1994) *Streetstyle*, London: Thames & Hudson.

Potter, J. (1996) *Representing reality: Discourse, rhetoric and social construction*, Los Angeles, CA: Sage Publications.

Potter, J. and Wetherell, M. (1987) *Discourse and social psychology: Beyond attitudes and behaviour*, Los Angeles, CA: Sage Publications.

Preble, E. and Casey, J. (1969) '"Taking care of business": the heroin user's life on the street', *International Journal of Addictions*, vol 4, pp 1–24.

Prieur, A. (2001) 'Respekt og samhold: unge innvandrermenn, kriminalitet og kjønnskultur', *Mannsforskning*, vol 1, pp 21–30.

Prieur, A. (2004) *Balansekunstnere: Betydningen av innvandrerbakgrunn i Norge*, Oslo: Pax.

Reimer, B. (1995) 'Youth and modern lifestyle', in J. Fornäs and G. Bolin (eds) *Youth culture in late modernity*, London: Sage Publications.

Roemer, M. (1997) *Telling stories: Postmodernism and the invalidation of traditional narrative*, Lanham, MD: Rowman & Littlefield.

Rogstad, J. (2000) *Mellom faktiske og forestilte forskjeller: Synlige minoriteter på arbeidsmarkedet*, Oslo: ISF.

Rogstad, J. (2004) 'Diskriminering som erfaring', *Søkelys på arbeidsmarkedet*, vol 21, pp 265–74.

Room, R. F., Fischer, B., Hall, W., Lenton, S. and Reuter, P. (2008) *The global cannabis commission report*, Oxford: The Beckley Foundation.

Roux, A. (2001) 'Investigating neighborhood and area effects on health', *American Journal of Public Health*, vol 91, no 11, pp 1783–9.

Roy, O. (2004) *Globalized Islam*, New York, NY: Columbia University Press.

Roy, O. (2006) 'The nature of the French Riots', http://riotsfrance.ssrc.org/Roy/ retrieved 7 September 2006.

Røed, M. and Bratsberg, B. (2005) 'Integrering av innvandrere i arbeidsmarkedet', in P. Schøne (ed) *Det nye arbeidsmarkedet*, Oslo: FAFO report 327, pp 29–49.

Sandberg, S. (2005) 'Stereotypiens dilemma: Iscenesettelser av etnisitet på "gata"', *Tidsskrift for Ungdomsforskning*, vol 5, no 2, pp 27–46.

Sandberg, S. (2008a) 'Street capital: ethnicity and violence on the streets of Oslo', *Theoretical Criminology*, vol 12, no 2, pp 153–71.

Sandberg, S. (2008b) 'Black drug dealers in a white welfare state: cannabis dealing and street capital in Norway', *British Journal of Criminology*, vol 48, no 5, pp 604–19.

Sandberg, S. (2009a) 'Symbolic capital and linguistic practice in street culture', PhD thesis, Department of Sociology, University of Bergen.

Sandberg, S. (2009b) 'A narrative search for respect', *Deviant Behavior*, vol 30, pp 487–510.

Sandberg, S. (2009c) 'Gangster, victim or both? The interdiscursive construction of sameness and difference in self-presentations', *British Journal of Sociology*, vol 60, no 3, pp 523–42.

Sandberg, S. and Pedersen, W. (2008) '"A magnet for curious adolescents": the perceived dangers of an open drug scene', *International Journal of Drug Policy*, vol 19, no 6, pp 459–66.

Sandberg, S., Viland, C. and Pedersen, W. (2007) '"Joint, joine, dele, være sammen": hasjmarkedets konsekvenser for bruk, risiko og avhengighet', *Sosiologisk Tidsskrift*, vol 15, no 4, pp 317–36.

Sarup, M. (1996) *Identity, culture and the postmodern world*, Edinburgh: Edinburgh University Press.

Schiffrin, D., Tannen, D. and Hamilton, H. E. (eds) (2001) *The handbook of discourse analysis*, Oxford: Blackwell.

Seale, C., Gobo, G., Gubrium, J. F. and Silverman, D. (eds) (2004) *Qualitative research practice*, London: Sage Publications.

Shakur, T. (1999): *The rose that grew from concrete*, New York: Pocket Books, a division of Simon & Schuster inc.

Shaw, C. and McKay, H. (1929) *Delinquent areas*, Chicago, IL: University of Chicago Press.

Sheridan, A. (1980) *Michel Foucault: The will to truth*, London and New York, NY: Routledge.

Silverman, D. (2001) *Interpreting qualitative data: Methods for analysing talk, text and interaction*, London: Sage Publications.

Silverman, D. (2004) *Qualitative research: Theory, method and practice*, London: Sage Publications.

Silverman, D. (2005) *Doing qualitative research*, London: Sage Publications.

Skardhamar, T. (2006) *Kriminalitet gjennom ungdomstiden blant nordmenn og ikke-vestlige innvandrere: Notat 33*, Oslo: Statistisk Sentralbyrå.

Smith-Solbakken, M. and Tungland, M. (1997) *Narkomiljøet: Økonomi, kultur og avhengighet*, Oslo: Ad Notam Gyldendal.

South, N. (1999) *Drugs: Cultures, controls & everyday life*, London: Sage Publications.

South, N. (2004) 'Managing work hedonism and the "borderline" between the legal and illegal markets: two case studies of recreational heavy drug users', *Addiction Research and Theory*, vol 12, no 6, pp 525–38.

SSB (2006) Statistics Norway, www.ssb.no (accessed 15 December 2006).

St John, C. and Heald-Moore, T. (1995) 'Fear of black strangers', *Social Science Research*, vol 24, no 3, pp 262–80.

Støren, L. A. (2002) 'Minoritetselever i videregående opplæring: en økende andel fullfører, men utfordringene er store', *Tidsskrift for ungdomsforskning*, vol 2, no 2, pp 109–18.

Storhaug, H. (2003) *Feminin integrering: Utfordringer I et fleretnisk samfunn*, Oslo: Human Rights Service.

Suttles, G. (1968) *Social order of the slum*, Chicago, IL: University of Chicago Press.

Swartz, D. (1997) *Culture and power: The sociology of Pierre Bourdieu*, Chicago, IL: University of Chicago Press.

Swidler, A. (1986) 'Culture in action: symbols and strategies', *American Sociological Review*, vol 51, no 2, pp 273–86.

Sykes, G. and Matza, D. (1957) 'Techniques of neutralization: a theory of delinquency', *American Sociological Review*, vol 22, no 6, pp 664–70.

Sznitman, S., Olsson, B. and Room R. (eds) (2008) *A cannabis reader: Global issues and local experiences*, Lisbon: EMCDDA.

Thornton, S. (1995) *Club cultures: Music, media, and subcultural capital*, Cambridge: Polity Press.

Thrasher, F. M. (1927) *The gang: A study of 1313 gangs in Chicago*, Chicago, IL: Chicago of University Press.

Tjersland, O. A., Jansen, U. and Engen, G. (1998) *Våge å leve: En bok om alternative veier i behandling basert på erfaringene fra Tyrili*, Oslo: Aschehoug.

Topalli, V. (2005) 'When being good is bad: an expansion of neutralization theory', *Criminology*, vol 43, no 3, pp 797–836.

Topalli, V., Wright, R. and Fornango, R. (2002) 'Drug dealers, robbery and retaliation: vulnerability, deterrence and the contagion of violence', *British Journal of Criminology*, vol 42, no 2, pp 337–51.

Torgersen, L. (2001) 'Patterns of self-reported delinquency in children with one immigrant parent, two immigrant parents and Norwegian-born parents: some methodological considerations', *Journal of Scandinavian Studies in Criminology and Crime Prevention*, vol 2, pp 213–27.

Tronstad, K. R. (2008) 'Experiences of discrimination', in S. Blom and K. Henriksen (eds) *Living conditions among immigrants*, Oslo: Statistics Norway.

Turner, G. (1990) *British cultural studies: An introduction*, London: Unwin Hyman.

van Dijk, T. A. (1997) *Discourse studies: A multidisciplinary introduction*, London: Sage Publications.

UNODC (United Nations Office on Drugs and Crime) (2006) *2006 world drug report*, Vienna: UNODC, www.unodc.org/unodc/en/data-and-analysis/WDR-2006.html

Venkatesh, S. (2006) *Off the books. The underground economy of the urban poor*, Cambridge, Mass.: Harvard University Press.

Venkatesh, S. (2008) *Gang leader for a day. A rogue sociologist takes to the streets*, New York: Penguin Press.

Vestel, V. (2004) 'A community of difference: hybridization, popular culture and the making of social relations among multicultural youngsters in "Rudenga", East Side Oslo', PhD thesis, Department of Social Anthropology, University of Oslo.

Vigil, J. D. (1987) 'Street socialization, locura behaviour, and violence among Chicano gang members', in J. Kraus, S. Sorenson and P. D. Juarez (eds) *Violence and homicide in Hispanic communities*, Washington, DC: National Institute of Mental Health, pp 231–41.

Vigil, J. D. (1996) 'Street baptism: Chicago gang initiation', *Human Organization*, vol 55, no 2, pp 149–53.

Vigil, J. D. (2002) *A rainbow of gangs*, Austin, TX: University of Texas Press.

Vigil, J. D. (2003) 'Urban violence and street gangs', *Annual Review of Anthropology*, vol 32, pp 225–42.

Vold, G. B., Bernard, T. J. and Snipes, J. B. (2002) *Theoretical criminology*, Oxford: Oxford University Press.

Wacquant, L. (2002) 'Scrutinizing the street: poverty, morality, and the pitfalls of urban ethnography', *American Journal of Sociology*, vol 107, no 6, pp 1468–532.

Wacquant, L. (2008) *Urban outcasts*, Cambridge: Polity Press.

Webster, C. (1996) 'Local heroes: violent racism, spacism and localism among white and Asian young people', *Youth & Policy*, vol 53, pp 15–27.

Webster, C. (1997) 'The construction of British "Asian" criminality', *International Journal of the Sociology of Law*, vol 25, no 1, pp 65–86.

Webster, C. (2007) *Understanding race and crime*, London: Open University Press.

Weinzierl, R. (2000) *Fight the power: A secret history of pop and the formation of new substreams*, Vienna: Passagen-Verlag.

Whan, L., West, M., McCLure, N. and Lewis, S. (2006) 'Effects of delta-9-tetrahydrocannabinol, the primary psychoactive cannabinoid in marijuana, on human sperm function in vitro', *Fertility and Sterility*, vol 85, no 3, pp 653–60.

WHO (World Health Organization) (1990) *International classification of diseases (ICD-10)*, Geneva: WHO.

Whyte, W. F. (1943) *Street corner society*, Chicago, IL: University of Chicago Press.

Wieder, D. L. (1974) *Language and social reality: The case of telling the convict code*, Lanham, MD: University Press of America.

Wilkins, C. and Sweetsur, P. (2006) 'Exploring the structure of the illegal market for cannabis', *De Economist*, vol 154, pp 547–62.

Wilkinson, D. (2001) 'Violent events and social identity: specifying the relationship between respect and masculinity in inner-city youth violence', *Sociological Studies of Children and Youth*, vol 8, pp 231–65.

Willis, P. (1977) *Learning to labour*, London: Saxon House.

Wilson, W. J. (1987) *The truly disadvantaged: The inner city, the underclass, and public policy*, Chicago, IL: Chicago of University Press.

Wirth, L. (1928) *The ghetto*, Chicago, IL: University of Chicago Press.

Wolfgang, M. E. and Ferracuti, F. (1967) *The subculture of violence: Towards an integrated theory in criminology*, London: Tavistock.

Wood, L. A. and Kroger, R. O. (2000) *Doing discourse analysis: Methods for studying action in talk and text*, London: Sage Publications.

Wright, R. T. and Decker, S. H. (1994) *Burglars on the job*, Boston, MA: Northeastern University Press.

Wright, R. T. and Decker, S. H. (1997) *Armed robbers in action*, Boston, MA: Northeastern University Press.

Yablonsky, L. (1966) *The violent gang*, New York, NY: Macmillan.

Young, J. (1999) *The exclusive society*, London: Sage Publications.

Zaitch, D. (2005) 'The ambiguity of violence, secrecy, and trust among Colombian drug entrepreneurs', *Journal of Drug Issues*, vol 35, no 1, pp 201–28.

Zinberg, N. (1984) Drug, set, and setting: The basis for controlled intoxicant use, New Haven, CT: Yale University Press.

Østbye, L. (2004) *Innvandrere i Norge*, Oslo: Statistisk sentralbyrå.

Index